Law and Visual Jurisprudence

Volume 9

Timothy D. Peters, University of Sunshine Coast, Sippy Downs, Australia

Andreas Philippopoulos-Mihalopoulos, University of Westminster, London, UK

Richard Powell, Nihon University, Tokyo, Japan

Marco Ricca, University of Parma, Parma, Italy

Julia J. A. Shaw, De Montfort University, Leicester, UK

Richard K. Sherwin, New York Law School, New York, USA

Mateusz Stępień, Jagiellonian University, Cracow, Poland

Kieran Mark Tranter, Queensland University of Technology, Brisbane, Australia

Farid Samir Benavides Vanegas, Ramon Llull University, Barcelona, Spain

Riccardo Vecellio Segate, University of Dundee, Dundee, UK

Denis Voinot, Lille University, Lille, France

Xu Youping, Guangdong University of Foreign Studies, Guangzhou, China

Frank Fleerackers
Editor

The Rearguard of Subjectivity

On Legal Semiotics—Festschrift in Honour of Jan M. Broekman

Springer

Editor
Frank Fleerackers
Leuven Centre for Public Law
KU Leuven
Leuven, Belgium

ISSN 2662-4532 ISSN 2662-4540 (electronic)
Law and Visual Jurisprudence
ISBN 978-3-031-26854-0 ISBN 978-3-031-26855-7 (eBook)
https://doi.org/10.1007/978-3-031-26855-7

This Springer imprint is published by the registered company Springer Nature Switzerland AG
The registered company address is: Gewerbestrasse 11, 6330 Cham, Switzerland

Preface

On the 18th of June 2021, in the midst of the COVID-crisis, an online conference on The Rearguard of Subjectivity was held in honour of Jan M. Broekman's 90th birthday. This book encompasses the conference papers and proceedings as well as a number of contributions by Jan's close friends and mentees. We also asked Jan to add his current thoughts on the subject.

Edmund Husserl's ideas, impressed by Kant's critiques, constituted a point of departure when rereading philosophical problems of subject and of subjectivity. Jan M. Broekman unveiled in his 1961/63 "Phänomenologie und Egologie" how Husserl analyzed the "Split Ego"—thoughts in Kant's vision, which became fundamental for his phenomenology. Form and function of subjectivity were likewise positioned in psychiatry and in literature as well as in aesthetics, as Broekman's texts on "Cubism" demonstrated. Problems of "language" unfolded in studies from texts of Ezra Pound to dialogic insights of Martin Buber, all participating in *significs* developing into *semiotics*. Two themes accompanied these insights: the notion and later Parisian mainstream entitled *structuralism* as well as the urgency to deepen insights into links between Marxism and Phenomenology. Central language concepts played a role: already in 1986 Broekman published on "semiology and medical discourse," in 1992 on "neurosemiotics," whereas in 1993 the link between speech act and (legal as well as social) freedom was exposed. In all these thoughts, both the subject and the atmosphere of subjectivity played a role. Broekman had been teaching parallel to actual philosophical issues, law and medicine until his 1996 retirement, and offered a synthetic view in his "Intertwinements of Law and Medicine" revisiting the subjectivity dimensions. In 1998, during his six years of visiting professorship at the Illinois Urbana-Champaign Law School, he developed his "A Philosophy of European Union Law." A 2004 study on "The Multicultural Self" brought him back to language and semiotics, especially when functioning several years as "Distinguished Visiting Professor" at the Penn State University, Carlisle Law School, establishing the "Roberta Kevelson Seminar on Law and Semiotics." Two issues of "International Journal for the Semiotics of Law" in 2009 en 2010 informed on these activities. The "Law and Semiotics" thinking brought in 2011 "The Semiotics of Law in Legal Education," in 2013 "Lawyers Making Meaning," in 2015 "Signs in Law-A Source Book," and in 2016 "Meaning, Narrativity, and the Real." The subject in law amidst a plurality of language types (especially analog and digital language) remained a major theme in Broekman's 2019 "Rethinking Law and Language. The Flagship 'Speech'." Core ideas were expanded upon in his "Springer Article in Law," published with F. Fleerackers in 2020, entitled "Legal Thoughts Convert. Rethinking Legal Thinking."

Contributions to the conference touched upon the analog/digital dichotomy in semiotics, the multicultural self in language and semiotics, semiology and legal discourse, the legal subject and the atmosphere of subjectivity, intertwinements of law and medicine, the semiotics of law in legal education, signs in law and legal discourse, making meaning in law, and legal speech acts.

Contributors include: José Manuel Aroso Linhares (University of Coimbra), Larry Backer (Pennsylvania State University), William Elliott Butler (Pennsylvania State University), Clara Chapdelaine-Feliciati (Xi'an Jiaotong Liverpool University), Lieven De Cauter (Leuven University), Ana Gaudêncio (University of Coimbra), Philip Grier (Dickinson College), Sarah Marusek (University of Hawai'i Hilo), Francis Mootz (University of the Pacific), Bart Nelissen (Erasmus University), Maria Lucrecia Rovaletti (University of Buenos Aires), Klaas Tindemans (Free University of Brussels), Antoon Vandevelde (University of Leuven), Anne Wagner (University of Lille) and, of course, Jan M. Broekman.

Book Publications Jan M. Broekman

- Phänomenologie und Egologie
- Hedendaagse Rechtsfilosofische Literatuur
- Mens en Mensbeeld van ons Recht
- Recht und Anthropologie
- Structuralism: Moscow.Prague.Paris
- Phenomenology and Marxism (4 volumes with B. Waldenfels & A. Pazanin)
- Recht en Taal
- Darstellung und Sinn (with H. Feldmann)
- Intertwinements of Law and Medicine
- Recht, Rechtsfilososfie en Rechtstheorie
- Bioetica Con Rasgos Juridicos
- A Philosophy of European Union Law
- Schizofrenie—Het Raadsel Opgelost
- Recht uit Woorden
- Ziektebeelden
- Encarnaciones
- Interacting Minds (with H. Foox)
- E-Education and the Web
- The Virtual in E-Education
- Binding Words, Unfolding Selves

- Prospects of Legal Semiotics (with A. Wagner)
- The Semiotics of Law in Legal Education (with J. Mootz III)
- Lawyers Making Meaning (with L. Catá Backer)
- Signs in Law—A Source Book (with L. Catá Backer)
- Meaning, Narrativity, and the Real
- Legal Signs Fascinate (with F. Fleerackers)
- Legal Conversation as Signifier (with F. Fleerackers)
- Rethinking Law and Language: The Flagship "Speech"
- Legal Thoughts Convert (with F. Fleerackers)
- Knowledge in Change—The Semiotics of Cognition and Conversion

Leuven, Belgium Frank Fleerackers

Contents

The Efficient Jurist as a Semiotician: A Dialogue with Jan Broekman and Larry Catá Backer

José Manuel Aroso Linhares

Abstract It is a very specific counterpoint between *utility* and *efficiency,* involving a stimulating understanding of the *lawyer as a semiotician* (conscious of the ways in which his/her role "must be necessarily subverted") that this chapter briefly explores. This means explicitly revisiting Jan M. Broekman's and Larry Catà Backer's *Lawyers Making Meaning,* but also returning to Hart's distinction between *internal* and *external* points of view, as well as considering different approaches of the connection between legal theory and semiotics. It means also defending the possibility of treating Law (or a certain Law) as an explicit cultural artefact and a specific occasion for the creation of meaning, involving a relevant claim of autonomy and a decisive civilizational conformation (inscribed in the *possibilities* of the Western Text).

1 Introduction

In the *Preface* to *Lawyers Making Meaning*, Jan M. Broekman and Larry Catà Backer introduce a very promising distinction between *utility* and *efficiency* which explicitly concerns the lawyer's *awareness* of his/her role and its possible degrees of reflection:

> A *useful* lawyer is one that is conscious of his/her role, and of the limits of that role. But the *efficient* lawyer is also the one conscious of the ways in which that role must be necessarily subverted through the application of forms of meaning that are at once a sign of fidelity to the structures of the legal system within which she operates and at the same time an effort to remake it... (Broekman and Backer 2013, p. ix).

It is the productivity of this distinction, in this stimulatingly unusual context, that this chapter endeavours to discuss: not exactly in order to reconstitute the "semiotic steps" which, as "steps to take in texts"—sensitive to their "multilayered

J. M. A. Linhares (✉)
University of Coimbra, Institute for Legal Research, FDUC, Coimbra, Portugal
e-mail: linhares@fd.uc.pt

F. Fleerackers (ed.), *The Rearguard of Subjectivity*, Law and Visual Jurisprudence 9,
https://doi.org/10.1007/978-3-031-26855-7_1

character"—(Broekman and Backer 2013, p. 196), legal work incorporates, even less to problematize the corresponding *modus operandi* (defining what we may call the *jurist's semiotic approach*)—these possibilities are, moreover, admirably explored in the book by Jan Broekman and Larry Backer (2013, pp. 195–197, 203 ff., 207 ff.)... --, rather in order to distinguish (and separate) the degrees (or gradations) of "awareness" or "self-awareness" (2013, pp. vii–viii, 7 ff., 12-14, 41 ff., 45 ff., 67–68, 80 ff., 116 ff., 122, 146-148, 195 ff., 200) which the *utility/ efficiency* binomial allows us to recognize in this assimilation process—not only when making the practical world of Law means inventing (more or less constitutively) its "substance", but also (and mainly) when making that world (as an authentic practical-cultural artefact) means determining its autonomy and limits, i.e. (in our Authors' words) "making and protecting the boundaries" which tentatively distinguish its field and its form of "compulsion" or "governance" from those which "not-law" worlds explicitly assume.[1]

2 The Questions Concerning the *Internal* and *External* Points of View: A Dialogue with Hart, Postema and Fish

The last accentuation regarding the problem of Law's autonomy and limits (whilst involving the constitutive role of legislators and judges[2]) not only purposely broadens the spectrum of operators to be taken into account (as *actants* and *acteurs* but also as *semiotic groups* or *interpretive communities* involved in legal relevant discourses), but also introduces the issue of the possible *two degrees*, concerning respectively the *useful* and the *efficient* jurist. This means generating a stimulating ensemble of questions.

We may eventually accept that the first of these two degrees matches a conscience of the jurist's role and its limits which is compossible with the deployment of an "internal point of view" (regarding the "inside" of legal materials and practices, or at least highlighting the "internal aspect of rules" whilst developing the indispensable "critical reflective attitude" which treats the "pattern of behavior" as a "common

[1]"To make a world requires two distinct actions. The first, the usual object of lawyers, is to fill the world with substance—and lawyers spend their time making meaning of this substance and sometimes making the substance itself. The second, sometimes the object of lawyers, and central to the tasks of judges and legislators in their engagement with law, is the task of making and protecting the boundaries of this world law makes. Beyond law exist other worlds, sometimes as complex as that of law, and always in communication with it; these other forms of compulsion—the "not-law" fields of governance with which lawyers have an increasingly uncertain relationship include, beyond religious, moral, and ethical "worlds", the worlds of psychology, of economics and philosophy. Lawyers make meaning, and a world, by making law; they also make meaningful boundaries that separate what is allocated to the law-world and everything else..." (Broekman and Backer 2013, p. vii).

[2]See the text quoted in the previous note.

standard"[3]) —in the sense in which Hart's analytical hermeneutics has taught us to recognize (Hart 1994, pp. 51 ff., 56–58, 88–90)—. . . and no less compatible with the "intensification of attention" (or the "heightened degree of attention while performing in the practice") which, considering the canons of *professional correctness*, Stanley Fish admits as the critical reflection integrable within the routines of practice and its *doing what comes naturally.*[4]

But what about the second step, the one which considers *efficiency* and where *semiotic sensitivity* is expected to play its indispensable role (Broekman and Backer 2013, pp. viii, 8)? How should we understand the critical "self-consciousness" and the "subversion"[5] it requires, not only whilst overlapping the tasks-roles of following and remaking, specifying and transforming, but also whilst sustaining simultaneous claims of "fidelity" and "opposition" to the "structures and logics" of the legal system (Broekman and Backer 2013, pp. ix, 196)? Is this specific critical reflectiveness still compatible with an internal commitment or engagement with the practical world of Law—and its *normal doing* or "its going along with things as they are"—or does it condemn the jurist to a hetero-referential exercise of distance, mobilizing—albeit briefly (as if in a reflective parenthesis!)—alien resources of *creative rhetoricity* or *theoretical calculus* (Fish 1999, pp. 215–216), when not external "forms of compulsion" (Broekman and Backer 2013, p. vii)?

And yet this is not the only alternative to be considered. To conclude for instance that the path to be pursued is unequivocally the second doesn't actually mean ensuring a single response and even less preventing a complex chain of new questions: very simply because the intended *external reflective distance* admits that it can be fulfilled from different perspectives and wearing the mask of different *observers.*

We should unavoidably begin with the possibilities of a *moderate external point of view ("moderate" EPOV),*[6] analytically describing the rules or the structures of

---

[3]"This internal aspect of rules may be simply illustrated from the rules of any game. (. . .) [P]layers (. . .) have a reflective critical attitude to this pattern of behaviour: they regard it as a standard for all who play the game. (. . .) What is necessary is that there should be a critical reflective attitude to certain patterns of behaviour as a common standard, and that this should display itself in criticism (including self-criticism), demands for conformity, and in acknowledgements that such criticism and demands are justified, all of which find their characteristic expression in the normative terminology of 'ought', 'must', and 'should', 'right' and 'wrong'. . ." (Hart 1994, pp. 56–57).

[4]The words are by Fish, included however in an interview leaded by Gary Olson: "Insofar as one is ever critically reflective, one is critically reflective within the routines of a practice. (. . .) What most people want from critical reflectiveness is precisely a distance on the practice rather than what we might call a heightened degree of attention while performing in the practice. (. . .) Insofar as critical self-consciousness is a possible human achievement, it requires no special ability and cannot be cultivated as an independent value apart from particular situations: it's simply being normally reflective. It's not an abnormal, special – that is, theoretical - capacity. . ." (Olson 1992).

[5]"Lawyers serve the structures within which meaning is made, but they also subvert those structures as they make meaning" (Broekman and Backer 2013, p. vii).

[6]"Statements made from the external point of view may themselves be of different kinds. For the observer may, without accepting the rules himself, assert that the group accepts the rules, and thus

language from the outside whilst giving full play to their internal dimensions and the normativity these involve—or rather, if we want, *acknowledging* but not *taking up* an *internal point of view* (*IPOV*) [Postema 2011, pp. 286–287]. Does this "moderate" EPOV suffice in order to ensure an authentic "sharpening of awareness" concerning the "multilayered character of texts" and the "unison structures of legal cases" (Broekman and Backer 2013, p. 196)? Or is the "radical" or "extreme" EPOV—and the *theoretical cut* it introduces—here absolutely necessary, whilst treating normativity and linguistic facts as components of empirically explainable regularities[7] (even though "organised in narrative terms" and "treated as narrative typifications of action"[8])? Shouldn't we however go beyond this approach (and overcome its theoretical calculus), in order to support the view that the reflective parenthesis in question needs the perspective which Postema (reading Hart) identifies as an "alienated external point of view" (Postema 2011, pp. 287–289, 316, 333)? I just recall that this one is a practically (rather than merely theoretically) oriented perspective, involving, however, the mask of an agent who, recognizing the rules as grounds, guides or standards in the practical reasoning of others, does not take them as guides for his own decisions and actions[9]...

may from outside refer to the way in which they are concerned with them from the internal point of view." (Hart 1994, p. 89).

[7]"[W]e can if we choose occupy the position of an observer who does not even refer in this way to the internal point of view of the group. Such an observer is content merely to record the regularities of observable behaviour (...). If, however, the observer really keeps austerely to this extreme external point of view and does not give any account of the manner in which members of the group who accept the rules view their own regular behaviour, his description of their life cannot be in terms of rules at all, and so not in the terms of the rule-dependent notions of obligation or duty. Instead, it will be in terms of observable regularities of conduct, predictions, probabilities, and signs. ..." (Hart 1994, p. 89).

[8]This treatment presupposes the aim is to locate the regularities and their "stock of social knowledge" within a Greimassian semiotic "framework" (exploring the so-called "thematic level"): see Jackson (1995), pp. 140 ff. 143, 152–154.

[9]"Like Holmes's mythical (...) "bad man" or "malefactor", agents of all these kinds may take an intense practical interest in the law, but they do not regard it as providing them with standards by which to guide or evaluate their behavior, but only as something likely to stand in the way of the pursuit of their projects. They are, we might say, "alienated participants," viewing the law within the frame of their practical reasoning, and in that sense "from the inside," but still external to its operation as a "shared standard." We might call this the "alienated EPOV"..." (Postema 2011, p. 287).

3 The CLS's Interiorization of the Semiotic *Modus Operandi*: An Exemplary Manifestation of the Possibilities and Limits of the *Alienated EPOV*?

The last question provides us with an irresistible cue to consider the important role that, regarding the interiorization of the *semiotic modus operandi* and the critical perspective that it provides—with its Janus-like performance of "forms of meaning" that are simultaneously a manifestation of "fidelity" to the "legal system" and "an effort to remake it" (Broekman and Backer 2013, p. ix) –, our Authors attribute to CLS's legacy. Instead of reconstituting the reasons that authorize them to recognize "an unexpected coherence between semiotics and CLS in law" (Broekman and Backer 2013, p. 94) – reasons which privilege two decisive thematic cores (social power and the construction of subjectivity[10])[11] –, I will rather return to the

[10]"Outlines of critical studies with particular semiotic relevance lead us to the phenomenon of law's social power and the position of the subject in that field of power..." (Broekman and Backer 2013, p. 123). For a development, see Broekman and Backer (2013), pp. 123–125 ("The CLS themes"), and very specially the chapters 10, 11 and 14, respectively pp. 127 ff., 135 ff., 195 ff.

[11]This intertwinement between an immanent conception of power and the recreation of the subject as a (decentred) instance of the discourse has its significant roots in a productive assimilation of a very specific *critical-philosophical approach* (involving significantly different trends "within" *Critical Legal Studies* and *Postmodern Jurisprudences*), the construction of which, whilst resisting the *metanarratives of totality* opened up by Hegelian and Marxist discourses (if not directly the possibilities of *dialectic-materialist critical theories*), reconciles with a *sui generis* return to Aristotle two major (surprisingly diverse) legacies (more or less selectively overlapping!)... attributable to Kant and Nietzsche respectively. It is as if this *new critical attitude* or the practical philosophy, if not anti-philosophy, it engenders—*un questionnement sur les fondements [qui] n'est ni fondationaliste ni anti-fondationaliste* (Derrida 1994, p. 22)—reinvents on the one hand a contemporary genealogy of the practical worlds and their *continuum*, whilst on the other hand inscribing (integrating) an autonomous (quasi transcendental) reconstitution of *conditions of possibility/impossibility* within this genealogy. The first dimension responds to Nietzsche's heritage whilst assuming a narrative reconstruction of cultural practices irradiating from their *pudenda origo* (concentrating on problems of provenience-*Herkunft* and emergence-*Entstehung*), as well as imposing a specific rethinking of perspectivism, concerned with the immanent experimentation of *Wille zur Macht* (and the circularity between genealogical reconstruction and reconstructed practices), but equally with the unconditional celebration of the "young virtue" of *Redlichkeit* and its return to the *Text als Text,* freed from pre-determined interpretations (Seibert 2006, pp. 32–43). The second dimension involves in contrast a selective re-writing of Kantian arguments (and his differentiation of *rationality types*), presenting (recovering) these arguments as an indispensable chapter in the chain of *plurality thinking* (Welsch ^{3}1991, pp. 291–294), as well as the forerunners (through the *aesthetics of sublime*) of a rational treatment of singularity (Aguado 1994, pp. 31–36). Whilst not forgetting certain decisive heterodox constructive mediations — which include Saussure's *arbitrariness of sign thesis* and Wittgenstein's *interpretive pluralism*, Heidegger's claim *to think against Humanism* and Levinas' *experience of infinite responsibility* (overcoming every *ontic* and *ontological* discourse), as well as Lacan's and Legendre's *decentring of subjectivity and life*—the full articulation of these two main legacies is, in fact, decided in the interplay of three major contributions. The first derives from Foucault's *microphysics of power* (Foucault 1976, pp. 117–127)—and involves his archaeological and genealogical re-writing of *l'Âge de l'homme*, if not his *aesthetics of existence*—, the second assimilates Lyotard's disputes between *phrases* and

counterpoint *internal/external* systematized by Hart and Postema. This means actually highlighting CLS's unmistakable critical ethos—and its intertwining of engagement and distance (assimilating two opposed strategic constellations)—as an exemplary manifestation of the possibilities and limits of the *alienated external point of view*. To realize the complexity and subtlety with which this point of view is here constructed, two major contributions, involving different communities of jurists, certainly deserve specific consideration. Let me just identify them, whilst alluding to the global possibilities they open up.

The first contribution is due to Duncan Kennedy's *ultra-theory* (Altman 1990, pp. 164 ff.) and has to do with the experience of a certain *constrained activist judge*—seriously taken as an ideological strategist (Kennedy 1997, pp. 180 ff., 194–196, 219–223)[12]—and with the way this is permanently wounded by the challenges of a gap, conflict or polarity between the common (more or less reified) perception of Law and legal materials and his initial sense of the desirable outcomes to be produced (and the correspondent ideological justification)[13]—challenges which justify an apparently (but only apparently!) enigmatic projection on the binomial *easy cases/hard cases*, for once decisively inverted...

> [A]n easy case in the conventional sense is a hard case from the point of view of the ideological strategist (...), in the sense that it will be difficult, it may take a lot of work, and it may be impossible to displace the obvious solution (...). A hard case in terms of the lawyers' typology is an easy case for the ideological strategist, since in a hard case there are two plausible rule choices, rather than only one obvious one. A hard case is by definition one in which the judge who prefers a particular rule choice won't have to confront an initial probability of failing to make a plausible legal argument for it — what makes it hard is

genres de discours—as well as his *incommensurability theorem* (Welsch [3]1991, pp. 251–256) and his *experience of community as a promise* (Lyotard 1990, pp. 61–84)—, the third assumes Derrida's *pragrammatological interpretation* (Derrida 1988, p. 159, note 16) and the way in which this (as a specific "intersection of a pragmatics and a grammatology") involves the *justice /deconstruction* connection, as well as a certain *economy of violence* (*une philosophie de la non-violence qui [choisit] la moindre violence*)[Derrida 1967, p. 136, note 1]. It is as if we were invoking the (reunited or separated) spells of a *political "morality"* (based on the Foucauldian experience of an immanent capillary network of *powers* and *resistances*), of an *aesthetics/anaesthetics of the sublime* (justified through a Lyotardian reinvention of Kant's *reflexive judgment*) and a radically autonomous *ethics of alterity* (committed to the Derridean translation of Levinas' *infinite responsibility*). For a less schematic exploration of this stimulating reflective puzzle (distributed among the different stages or generations of CLS scholarship), see Linhares 2016b, pp. 88–98, 98 ff. For a synthesis of this complex heritage, as well as a critic consideration of its projection in law and legal thinking regarding the binomial *singularity/concreteness* (with the formulations reproduced in this note), see Linhares (2020), pp. 86–90.

[12] "[A] judge with an ideological preference for an outcome can work to make that outcome law. (...) I suggest three typical postures that judges adopt as workers conscious of the possibility of pursuing ideological strategies. These are the postures of the constrained activist, the difference splitter, and the bipolar judge..." (Kennedy 1997, p. 180).

[13] "This is a conflict(...) or polarity (...) or gap (...) between "the law"(...) or the common perception of "the law" and HIWTCO (...), between my initial impression of the law and my initial sense of 'how I want to come out'..." (Kennedy 1986/92, pp. 45, 46, 86).

that with minimum work or at first blush it is obvious that there is no obvious answer... (Kennedy 1997, p. 166).

The second contribution, due to Roberto Mangabeira Unger's (explicitly assumed) *super-theoretical* approach, focuses on the territory of legal dogmatics and on the critique of *formalism* (Unger 1983/86, pp. 2–4, 8–14) which, exploring the binomial *center/periphery*, allows an *expanded* version of legal doctrine, presented as *deviationist doctrine* (Unger 1983/86, pp. 14–22, 43 ff., 88–90; Linhares 2008, pp. 469–470). The issue at stake is not actually just about an internal dynamic exercise—moving peripheral doctrines toward the centre and core doctrines toward the periphery—, it reflects also the experience of a decisive macroscopic counterpoint "between a dominant ideology" and "a day-to-day experience"—the first one putting "impersonal law at the center of society", the second restituting "such law" to the "periphery" (Unger 1976, p. 44).[14]

The simple allusion to these possibilities and their argumentative intertwinement—if not their *nested oppositions,* in the productive deconstructive sense we owe to Jack Balkin (Balkin 1998, pp. 221–235)—suffices in fact to understand the main problem-challenge which, according to CLS's reconstitution (and its assimilation of a immanent experience of power), every *jurist* (whatever role he/she plays) unavoidably faces: the problem-challenge of exploring a (smaller or wider) spectrum of *possibilities of decision* (or *decision-performance*), whilst assuming on one hand the compossibility with the binding legal materials and on the other hand the unavoidability and transparence of an *ideological choice*. Justified (unified) through the reference to a common (more or less undetermined) legally binding frame, but no less distinguished (autonomized) as alternatives from the perspective of their predictable political-societal *outcomes*—outcomes which are not only relevant in legislative production but also in adjudication and doctrinal creation—, these possibilities are actually conceived of as if they were disputed by two polarized strategies, a dominant one (covered by the *formalist* mask)—tending towards the conservative reproduction of "entrenched divisions and hierarchies" (Unger 1996, p. 163)—and an alternative critical one, committed to the progressive "moderation" and dismantling of these "divisions" (Kennedy 1983/92, pp. 427 ff.). Regardless of the critical-interpretive problem that, concerning the reconstitution *qua tale* (and its meta-discursive approach), the rigorous identification of these two strategies (and their opportunities of balancing and practical effectivity) indisputably raise, the possibility of treating the leading perspective as an *alienated external point of view* (creating a kind of an intentional *continuum* between a meta-discursive critical interpretation and the legally relevant reconstituted practices) only becomes understandable in its complexity (in its *nested* intertwinement of signifiers, as well as powers and resistances) when we pay attention to a pair of fundamental (more or less implicit) assumptions: the first referring to a constitutive overlapping of explanatory and transformative intentions—which, with Dworkin, we could say that involves

[14]For a detailed reconstitution of the steps involved in this critical approach, see Linhares (2016b), pp. 102–105 and Gaudêncio (2011), pp. 63–89.

two types or genres of interpretation or interpretive enterprise, named *explanatory* and *collaborative* (Dworkin 2011, pp. 135 ff.)[15]—, the second developing a basic *indeterminacy* (and *indeterminacy-generating*) *thesis* concerning legal materials and their *communication modes*, the peculiar complexity of which is less in the different versions it allows—going from aggravated uncertainty and *underdeterminacy* (Solum 1987, pp. 472 ff.) to full *undecidability* (Linhares 2017, 138–143)—than in the way it overlaps diverse reflective attitudes, which (using again Dworkin's formulations) we could identify as *internal* and *external* modes of *skepticism* (Dworkin 2011, pp. 90 ff.). It is as if we should conclude that, just as a "demystifying explanatory interpretation" can only successfully achieve its objective (its "proper role) of "radically" changing "opinion and practice" when it wears a "collaborative clothing" (Dworkin 2011, p. 144), so too the attitude of *internal skepticism (within the enterprise of interpretation)* does provide a condition of an *efficient* jurist's game (and his/her Janus-like performance of fidelity and subversion) only when this skepticism is able to appear convincingly masked as a *default thesis* (or *default position*) and as such meta-discursively legitimized or protected (if not disguised) as a plausible manifestation of *external skepticism (outside and about the enterprise of interpretation)* [Dworkin 1986, pp. 78–79, Dworkin 2011, pp. 44, 91]... Aren't these however good reasons to admit that this Janus-like identity (and its productive practical *circularity*, involving commitment and critical reflection) should also be *searched for* outside of this specific ground, if not rejecting its *sui generis* EPOV (and the reductive treatment of *law as politics* that it demands)? I think they are.

4 Answering Paths

The search for a "safe place" (freed from "the din and confusion of partisan struggle")[16] is certainly not an easy task, since the intended answers or answering paths (concerning the possibilities of criticisms and their connections to internal or external points of view) are not separable from the limit-situation which we experience, a *Grenzsituation* in which the paradoxical conjugation of self-celebrating plurality (if not incommensurability) and homogenizing globalization (with its detersive standardization) permanently challenges the possibilities of Law and the plausibility of juridically relevant argumentation.

[15]"Collaborative interpretation assumes that the object of interpretation has an author or a creator and that the author has begun a project that the interpreter tries to advance. (...) Explanatory interpretation pressuposes something different: not that interpreters are in partnership with those who created some object or event, but that an event has some particular significance for the audience the interpreter addresses." (Dworkin 2011, pp. 135–136).

[16]These words are evidently by Fish, in his well-know diagnosis on political correctness: "It is not that there are no choices to make or means of making them; it is just that the choices as well as the means are inextricable from the din and confusion of partisan struggle. There is no safe place" (Fish 1994, p. 115).

4.1 Considering the First Ensemble of Questions

I would start by stating the obvious: in a time of many and varied crises, in which we witness (also at the microscopic level of the case) an uncontrolled *emergence of complexity* (which is also the loss of naturalness concerning discourses and their borders or, more strictly, the loss of the possibility of recognizing a univocal *doing what comes naturally*), hetero-referential approaches and other external gazes (considering legal relevant discourses and practices, if not *juridicalness* as such, as plausible objects to be described or explained or reconstituted) offer certainly a crucial *information base*, the need for which (or the indispensability of which) the claim for *professional correctness*, although very persuasively defended—as it happens with Fish (1995)...—, is today in no position to discuss, let alone reject. The disagreement with Fish goes further, however. Whilst defending the inevitability of *external* contributions and the resources they make available, I certainly also defend (and certainly no less vehemently) the point that the corresponding *external points of view* do not replace an *internal critical perspective* nor satisfactorily compensate for its eventual absence; in saying this, however, I am presupposing and demanding an *internal critical approach* which (versus Fish) is certainly irreducible to the mere intensification of attention required by the game and its discursive routines.

With regard to the possible intention of substitution or compensation, what I mean is not so much that external approaches should avoid constitutive claims justifying regulative interferences (conforming or shaping the discursive practices which they describe, explain or reconstitute), but rather that these approaches (no matter what they are or what their relevant contribution is) should unambiguously preserve their *external identity*—not only in themselves but also when they are selectively (and properly) assimilated. In order to preserve this identity (either as such or in its eventual reception process), it is not necessary to reject every *one-sided projection* (entirely deployed from *external* categories of intelligibility and their presuppositions), it is only and in contrast indispensable to avoid unilateral projections *which are not immediately recognized or recognizable as such* (and which thus introduce the risk of treating law and legal thinking as apparent interlocutors or as pieces of a dialogical structure that does not actually exist).

This simple constructive recommendation, albeit roughly formulated, brings us the *first answer* or *answering path*, since what has just been said about external perspectives in general is certainly also valid for legal semiotics in particular: valid for legal semiotics when we admit that we must contain it within a more descriptively analytical trend (justifying a *moderate external point of view*), but also when, in the name of a naturalistic epistemology and a realistic ontology of the modes of meaning, we attribute to its perspective-subject a dominantly empirical and explanatory intention (deploying an *external radical point of view* addressed to the facts of the language); but also and still when, on the border with the exercises of Deconstruction, we associate legal semiotics to an immanent critical reflection, unveiling every microscopic manifestation of practice and discourse as a multidirectional web of powers and resistances or celebrating singularity from the perspective of contextual instability or incommensurability (opening up the doors to an *alienated external point of view*).

4.2 Considering the Second Ensemble of Questions

What about the second answering path? Two brief remarks must suffice here.

I begin identifying the *internal critical approach* which (I think) contemporary legal discourse should not *do without*—the urgency of which our context of crisis has exemplarily accentuated (Neves 2008, pp. 9 ff., 101 ff., Linhares 2012b, pp. 497–501, Linhares 2016a, pp. 432–443). I mean a jurists' reflection, developed (lived) *from the inside* by those who take Law as their *form of life*—i.e. as a specific way of creating intersubjective meanings, following a persistent, albeit permanently reinvented, *claim to autonomy*—, but no less a *radical critical reflection* (and with a manifest potential of *subversion*). This intertwinement of *commitment* and *critic* has certainly to do with the persistent recreation of a microscopic community (made of *comparable* equals and an analogically conceived experience of *concreteness*), but it has mainly to do with the constitutive awareness, pursued at different dogmatic and meta-dogmatic levels, of the identity and limits of this Law—seriously taken as a *certain* Law (*inscribed* in the *possibilities* of the Western Text) and as such experienced as a *non universal* (culturally plausible and civilizationally moulded) artefact [Linhares 2020, pp. 90–98 ("The invention of concreteness and its argument of continuity")]. To explore this *internal practical ethos* means actually considering a complex relationship between *dogmatic stabilizing* and *problem-solving* practices, as well as acknowledging the challenges of plurality and fragmentation or the way these wound or fragilize the claim to *communitarian validity* and with it the practical consonance of principles, conceived of as *foundational warrants* and incorporated or «objectified» *jus* (Linhares 2018b). It means however also questioning the plausible contemporary endurance or congruence of the form of life itself, exploring the meaning of an *argument of continuity* and as such discussing the persistence or the survival of *jus* and its practical world (Linhares 2018a, pp. 244 ff., 248-253, 254 ff., 259–262).

If on the one hand I insist that this *internal critique* is truly precious and cannot be successfully replaced by an *external perspective* (whatever it may be), I cannot, on the other hand, fail to recognize the productivity of the semiotic *modus operandi* and its contributions, when properly assimilated by that perspective. If this *internal ethos* needs these resources (and if it assimilates *them* successfully), it is not actually to develop a *legal semiotic work*, it is rather to pursue its own path and thus participate in the experience of its *form of life* and in the reinvention of its *system of meaning*.

As this is basically the second remark I would like to introduce, allow me to conclude by completing it with two possible examples, both of them inspired by Greimasian narrative grammar.

With the first I want to emphasize the importance of the counterpoint between *communications sociales généralisées* and *communications sociales restraintes* -- associated with the notion of semiotic group and the process of narrativization of shared structures of understanding (Greimas 1976, pp. 45 ff., 53–60, Jackson 1995, pp. 93–98, 154–158, 393–397, 424 ff.). This counterpoint is certainly very productive when we develop a semiotic description or explanation of legal phenomena (led either by a still moderate or an already radical EPOV), it is however also a precious resource when we explore *legal reality* and its *law in action* from a *critical-reflective internal point of view.* Following Castanheira Neves, this means in fact treating this reality and its ensemble of institutional situations not as a simple *material presupposition* or *application field* (where legal normativity should be projected), but as an authentic specifying *stratum* or *layer* of the *legal system*, seriously taken as a decisive component of its content (Neves 1971–1972, pp. 347–351, Neves 1995, pp. 56–58, 172–174). The internal reflexive opportunity which this resource (when properly assimilated) stimulates has certainly much to do with the methodological implications of a *judgement of (global or partial) obsolescence*—assuming in concrete the lack of effectiveness of formally binding statutory rules, i.e. the lack of correspondence of these rules with the institutional situations of juridically relevant or juridically assimilated reality (Neves 1993, pp. 149, 151ff, 157 ff., 176 ff,. 182–184) –, its main autonomous relevance concerns however another (much less explored) issue, this one explicitly considering the impact which different *internal perspectives*—justifying, the multiplication of *interpretative communities* or the stabilisation of differentiated *sociolects,* projected in diverse ensembles of *legally relevant canons*—*do* effectively *have* today in the determination of Law in general and principles in particular (Linhares 2018b, pp. 118–120)[17]...

The second example is about proof in legal context, or more precisely about the need to explore a radical alternative to the *correspondence theory of truth* which allows us to understand an internally relevant *thesis for methodological unity* between evidentiary adjudication and adjudication tout court, if we want between *quaestio facti* and *quaestio juris* (Linhares 2012a). The resources are concerned here with the way that Bernard Jackson refines the claim for narrative coherence, freeing

[17]This possibility of determination, with its «local contexts, that are stabilized, if only temporarily, by assumptions already and invisibly in place (Fish 1994, pp. 190–191) is particularly interesting, since its *doing what comes naturally*, regarding the internal point of view of differentiated communities of jurists (judges, lawyers, prosecutors, academics, etc), all pursuing *disciplinary identity* in their own way (whilst confronting the coherence issues which this identity demands) seems, for once, directly accessible, both from a *moderate external point of view* considering *interpretive communities*—i.e. giving the stabilized practices the regulative intelligibility of flexible (*non-monolithic*) codes, canons, textualization and re-textualization procedures and standard examples that can be *confidently followed* and are also *capable of being transformed* coherently, as long as the game is played (Fish 1989, pp. 141ff., 150–153)—or from a *less moderate* (or even a *radical* or *extreme*) one involving *semiotic groups*—reconstituting those practices less as *rules* or *canons* than as *regularities*, albeit preserving a significant sensitivity to their explicit *narrative configuration*, i.e. giving them the productive shape of falsifiable "narrative typifications of action", operating within their own system of semantic values (Jackson 1995, pp.154 ff.).

it from compromises with a *triadic* realistic-referential epistemology (and even from the pragmaticist version justified by Peirce), and restoring it unequivocally to the horizon of a purely *intensional* understanding of meaning.[18] They concern also the possibility of treating "truth" not as "a function of discourse" but of the "enunciation of the discourse", which means "narrativising the pragmatics of the act of enunciation" ("the act of making a truth-claim") or, if we want to defend the notion that "basic structures of signification must apply to the intelligibility of the pragmatics of discourse, as much as to its semantics" (Jackson 1988a, pp. 33–36, 71 ff., 76 ff., 84–88, 112–129, 143 ff., Jackson 1988b, pp. 227 ff., 244 ff., Jackson 1995, pp. 159 e ss, 356, 432 ff.). It is precisely this need to pay attention either to the *narrativised semantics of the case* or to its *narrativised pragmatics*—projected in the indispensable counterpoint between *the story in the trial* and *the story of the trial*, i.e. between "the events in the outside world which are to be adjudicated in the trial" and "the events in the trial process which make sense as meaningful acts of enunciation and other forms of meaningful behaviour"—that opens up the opportunity to explore the evidence discourse (and the referential uses it institutionalises, combined with constitutive claims to *juridicalness* or *juridicity*) as a "participated texture",[19] if not explicitly as a juridical dispute involving opposing different stories or, rather, *rival versions of one story*, "vying for supremacy"(Jackson 1988b, pp. 226–227 (1.), 232–234, 1988a, pp. 58, 82–88, 1995, 390 ff (cap. XI), 424 e ss, 441–442, 445–452)—with the certainty that the defence of this claim does not deny (or dilute) the specificity of the evidence problem, but instead provides this specificity with new opportunities to be understood and experienced in direct connection with the (increasing!) need to identify law's specific *project* and its autonomous *practical world* as an unmistakable cultural acquisition, whilst simultaneously discussing its practical-cultural continuity. To condense the argument, I would say that *methodological unity* has to do with the priority of controversy—as a specific practical structure demanding *judgment* and the constitutive entrance of the *comparing Third*—, whereas the specificity of evidential judgment corresponds to the irradiance of the referential claim and the *narrative intelligibility* that identifies it. Is this an approach that only a *critical internal point of view* can productively develop and argumentatively justify? I would say it is, without forgetting however that the mobilized analytical resources (effectively assimilated, even though preserving their original identity) owe their transparency and rigor to the fruitful stimulus of the *external semiotic modus operandi* which has created them.

[18]This means that "sense" is here "a function of the relationships within a system of meaning of individual sense-bearing elements, sometimes called signs, while *reference* is something that human beings do with that already-established 'sense' of the signs, including, modifying it" (Jackson 1996, p. 248).

[19]The expression *textura discursiva participable* is not from Jackson but from Calvo González (1993), pp. 28, 30–34, 39, 52, 77, 87–88, 91–92.

References

Aguado MP (1994) Ästhetik des Erhabenen. Burke, Kant, Adorno, Lyotard. Passagen Verlag, Wien
Altman A (1990) Critical legal studies. A liberal critique. Princeton University Press, Princeton
Balkin J (1998) Cultural software. A theory of ideology. Yale University Press, Yale
Broekman J/Backer LC (2013) Lawyers making meaning. The semiotics of law in legal education II. Springer, Dordrecht
Calvo González J (1993) El discurso de los hechos. Narrativismo en la interpretación operativa. Editorial Tecnos, Madrid
Derrida J. (1967) L'écriture et la différence. Éditions du Seuil, Paris
Derrida J (1988) Limited Inc. Northwestern University Press, Evanston
Derrida J (1994) Force de loi. Le "fondement mystique de l´autorité". Galilée, Paris
Dworkin R (1986) Law's Empire. The Belknap Press of Harvard University Press, Cambridge Mass
Dworkin R (2011) Justice for Hedgehogs. The Belknap Press of Harvard University Press, Cambridge
Fish S (1989) Doing what comes naturally. Duke University Press, Durham/London
Fish S (1994) There's no such thing as free speech and it's a good thing, too. Oxford University Press, Oxford/New York
Fish S (1995) Professional correctness: literary studies and political change. Harvard University Press, Cambridge
Fish S (1999) The trouble with principle. Harvard University Press, Cambridge
Foucault M (1976) L'Histoire de la sexualité, I, La volonté de savoir. Gallimard, Paris
Gaudêncio AM (2011) Entre o centro e a periferia: a perspectivação ideológico-política da dogmática jurídica e da decisão judicial no Critical Legal Studies Movement., Lumen Juris, Rio de Janeiro
Greimas A (1976) Sémiotique et sciences sociales. Éditions du Seuil, Paris
Hart HLA (1994) The concept of law, 2nd edn. with Postscript. Clarendon Press, Oxford
Jackson BS (1988a) Law, fact and narrative coherence. Deborah Charles Publications, Liverpool.
Jackson BS (1988b) Narrative models in legal proof. Int J Semiot Law I(3):225–246
Jackson BS (1995) Making sense in law. Deborah Charles Publications, Liverpool
Jackson BS (1996) Making sense in Jurisprudence. Deborah Charles Publications, Liverpool
Kennedy D (1983/92) The politics of hierarchy. In: Boyle (ed) Critical Legal Studies. New York University Press, Dartmouth, pp 427–446
Kennedy D (1986/92) Freedom and constraint in adjudication: a critical phenomenology. In: Boyle (ed) Critical legal studies. New York University Press, Dartmouth: 45-89
Kennedy D (1997) A Critique of Adjudication (fin de siècle). Harvard University Press, Cambridge
Linhares JMA (2008) Rechtsdogmatik, Autonomie und Reduktion der Komplexität. Brauchen die Gerichte eine Sicherheitsnetz ? In: Schweighofer et al. (ed) Komplexitätsgrenzen der Rechtsinformatik. Tagungsband des 11. Internationalen Rechtsinformatik Symposions Iris 2008. Boorberg Verlag, Stuttgart, pp 463–472
Linhares JMA (2012a) Evidence (or Proof?) as Law´s Gaping Wound: a Persistent False Aporia? Boletim da Faculdade de Direito, 88, tomo 1: 65–89
Linhares JMA (2012b) Law's cultural project and the claim to universality or the equivocalities of a familiar debate. Int J Semiot Law 25:489–503
Linhares JMA (2016a) In defense of a non-positivist separation thesis between law and morality, Rechtsphilosophie. Zeitschrift für Grundlagen des Rechts 4:425–443
Linhares JMA (2016b) A identidade na pluralidade dos Critical Legal Scholars. Um discurso da dialéctica societas/communitas? Revista da Faculdade de Direito da Universidade Lusófona do Porto 8(8):83–130
Linhares JMA (2017) O binómio casos fáceis/casos difíceis e a categoria de inteligibilidade sistema jurídico. Um contraponto indispensável no mapa do discurso jurídico contemporâneo? Imprensa da Universidade de Coimbra, Coimbra

Linhares JMA (2018a) Law and Opera as practical-cultural artefacts, or the productivity and limits of a plausible counterpoint. In: Manzin et al (eds) Multimodal Argumentation. Pluralism and Images of Law (Studies on Argumentation and Legal Philosophy). Università degli Studi di Trento, Trento, pp 241–266.
Linhares JMA (2018b) The Claim for "Consonance" between Principles and Problem-Solving Practices: The Challenge of Plurality and the Indispensable Mediation of Juristenrecht. In: Linhares et al (ed) Jurists' Law and European Identity. Dogmatic-institutional, Methodological and Legal-philosophical Problems. IJ (UCILeR), Coimbra, pp 107–127
Linhares JMA (2020) Exemplarity as concreteness, or the challenge of institutionalising a productive circle between past and present, old and new. In: Condello A (ed) New rhetorics for contemporary legal discourse. Edinburgh University Press, Edinburgh
Lyotard JF (1990) Pérégrinations. Loi, forme, évènement. Galilée, Paris
Neves AC (1971–72) Curso de Introdução ao estudo do direito. Lições proferidas a um curso do 1° ano da Faculdade de Direito de Coimbra, no ano lectivo de 1971-72. Coimbra: Policop.
Neves AC (1993) Metodologia jurídica. Problemas fundamentais. Coimbra Editora, Coimbra
Neves AC (1995) Digesta – escritos acerca do direito, do pensamento jurídico, da sua metodologia e outros, vol 2. Coimbra Editora, Coimbra
Neves AC (2008) Digesta – escritos acerca do direito, do pensamento jurídico, da sua metodologia e outros, vol 3. Coimbra Editora, Coimbra
Olson G (1992) Fish tales: a conversation with "The Contemporary Sophist". J Adv Composit 12(2):253–277. Retrieved July 23, 2021, from http://www.jstor.org/stable/20865856
Postema G (2011) Legal philosophy in the twentieth century: the common law world (A Treatise of Legal Philosophy and General Jurisprudence), vol 11. Springer, Dordrecht
Seibert ThM (2006) Dekonstruktion der Gerechtigkeit? In: Buckel et al (ed) Neue Theorien des Rechts. Suhrkamp, Stuttgart, pp 29–55
Solum L (1987) On the indeterminacy crisis: critiquing critical dogma. Univ Chicago Law Rev 54(462):462–503
Unger RM (1976) Law in modern society. Toward a criticism of social theory. The Free Press, New York
Unger RM (1983/86) The critical legal studies movement. Harvard University Press, Cambridge Mass
Unger RM (1996) What Should legal analysis become? Verso, London
Welsch W (^{3}1991) Unsere postmoderne Moderne. Acta Humaniora, Weinheim

On the Life and Work of Tikhon Fedorovich Stepanov

William E. Butler

Abstract This article addresses for the first time in English the life and career of Tikhon Fedorovich Stepanov (1795–1847), author of the first treatise/textbook in the Russian Empire devoted to public international law but never published in full to this day.

It is entirely appropriate in the world of semiotics to note that the 90th year of Professor Jan Broekman coincided with the ninetieth anniversary of the birth of Roberta Kevelson (1931–1998), whose legacy in the field of legal semiotics Jan commemorated through the establishment of the Roberta Kevelson Seminar on Law and Semiotics at Penn State Dickinson Law. Kevelson was a professor at one of the commonwealth campuses in the University, not at Dickinson Law. When I learned from Jan several years ago that Kevelson's personal archive had been discovered in a Texas storage unit and could be acquired for the back rental costs, I persuaded the Dean of the Law School to acquire them. Jan processed the archive, which was later transferred to the custody of Professor Larry Backer at Penn State Law in University Park, within the same University.

When Jan arrived at Dickinson Law in Carlisle, I attended his inaugural seminar over the entire semester. He had a loyal following of bright students who produced excellent seminar papers. The subject of legal semiotics is daunting, deeply philosophical and jurisprudential, intellectually challenging, with its own vocabulary and concepts—many of which originated with Jan. He taught the seminar well and then

An earlier version of this article appeared in Jus Gentium: Journal of International Legal History, II (2017), pp. 607–686, together with an English translation of Chapter 1 of the Stepanov treatise.

W. E. Butler (✉)
Penn State Dickinson Law, Carlisle, PA, USA

University College London, London, UK

National Academy of Sciences of Ukraine, Kyiv, Ukraine

National Academy of Legal Sciences of Ukraine, Kyiv, Ukraine
e-mail: web15@psu.edu

F. Fleerackers (ed.), *The Rearguard of Subjectivity*, Law and Visual Jurisprudence 9,
https://doi.org/10.1007/978-3-031-26855-7_2

instituted a series of conferences, to which I contributed a paper on the founder of Dickinson Law, John Reed (1786–1850), later published in one of his volumes. Until I listened to Jan, I would not have imagined that my piece was relevant to legal semiotics—but I underestimated the field, which was a lesson in itself.

Just as many continental colleagues, Jan was a connoisseur of fine wine. I learned this the hard way, being assigned by the Faculty to take Jan for lunch to a local restaurant, where he ordered and promptly, upon tasting, rejected the house white wine with some rude comments to the waiter. The restaurant has now disappeared.

Turning to the subject at hand, in 1847 a two-volume treatise on public international law was completed by a Russian/Ukrainian international lawyer, Tikhon Fedorovich Stepanov (1795–1847), but never published. Although the Russian censor had approved the manuscript for publication, it is presumed that Stepanov's untimely death precluded its appearance. For decades the manuscript was believed to have been lost or to have been destroyed during the Second World War and was so recorded in Grabar's history of the literature of international law in Russia published in 1958.[1] In 1960 the manuscript was reported to have been discovered and identified in the Archive of Kharkov University in Ukraine.[2] At present the manuscript is held by the Central State Historical Archive of Ukraine in the City of Kyiv, fond 2055, delo 5.[3]

More recently, an earlier manuscript, believed to date from 1844 and possibly compiled by a student(s) who attended the Stepanov lectures, was located by Oleg Tarasov at Kharkov in the Archive of Rare Publications and Manuscripts of the Library of the V. N. Karazin Kharkov National University.[4] The first and last pages of the manuscript are lacking, which complicates the determination of authorship, and the place and year of composition are absent. On the basis of internal evidence, however, the 1844 manuscript most certainly is the earliest extant version of the Stepanov treatise, notwithstanding early doubts.[5]

Stepanov was born at Voronezh, Russia.[6] After completing studies at the Voronezh Theological Seminary in 1814, he enrolled at Kharkov University in the

[1] See Grabar (1990), p. 303.

[2] Semenov and Ul'ianova (1961), pp. 243–254.

[3] Denysov and Savchuk (2004), p. 38. Denysov and Savchuk transcribed the first chapter of the manuscript, composed in the Russian language, for the aforementioned Anthology. The translation in *Jus Gentium* is based on their version in ibid., VIII, pp. 39–72.

[4] Право народов и Дипломатия: рукопись (1844) 476. Bound in paper boards. Gift of Professor Andrei Nikolaevich Stoianov (1831–1907). Without indication of authorship, place, year or final page(s). Classification number in Library catalogue: 938 1841/C. See Tarasov (2020), pp. 641–647. Tarasov transcribed the Table of Contents of the manuscript together with fragments of the text; these were translated by W. E. Butler to accompany Tarasov's Note in *Jus Gentium.*

[5] See Tarasov (2001), pp. 169–175.

[6] This biographical sketch draws upon Grabar (1990); Semenov and Ul'ianova (1961); Denysov and Savchuk (2004); Levitskii (2007), pp. 277–279; F. K. (1999), pp. 398–399; Savchuk (2004a), pp. 284–288; Savchuk (2004b), p. 646; Savchuk (2019), pp 779–781; Savchuk (1980), p. 62; Savchuk (1901), p. 596.

Faculty of Morals and Politics. During his early years at University, he attended lectures on politics and language, and during his 3rd year, on Roman law and physics. He graduated in 1819 with the degree of kandidat "with distinction", only to see the degree retracted, together with several other students, as a result of a denunciation of the University by a trustee. He resat the examinations in 1821 and received the degree of kandidat of legal sciences.

In 1823 he found employment as an instructor in universal history and geography at the Kharkov Institute of Noble Maidens and took various part-time appointments in local boarding schools, including the De Roberti boys boarding school. He defended a dissertation on political equilibrium for which the degree of magister of political history and statistics was conferred in 1824 by Kharkov University. At about this time, the Rector of Kharkov University offered Stepanov appointment to the Chair of Russian Law; the offer was declined partly because Stepanov was not interested in this subject and partly because he intended to pursue a civil service career. From July 1830 to 1831 he removed to St. Petersburg to take up a civil service position in the State Commission for the Repayment of Debts.

During his years in Kharkov and St. Petersburg, Stepanov did not produce works of scholarship in the disciplines of economics, political economy, or law; however, he did devote himself energetically to a large number of journal and newspaper articles on philosophical topics and matters of political economy during the 1820–1830s.[7] Those published between 1830 and 1832 he deployed to advantage to seek appointment to a University position.

So it was that in 1832 he returned to Kharkov University in the position of professor *extraordinarius* in the Chair of Political Economy and once more a lecturer at the Institute of Noble Maidens; he was elevated to professor *ordinarius* in 1836. He served as a Syndic of Kharkov University from 1833 to 1834.[8] He was elected Dean of the Faculty of Morals and Politics in 1835 and in 1837 became Pro-Rector of Kharkov University. In 1839 he was assigned to supervise the instructional component in the Pedagogical Institute formed within the Kharkov University with the rank and title of Director.

The 1835 General Statute on Imperial Russian Universities enhanced the status of international law or the law of nations ("all-people's law", or "people's law")[9] in the University curriculum. Stepanov was assigned to lecture on this subject as from 1837. This doubtless became the occasion for writing his treatise on the subject. It is

[7]These all seem to be devoted to political economy. An extensive list is given by F. K. (1999), p. 399. Reference is made to an unpublished manuscript attributed to the period 1824 to 1826 "On Philosophical and Political-Diplomatic Principles", whose whereabouts is unknown.

[8]Under the 1804 Statute on universities in the Russian Empire, a Syndic was an administrative position filled by a member of the professorial staff to assist with judicial matters within the University, including the preparation of decisions by a University court in accordance with University statutes and State laws. A Syndic served on the Board of the University with the right of a consultative vote and might be delegated to represent the University in administrative or judicial proceedings connected with the University.

[9]The term "international law" was not introduced until the 1863 University Statute.

confirmed that Stepanov offered the course on international law during the academic year 1844/1845 at Kharkov University.[10]

Stepanov taught at Kharkov until 1845, when ill-health forced him to retire. He died in 1847 not long after completing his treatise on international law. An autobiography completed in 1845 or 1846 (the sources differ on the date) remains unpublished. Levitskii had access to this material when he prepared his history of the Kharkov law faculty.[11]

Stepanov's intellectual legacy in the field of international law will not be fully appreciated until the publication of the complete text of his two-volume treatise. Grabar had a high opinion of Stepanov on the basis of what was known about his approach to the law of nations. Stepanov was, Grabar wrote, an ". . . original thinker" who equal was "difficult to find . . . among foreign international lawyers". Among Russian international lawyers, Grabar believed that Stepanov occupied ". . . a place second only to V. A. Nezabitovskii".[12] F. K., on the other hand, commenting principally on the basis of Stepanov's contributions to political economy rather than public international law, described Stepanov as more an ". . . eclectic and gifted publicist than an independent and profound scholar", although acknowledging that Stepanov was rightly considered to be the best specialist on political economy, an outstanding and talented lecturer who had a significant influence upon his audience, a man deeply sincere, eloquent, and honorable, and of enormous impact in his discipline.[13] His former student, M. De Poulet, described Stepanov as a talented and eloquent lecturer who treated critically the realities of the time, "opposing them in a most courageous and passionate way".[14]

Until the publication of the excerpt from Stepanov's treatise, what little we have known about his approach to the law of nations was based upon the inaugural lecture which he delivered upon his appointment to the Chair of Political Economy in 1832. This lecture addressed the essence, importance, and purpose of the political sciences and was plainly drawn upon by Stepanov when composing the first chapter of his

[10] See Обозрение преподавания предметов в Императорском Харьковском университете на 1844/45 учебный год [Survey of Teaching of Subjects in the Imperial Kharkov University in 1844/45 Academic Year] (1844), pp. 15–16; Обозрение преподавания предметов в Императорском Харьковском университете на 1845/46 учебный год [Survey of Teaching of Subjects in the Imperial Kharkov University for the 1845/46 Academic Year] (1845), p. 16; Отчет о состоянии Императорского Харьковского университета за 1844/45 академический год и Речи, произнесенные в торжественном собрании 30 августа 1846 года [Report on the State of the Imperial Kharkov University for the 1844/45 Academic Year and Address Delivered at the Ceremonial Assembly on 30 August 1846] (1846), p. 9; Отчет о состоянии Императорского Харьковского университета за 1845/46 академический год, составленный по поручению Совета, Орд. Проф., доктором прав, Иваном Платоновым [Report on the State of the Imperial Kharkov University in the 1845/46 Academic Year Compiled on Behalf of the Council by Professor Ordinarius, Doctor of Laws, Ivan Platonov] (1846), p. 15. See Tarasov (2020).

[11] Levitskii (2007), p. 277.

[12] Grabar (1990), p. 303.

[13] F. K. (1999), p. 399.

[14] De Poulet (1874a), pp. 75–115; De Poulet (1874b), pp. 565–588.

treatise some years later.[15] Many passages in the texts are nearly identical; the views which he expressed in 1833[16] had not been significantly revised.

It should be noted that Stepanov anticipated Nezabitovskii in treating as subjects of "all-people's law" not only peoples, but people; that is individuals or natural persons (whom he calls "inseparables" throughout his text). He actually used the expression human rights in connection with their belonging to natural persons as subjects of all-people's law. The translation distinguishes sharply between the two expressions used in the time of Stepanov and earlier in Russia: "people's law" [народное право] and "all-people's law" [всенародное право], which later became, inspired by Jeremy Bentham (1748–1832), "international law" [международное право]. Many translate all of these terms as the law of nations [право народов] or as international law, but to do so would lose the nuances embodied in the original Russian terms (one of which may be that natural persons are subjects of "people's law" or "all-people's law") or deprive us of the ability to draw distinctions based upon the use of these four terms. There can be little doubt that in each case the Russian (or Ukrainian) author is offering a Russian language version of the *jus gentium*.

In general, Stepanov is using the views of Professor Georg Friedrich Martens (1756–1821), of Gőttingen University, as a foil for his remarks. Martens often was referred to in Stepanov's manuscript as the "writer" or the "publicist".

The passages from the two-volume treatise have little to say about diplomacy. Something of Stepanov's views, however, can be gleaned from his 1833 lecture, where he wrote: "Diplomacy is concerned with the laws of physical and moral life of nations in their mutual relations; it should demonstrate the rules which nations are obliged to follow in their constant interactions".[17]

As Grabar observed,[18] Stepanov used the word "diplomacy" in two senses:

> By diplomacy I understand the conditional law of nations in general. The authorities usually treat Europe only and consider it in this respect the positive law of the nations of Europe.
>
> . . . I call diplomacy conditional law if we separate it from the natural law of nations. In this event politics and political economy will also constitute conditional sciences, and natural law will embrace that unconditional science which expounds the purely unconditional principles and rules which serve as the basis for uncovering the life of societies and nations.[19]

The full measure of Stepanov will be appreciated only when the complete text of his two-volume treatise becomes available. In the meantime, we now have accessible to an international readership portions of what is to date the earliest known original

[15] Stepanov (1833), 64 p.

[16] The address was delivered at a solemn meeting of Kharkov University on 30 August 1833. The printed text of the address a decade later had become a veritable *cours* on political economy "unique in Russian literature". See Levitskii (2007).

[17] Stepanov (1833), pp. 41–42.

[18] Grabar (1990), p. 301.

[19] Stepanov (1833), p. 42.

manual on positive international law in the Russian language. The distance in time between the treatise of P. P. Shafirov (1717) as the first original work in the Russian language on public international law and the first proper manual on the subject (1847) was 130 years.

References

De Poulet M (1874a) Харьковский университет и Д. И. Каченовский: Культурный очерк и воспоминания из 40-х годов [Kharkov University and D. I. Kachenovskii: cultural essay and memoir from the 1840s]. Вестник Европы [Herald of Europe] (1):75–115

De Poulet M (1874b) Харьковский университет и Д. И. Каченовский: Культурный очерк и воспоминания из 40-х годов [Kharkov University and D. I. Kachenovskii: cultural essay and memoir from the 1840s]. Вестник Европы [Herald of Europe] (2):565–588

Denysov VN, Savchuk KO (2004) Степанов Тихон Федорович [Stepanov, Tikhon Fedorovich]. In: Shemshuchenko IS (ed) Антологія української юридичної думки [Anthology of Ukrainian legal thought], vol VIII. Kyiv, p 38

F. K. (1999) Степанов Тихон Федорович [Stepanov, Tikhon Fedorovich]. In: Русский биографический словарь [Russian biographical dictionary], vol. Smelovskii – Suvorina (reprint ed). Moscow, pp 398–399

Grabar VE (1990) In: Butler WE (ed and transl) The history of international law in Russia 1647–1917: A bio-bibliographical study. p 303

Levitskii V (2007) Степанов [Stepanov]. In: Bagalei DI (ed) Юридический факультет Харьковского университета за первые 100 лет его существования (1805–1905) [Law Faculty of Kharkov University for the first hundred years of its existence (1805–1905)] (reprint ed). Kharkov, pp. 277–279

Savchuk KO (1901) Степанов Тихон Федорович [Stepanov, Tikhon Fedorovich]. In: Arsen'ev K, Petrushevskii F (eds) Энциклопедический словарь [Encyclopedic dictionary], vol XXXI, p 596

Savchuk KO (1980) Степанов Тихон Федорович [Stepanov, Tikhon Fedorovich]. In: Rumiantsev A (ed) Экономическая энциклопедия. Политическая энциклопедия [Economic encyclopedia. Political economy], vol IV, p 62

Savchuk KO (2004a) Внесок професора Т. Ф. Степанова в становлення вітчизняної науки міжнародного права [Contribution of Professor T. F. Stepanov to the development of the Fatherland Science of International Law]. Правова держава [Rule-of-Law State] (15):284–288

Savchuk KO (2004b) Степанов Тихон Федорович [Stepanov, Tikhon Fedorovich]. In: Shemshuchenko IS (ed) Юридична енциклопедія [Legal encyclopedia], vol V, p 646

Savchuk KO (2019) Степанов Тихон Федорович [Stepanov, Tikhon Fedorovich]. In: Shemshuchenko (ed) Енциклопедія міжнародного права [Encyclopedia of international law], vol III, pp 779–781

Semenov VS, Ul'ianova NN (1961) Первый русский курс международного права [First Russian Course of International Law]. Советский ежегодник международного права 1960 [Soviet Yearbook of International Law 1960]. Moscow, pp 243–254

Stepanov TF (1833) Речь о сущности, важности и назначении политических наук [Address on the essence, importance, and purpose of the political sciences]. Kharkov, 64 p

Tarasov O (2001) О рукописи «Право народов» (середина XIX в.) [On the manuscript of the course 'Law of Nations' (mid-nineteenth century)]. Проблеми законності [Problems of legality] (48):169–175

Tarasov O (2020) Fragments from the 1844 Stepanov manuscript on the 'Law of Nations and Diplomacy': from the legacy of the Kharkov School of International Law. Jus Gentium V:641–647

Describe, Predict, Intervene!—On Objective Subjectivities and the Simulacra of Semiotics in the New Era; Simulated Signification and Mechanical Meaning Making in Managing Post-COVID Human Society

Larry Catá Backer

Abstract This contribution considers the challenges for semiotics, for the understanding of the conditions of meaning in relation to the human that is posed by a global obsession with the control of reality and its instrumentalization through the mechanics of simulation. Simulation describes, predicts, and intervenes to manage a situation, context, or process it imitates. While simulation is meant to imitate an environment, through a process of replication made possible by reducing the imitated environment to its essence, semiotics suggests that simulation has a more profound effect. The decisive move toward the objectification of reality and its meaning through its simulation (present) and its modeling (future)—that is the quantification, and digitalization of humanity—has brought humanity to a great transformative moment. If a situation, context, or process is now comprehended as and by its own simulation, then the modalities of objectification, of signification, and ultimately of the encounters with meaning and its making, have now (again) removed themselves from an immanent to a transcendent condition. That is, that human activity becomes centered in and manifested through its simulation rather than in the world itself. This, in turn, processes assets of challenges for human institutions and their utilization—law, governance, politics, and culture are now more real in simulation than in the reality they were meant to imitate. The essay starts with an examination of the problem. To make the discussion more concrete, the analysis is undertaken in the framework of the challenges for simulating humanity

International Roundtables for the Semiotics of Law—IRSL 2021
The Rearguard of Subjectivity
In Honor of Jan M. Broekman's 90th Birthday
Hosted by Leuven University Faculty of Law
17–18 June 2021 (Online)

L. C. Backer (✉)
W. Richard and Mary Eshelman Faculty Scholar Professor of Law and International Affairs, Pennsylvania State University, University Park, PA, USA
e-mail: lcb11@psu.edu

F. Fleerackers (ed.), *The Rearguard of Subjectivity*, Law and Visual Jurisprudence 9,
https://doi.org/10.1007/978-3-031-26855-7_3

(and thus of saving it from its predicted barbaric fate) created in Isaac Asimov's "Prelude to Foundation" and the more ancient insights taught in the interpretation of dreams. Asimov's recounting of the effort to use a planet to simulate the human universe, and of Joseph's modeling of Pharoah's dream nicely frame the central problems of simulation today. The essay then applies these insights to its manifestation in the use of simulations in the early efforts to describe, predict and intervene in the course of the COVID-19 pandemic. It considers the way that Jan Broekman has pointed a way forward for semiotics, or at least that branch of its study that points to an understanding of the objectification of subjectivity and the instrumentalization of the "Human, All-Too-Human" essence of the reductionist model. The essay ends with a look at some of the areas of human self-governance in which modeling is now displacing the situations it was meant to imitate and considers what semiotics may bring to this emerging reconstruction of reality and the challenges that it may pose for traditional approaches to understanding the making of meaning.

1 Introduction

In his after-the-fact prequel to his famous *Foundation* series, *Prelude to Foundation*,[1] Isaac Asimov attempted a novelistic construction of a taxonomy of collective meaning-making, and to give it life apart from the objects out of which it was formed.[2] In the process, Asimov considered the *problematique*[3] at the heart of the post-1945 drive toward the systemization of the meaning of the world, its ordering, and the individual's role in it—to remake the world in its own image.[4] That *problematique* centered on the *reduction* of the qualitative element of signification to its *essence*, and then the reconstitution of that essence as the reality of its own representation. Asimov starts with the problem of simplification in the face of

[1] Asimov (1988).

[2] This effort was, in turn, embedded within a lifelong construction of a chronology of a human-centered universe the complexities of which have produced some interesting studies touching on chaos and fractal theory. See, e.g., Palumbo (1996), pp. 27–34.

[3] See Warfield and Perino (1999), pp. 221–226.

[4] This remaking of the world was meant to mimic another remaking of the totality of a thing in its own image—as something complete but apart; as something that simulated that from which it was made but in a derivative sense. "So God created man in his own image, in the image of God created He him; male and female created He them." Gen.1:27 (KJV). This was a remaking that provided a way for experimenting without affecting the creator directly. That, at any rate, is the essence of the proposition at the heart of Job: with which it was possible to experiment.

> Now there was a day when the sons of God came to present themselves before the Lord, and Satan came also among them... And the Lord said unto Satan, 'Hast thou considered my servant Job, that there is none like him in the earth, a perfect and upright man'... Then Satan answered the Lord and said, 'Doth Job fear God for nought? ... But put forth thy hand now, and touch all that he hath and he will curse thee to thy face.' And the Lord said unto Satan, 'Behold, all that he hath is in thy power.' Job1:6-12 (KJV).

dynamic complexity; that is of the perversities of modeling as a Platonic exercise,[5] what Asimov has his hero Hari Seldon call 'psychohistory'—the rationalized quantification of intuition.[6]

Through this science, Asimov toys with the idea of rationalizing intuition—and thus of democratizing it, of detaching a rarified talent for intuiting future paths into an everyday tool that anyone can use.[7] That required a change in the language of prediction from intuitive and qualitative to rationalized and quantitative: As Asimov had the none-too-bright Emperor Cleon intuit: "A mathematician, however, who would back his prophecy with mathematical formulas and terminology, might be understood by no one and yet believed by everyone."[8] That rationalization of intuition, and its quantification, were built on two core premises. The first was that the data set was both robust and large enough; the second those (people and collectives) from whom data is extracted remain unaware.[9] The first speaks to the integrity of modeling; the latter to the prevention of strategic behavior.

Yet initially, there is a rejection of the idea that one can model reality, much less reliably predict the future states of its component parts, as well as the while. Using the human voice of his hero, Asimov suggests the inherent fallibility of models that are mere incomplete reflections of the objects they are designed to reduce to a true essence, a fallibility that inherently defeats the objective of simulation.[10] It is one

[5]Weissman (2021), pp. 650–654. He note (ibid., 651):

> Plato argued in the *Cratylus* that signifiers embody the natures of their referents. .. The word signifying goats embodies in some way the nature of goat... Yet the *Cratylus* is thought to be earlier Plato; the allegory of the cave is middle Plato and a different account of linguistic meaning. There, in its opening stage, words are used projectively by prisoners who make shadows intelligible by telling stories about them. The fictive "objects" evoked by their stories have no other reality.

[6]Psychohistory was defined by Asimov as a language of mathematics, a "branch of mathematics which deals with the reactions of human conglomerates to fixed social and economic stimuli." Asimov (1951), p. 14. See, also, Asimov (1988), Asimov, himself, in a later interview suggested the tensions meant to be modeled through psychohistory: "It seemed to me that if we did have a galactic empire, there would be so many human beings-quintillions of them-that perhaps you might be able to predict very accurately how societies would behave, even though you couldn't predict how individuals composing those societies would behave." Ingersoll et al. (1987), p. 70. The fiction here has not obscured to science. See, e.g., Cullenwood and Sudarshan (2011), pp. 457–472.

[7]"'With the proper mathematics, anyone would be able to assess the probabilities. It wouldn't take the rare human being who is successful because of a remarkable intuitive sense.'" Asimov (1988), pp. 10–11. u

[8]Ibid., p. 5.

[9]Asimov (1951), p. 14.

[10]Asimov (1988). Speaking through the voice of Hari Seldon, the "inventor" of "psychohistory", Asimov argues:

> "Well--" He retired into himself to choose a method of presentation. Then he said, "If you want to understand some aspect of the universe, it helps if you simplify it as much as possible and include only those properties and characteristics that are essential to understanding ... The simplification you can call a model or simulation... Such simplified simulations make it far easier to grasp a phenomenon than it would be if we had to study the phenomenon

mindful of Wittgenstein's early critique that "to say of two things that they are identical is nonsense, and to say of one thing that it is identical to itself is to say nothing at all."[11] At the same time, it is a process that requires overcoming the error of oversimplification, even of the problemmatique itself.[12] In effect—to answer the question: 'is it possible to predict the future?' it is only necessary to thoroughly understand the past and present as expressed in multi-generational interactions under conditions of change. But to do that, one would have to acquire data about everything. That is, in order to predict the future, one would have to recreate the world as it exists in time. The model, in effect, is itself.[13]

But then he is challenged by a robot—the ultimate simulation of the fundamental complexity at the heart of meaning for humanity, a robot, we learn later, has been guiding humanity toward its perfection (or at least away from disaster) for eons. The ultimate simulacrum of humanity asks the human about the possibility of simulating simulation to avoid the fatal trap of reductionism—that reduction is inherently impossible because it was inconceivable that such an effort was possible without fracturing the whole of the object simulated.[14] That is, the project takes as its starting point the possibility of detaching selfness and identity from its object[15]—of making it portable and practical. Hidden within this exercise is its ultimate power—not to see into the future but to mold it; to instrumentalize time by transforming the possibilities of prediction into a science of molding the future to achieve the objectives of the present.

Asimov then has his hero reconsider. A reduction of a reduction was not merely possible but could also appear to distill its signification in ways that mattered to those signifying.[16] In this case, a planet that reflected and contained within it a significant

itself... Now, as you wish to know more and more about any phenomenon, or as a phenomenon becomes more complex, you need more and more elaborate equations, and more and more detailed programming, and you will end with a computerized simulation that is harder and harder to grasp." "Can't you form a simulation of a simulation?" asked Hummin. (Ibid., pp. 146–147).

[11] Ludwig Wittgenstein, Tractatus logicus-philosophicus, in Workausgabe Vol. 1 (Frankfurt, 1984); ¶5.5303.

[12] Régis Meissonier, 'De la problématique â la problématisation,' (2021) Revue française du gestion No. 297 73–80 ("Ainsi, notre société, habituée à résoudre les problèmes en les décomposant et en les simplifiant comme cela est enseigné dans les écoles, comprend de moins en moins le monde dont elle fait pourtant partie.").

[13] Ibid., p. 11.This is a problem that bedevils modern predictive science. In the context of climate change models , see, Cullenwood and Sudarshan (2011), pp. 458–459.

[14] Asimov (1988). Here Asimov speaks through the voice of his ancient robot hero R. Daneel Olivaw, who has disguised himself in a way that both plays with and reveals his simulated (hyper)humanity—Chetter Hummin, who asks: "'Can't you form a simulation of a simulation?' asked Hummin. 'You would go down another degree.'? (Ibid., p. 147).

[15] Consider the problemmatique in Wagner (2002), pp. 32–55 and the issue of the identity-selfhood complex in interaction between the collective and individual self.

[16] Kralemann and Lattmann (2013), pp. 3397–3420 (mapping models in semiotic spaces; "that which makes something a model is not to be found within the model itself, but that this rather

quantum of the variant in the universe could itself serve as the basis for the simulation of the simulation of the galaxy.[17] Yet, the model has escaped its nineteenth and twentieth-century semiotic confines as an icon;[18] as predictive or manipulative instruments it has become the thing it represents, it has become its own object the interpretation of which is written into the success of its predictions and intervention (control). This is not just science fiction. This is the foundation of the post-1945 international order and the reconstitution of the United States as the simulation of the world, the modeling of which could be tested and refined, and thus refined, exported, and generalized as a global order. The United States as the simulation of the world assumed a much great power when it moved from the traditional semiotics of word and meaning to its quantification and reduction to objectifiable subjectivities. It is a model that now finds its analog in the reconstitution of socialist society through the simulacra that in the aggregate constitutes the Chinese social credit system.[19]

The simulated object, corporeal or virtual, becomes less objective than its avatar. It is decentered. The operative element of social semiotics moves from the thing itself to its simulation, fed by the data that simulation may stimulate. Yet what occurs in the reality space inhabited by the avatar is felt with greater force by the object. The semiotic object (the thing simulated) exists only as a projection of simulated reality outward. Modeling is signification, and its manipulation becomes the form of meaning-making for a new era of human development—one in which the driving force is no longer humanity but humanity's detritus, and one in which the operative force is not natural but artificial persons representing the simulated perfectibility of the human object. This is Pharoah's Dream[20] as much as it is the Galactic Empire that serves as the novelistic simulation in Asimov's Foundation series. Both provide significant clues about the reshaping of semiotics and its expression in governance and politics.

Trantor—the planet—is both real (a planet full of people) and a simulation of a larger reality the operations of which it simulates (humanity as a whole spread across the galactic empire). Pharoah's dream of the seven lean cattle consuming the seven fattened ones, and of the seven withered ears consuming the seven full[21] is both real (Pharoah) and a simulation (Egypt). Psychohistory—the modeling—is descriptive

belongs to the specific outer context into which something is placed by a pragmatic act of a subject in order to use this object as a model: the ontological question of what a model is thus becomes "a question about reasoning of a judgement on model-being"" ibid., 3399).

[17]Asimov (1988), p. 413. (the planet "was itself a system complex enough to make [simulation] meaningful and yet it was simple enugh, compared to the Empire as a whole, to make [simulation] perhaps practical."].

[18]Kralemann and Lattmann (2013), pp. 3404–3410.

[19]Larry Catá Backer, 'Next Generation Law.

[20]Gen Chapter 42 (KJV).

[21]Gen 42:17–24.

and predictive; It objectifies ideology in the habits and behaviors of collectives.[22] So is dreaming where God is the Shepard of the simulation the description of the future shape f which is communicated through dreams.[23] The greatest force of both is in their reality-making—the power to project description and prediction into the future permits altering that future in simulated space—and then transposing that outward to the simulated world.

Here one moves from the semiosis of text and individuals to the semiosis of the collective expressed in the interrelation of description, prediction, and intervention (control). The descriptive model-simulation observes; it is how the semiotic construction of Trantor (as the simulation of humanity) is undertaken; it is the signification of Egypt as cattle and corn in a fertile Nile Valley. The descriptive model serves as the signification of the essentialized reduction of a constantly changing present. The predictive model-simulation projects observation forward; it is passive—in the sense that it teases out the future from the present. It is also reactive—it provides a means of mitigating and remedying what cannot be prevented. Joseph's plans for the storage of grain during the years of plenty; Asimov's construction of the 1st Foundation and the preservation of knowledge. Both make the most powerful vision of the simulation-model operative—where the simulation becomes the space where description and prediction are deployed to prevent, change, and control what is observed in the future by changing the pathways of the present. The object here is to manage the simulation by changing the variables that produce description and lead to prediction. Here one does not change meaning—one reframes the basis on which meaning is made. In Asimov's world, one changes societal variables enough to reduce the age of barbarity from 30 to a single millennium. In Pharoah's world that is undertaken by building the Aswan Dam, or by inducing God to change Divine intention. The lifeworld of semiotic meaning moves from the objects modeled to the model and from the present to a set of multiple possibilities in the future, the possibilities of which are a function of the power to direct the present—at least to the extent it can be grasped and mapped.[24]

This contribution considers the challenges for semiotics, for the understanding of the conditions of meaning in relation to the human that is posed by a global obsession with the control of reality and its instrumentalization through the mechanics of simulation. Simulation describes, predicts, and intervenes in (controls) a situation, context, or process it is imitating. While simulation is meant to imitate an environment, through a process of replication made possible by reducing the imitated environment to its essence, semiotics suggests that simulation has a more profound effect. The decisive move toward the objectification of reality and its

[22] Jeremy Campbell, The Improbable Machine (New York, 1989) (noting the incomprehensibility of the completely open mind in a collective the ordering of which is grounded on complex systems of biases; ibid., 35, 151, 158); DeLeon (2008), pp. 256–277.

[23] Gen 42:28 (?"What God is about to do he showeth unto Pharoah").

[24] See Buttimer (1976), pp. 277–292 (on the need to bring intellectual knowledge closer to lived experience presaged the sensibilities of dynamic simulation).

meaning through its simulation (present) and its modeling (future)—that is the quantification, and digitalization of humanity—has brought humanity to a great transformative moment. This, in turn, processes assets of challenges for human institutions and their utilization—law, governance, politics, and culture are now more real in simulation than in the reality they were meant to imitate. After this introduction to the problem, the essay employs the imagery and insights of Asimov's "Prelude to Foundation" and of Joseph's modeling of Pharoah's dream to frame the central problems of simulation today. The essay applies these insights to its manifestation in the use of simulations in the early efforts to describe, predict and intervene (control) the course of the COVID-19 pandemic. It considers the way that Jan Broekman has pointed a way forward for semiotics, or at least that branch of its study that points to an understanding of the objectification of subjectivity and the instrumentalization of the "Human, All-Too-Human"[25] essence of the essential Ing model. The essay ends with a look at some of the areas of human self-governance in which modeling is now displacing the situations it was meant to imitate and considers what semiotics may bring to this emerging reconstruction of reality and the challenges that it may pose for traditional approaches to understanding the making of meaning.

2 Mathematical Intuition for the Masses

Simulation is semiotic. It is a semiotics that inverts the usual human individual-based lens, effectively inverting the polarity of the semiotic lens. What is simulated is actually unaware of the use to which it is put even as it feeds its own simulation: computer games, insular communities, and identity groups. The simulation exists in virtual space and yet represents an incarnate community with desired characteristics and habits. The others are subsets of a larger community exhibiting a set of characteristics in the world that may be useful to understand and perhaps manipulate. Each provides the data vat which, when properly stirred—that is when appropriate social stimulation is applied—provides the information necessary to either shape or shape the meaning or signification of the greater object for which the simulation serves as a manageable space for observation and social engineering. In semiotic terms, the space where objects represent other objects which contain their own signification and a representative signification for the other object for which it is a placeholder. At the same time, they provide a space where the ideology structuring the simulation can be exposed and instrumentalized in its own service or for its management.

[25] Nietzsche (1908); Project Gutenberg November 26, 2011 [EBook #38145]); available <https://www.gutenberg.org/files/38145/38145-h/38145-h.htm> ("In the dream, mankind, in epochs of crude primitive civilization, thought they were introduced to a second, substantial world: here we have the source of all metaphysic. Without the dream, men would never have been incited to an analysis of the[25] world." Ibid., Of First and Lat Things ¶5).

What appeared impossible—the reduction of object-signs into systems of signification that could be read, and managed—becomes possible where reality itself can be reconstructed as a model of itself. Thus simulated, it could be vested with meaning.[26] But more than that, it could be directed and changed. The project becomes possible when the entire body of a macro-model is constructed from out of the rationalized organization of sub-models. One constructs a modeled universe like any other self-reflexive system, one component at a time. That is, Asimov pointed to what would become commonplace by the time of his death near the end of the twentieth century: that the solution to the problem of signification was grounded in the *reconstitution of signification as an object which is at once both identical to the original object signified and something else again.* That, in turn, requires both the ability to understand the disaggregated subparts of the whole—simulating each; and then to aggregate these subparts into an ordered whole. And the simulation is infinitely practical, it can reconstruct reality in its own image. But for this purpose, humanity requires a simulation of itself to bring it to simulate its own surroundings and through this simulation reconstruct it also in humanity's own image.[27] "Visualization and quantification: together they snap the padlock—reality is fettered (at least tightly enough and for long enough to get work out of it and possibly a law of nature or two).[28] That simulation, though, is a Golem—a system that reflects its creator but the inner workings of which remain obscure to those who can only look at but not in the Golem.[29]

2.1 From Model to Subject . . . And Back Again

At this point, one might usefully take up the challenge of partitions that Jan Broekman issued in Chapter 5 of his *Meaning, Narrativity, and the Real.*[30] This, then, is how signs now fascinate[31] simulating law through nudging. This is a first-

[26]Ciula and Øyvind (2017), pp. i33–i46 ("modelling as a creative process to gain new knowledge (meaning) about material and immaterial objects by generating and manipulating external representations of them" Ibid., p. i33; p. I34 ("modelling as a means to create 'tools for thinking'. . . and "as a process of signification and reasoning in action.").

[27]Here one hears echoes of the four stages of Jean Baudrillard's sign-order which progresses from faithful copy (the sacramental order), to a perversion of the reality once faithfully represented, to the reconstitution of the copy as something that pretends to be a faithful representation (the order of sorcery where meaning is made to appear as a reference to some truth, and finally to pure simulacrum where the copy has no relation to any reality from which it had started out to faithfully represent. See Baudrillard (1994), p. 6.

[28]Crosby (1997).

[29]A Golem story fragment of Kranz Kafka perhaps captures this best. See, Dekel and Gurley (2017), pp. 536–551. For its application in the universe of models and analytics, see, e.g., Bird et al. (2021), pp. 1–19.

[30]Broekman (2016).

[31]Broekman (2017).

order simulation projecting interiority outward in the form of communication—and then rationalizing that exteriority so that it connects multiple individuals—in the process of reshaping the way the individual approaches exteriorization through communication. And the signage of language becomes more interesting when projected back within the individual whose body and consciousness inhabit language worlds. In that case, one might think of the body as the common simulation for the operation of lingual realities that both occupy and avoid the same physical space. One here is reminded of Luc (now Lucy) Sante's semi-autobiographical reminiscences about growing up in a single body as two persons, united and divided by the languages of self-awareness and self-construction;[32] in order to speak of his childhood, he has to translate.[33] But more than that; there is a temporal element as well: "In Belgium, I am an oddity. Having been raised abroad in a bubble of the old culture, I've retained curious verbal archaisms."[34] That in-betweenness appears also as a data point in its larger simulation—Belgium itself—an "ill-fitting suit of a country."[35]

Jan here also reminds us of another galaxy of simulation—of the simulacra of "tongues" in the incarnation of the self and its projection outward. That simulation is Janus-faced—as Jan reminds us with the language of emoticons.[36] On the one hand, it serves as a condensation of language—a simulation of language as well as a reduction to essentials that takes language—already an abstraction and produces its own simulation. Emoticons are simulations of simulations of meaning objects now packaged so that their interpretation requires a different approach to unlocking meaning. It works in the same way that coding produces a symbolic rendition of instructions for the extraction of meaning or the construction of command that can be read by a machine, as well as by a human. And for both, "Language not only functions as a means of communicating our thoughts but plays an active role in shaping them. Rather than passively reflecting the joints of nature, words and larger constructions help carve joints into nature."[37] On the other hand, it follows that the simulation of simulation has acquired a substance of its own. Emoticons, like coding, acquire their own autonomy even as they serve as the blocks for the operation of other systems. To create a simulation, to use it, is to understand that

---

[32] Sante (1998).

[33] Ibid., p. 261.

[34] Ibid., p. 268.

[35] Ibid., p. 269 ("And it unnaturally couples two language groups that are both right and wrong... And both principal language groups have ambiguous ongoing relationships with the majority stockholders of their languages, that is, the Dutch and the French." Ibid., 269–270).

[36] Broekman (2020), pp. 415–429 ("nobody ever studied the language of those signs, and nobody has ever acquired a precise and total oversight of their number and their meanings – let alone an opinion about the question whether they are really signs or are better characterized as symbols." Ibid., 416).

[37] Lupyan and Clark (2015), p. 282. Emoticons are a new language with physiological effects as well—changing our brains—the simulation affecting the object from which it is produced and to which it provides tools for self-expression. Salleh (2014).

it, like that in whose image it was created, are not identical. And it is in the spaces between simulation and simulated that meaning can be trapped. This becomes a more profound problem where the simulation is itself a simulation that is drawn from a more manageable simulation—from a subset that is meant to stand in for the whole. That is the essence of the emoticon as well—a partial language complete in itself but hardly reflecting the complexity of the simulation of communication from which it is drawn. Jan suggests that a "“digital sociability" is not yet conceived, despite the fact that its social techniques flower on a global scale, and economists calculate milliards of Dollars, Euros, Yans, and Yens spend via and on them."[38] And yet the pathway toward a simulation of sociability is certainly opened between word and meaning—or better understood in the dynamic constant shifting between word and meaning and between meaning and word.

Reading Jan's "Rearguards of Subjectivity"[39] brought to mind at first not the philosophical anthropology of Helmuth Plessner and Adolf Portmann,[40] but that of Genesis: "And out of the ground the LORD God formed every beast of the field, and every fowl of the air; and brought them unto Adam to see what he would call them: and whatsoever Adam called every living creature, that was the name thereof."[41] If in the Biblical account of creation, God created the Earth and all in it, it was humanity to whom He delegated the power to give each meaning. This meaning by naming also has ancient roots in Chinese rhetorical principles from the time of the Pre-Socratics. Guiguzi speaks of *ming* (名)—of naming, of defining accurately, and of drawing distinctions,[42] a concept that itself was closely though controversially tied to that of *shi* (实) of actuality, truth, or essence of the thing names.[43] Intersubjectivity was a divine prerogative, at least until humanity took for itself (at the instigation of another divine form), the fruit of the knowledge of the tree of good and evil; "For God doth know that in the day ye eat thereof, then your eyes shall be opened, and ye shall be as gods, knowing good and evil."[44]

In the process, one adds a layer to the eccentricities of the human condition.[45] That eccentricity—that humans are trapped in their bodies and all other life forms are their bodies—produces a dynamic semiotic state. For humans, the state of confined detachment produces the conditions of semiosis—objectification that produces significance that is portable and transposable, and that is amendable to

[38] Broekman (2020), p. 418. ("Emojis do not create specific positive or negative colorings of words (linguistics teaches us that all words are constantly in motion) but they are energized by conversions. These complex processes focusing on meaning are an outstanding semiotic issue and create attitudes, which one encounters in all forms of communication respectively connectivity." Ibid. 420)

[39] Broekman (2023).

[40] Ibid., citing Plessner (1928), p. 289 f.; Portmann (1956). See also: Theunissen (1965), p. 156 f.

[41] Genesis 2:19 (KJV).

[42] Guiguzi (2016), p. 156.

[43] Ibid., p. 60 n. 26.

[44] Genesis 3:5.

[45] See discussion of Plessner and Portmann in Broekman (2023).

communication by a consensus of meaning. That applies to language, as well as to the playthings of humans—their technology, their language, and their obsession with themselves. Humans are the unpunished Narcissus aware of the greatest threat to their own sense of themselves is their own self-reference—signification can reduce the consciousness to a pretty flower that is consumed by itself,[46] a closed loop in endless hypercyclidity.[47] That is a great insight of computational language.[48]

Nonetheless, as Jan points out quite clearly in *Rearguards of Subjectivity*, something odd happens both to language and to the philosophical anthropology of a mechanical age. Guiguzi's naming-truth (ming/shi 名/实), Genesis' Tree of the knowledge of good and evil, and philosophical anthropology all mean to account for the margins that are the individual human, and their recognition in the reflection of the others—not just other people, but other things as well. Thus Plessner and Portmann may look to eccentricity tied both to the bodies of a human person and that body's 'person-ality.' The mechanics of that double birth structure, again as Jan astutely develops, may be bound up in language, and language bound up in meaning (again we come back to Genesis and Guiguzi), but technology has shifted the parameters of analysis and the primary objects of signification. We are no longer in a world the humanity of which is signified by "consciousness and completeness ... intertwined with physiological process"[49] nor one bounded by the constraining technologies of language to communicate its insights.[50] Instead, technology has now relegated *eccentricity* of the self, which is the foundation of philosophy as networked, intersubjective, deviations from a mean against which eccentricity is possible, to a second-order product. To be human today is an expression of the simulation of the human, which is itself constructed from out of the absorption of eccentricity and its rationalization against the ideal which is itself a product of this aggregation. The semiotics of identity has reversed polarity—the human is manufactured, but not quite in the way that critical theorists of a receding generation surmised who still believed in an ordering foundation, a true ideal state of some sort.[51] But like them, modelers understand that identity can both have its false consciousness,[52] and its corrective measures; it is just that this consciousness can be true or false at the instance of those who supply its measure.

To center the human is to engage in a resistance to the objectification of subjectivity within its own simulation. To center the human, the singular

---

[46] Olteanu et al. (2021), pp. 45–68 ("Of particular importance is that social media forces newspapers to change as a medium by collapsing the media content producer/consumer dichotomy of broadcasting." Ibid., p. 59).

[47] Eigen and Schuster (1978), pp. 7–41.

[48] Tanaka-Ishii (2008), pp. 299–311.

[49] Jan Broekman (2023) draft text at p. 5.

[50] Ibid.

[51] Derick Bell, And We Are Not Saved (1987); Lawrence (1987), pp. 317–388; Unger (1983), pp. 561–675.

[52] Matsuda (1990), p. 1763.

eccentricity, in an age of technology that has incorporated the individual eccentricity of the subject as a statistic[53] in the construction of a collective humanity through which eccentricity is only possible within its simulation. Simulation decenters the human and places humanity again within its ecology in which it is one of many subjectivities and where the eccentricities of component parts are far less interesting than the collective eccentricity of humanity as a distinctive psycho-physiological being in an environment populated by a number of other quite distinct collections of eccentricity (or of marginalia producing a unity capable of essentialization). The semiotics of the human thus operates at two simultaneous and distinct levels of intersubjectivity (meaning-making, signification, and consciousness).[54] The first is internal—which has been the object of philosophy for millennia—remains the relation between the body of the individual within and against the body of humanity. The second is external, which has been an object but of politics and biology—centers the human against their collectives of living and non-living things among which humanity exists.

Here one encounters the insights of both biosemiotics and more interestingly, of cybersemiotics.[55] It reminds one, in the manner of Hari Seldon, that language has morphed in form and expression—from text to hypertext, from words to data, and from grammar to modeling. If language constitutes the observer, and if we are all both object and observer, who collectively converge on meaning (communication), then the language of modeling becomes the modeling of language, and with it the shaping of those modeled. Intersubjectivity and lifeworlds do not so much collapse as disappear into the imagined intersubjective lifeworld of the possible and the predictable in the model.[56] And, in the process of this transformation from word to model, and from text to simulation, the character of agency as a semiotic category has also changed from motivation and consciousness as inherent in the individual and as a series of external stimuli that produce internal effects. Neither is apparent where the traditional language of text is proffered; more may be revealed where these are transposed from the bodies of the motivated to their modeled avatars. And yet the exercise of modeling—of transposing semiotics from its original to its hypertextual

[53] Foucault (2004).

[54] For an interesting discussion through a related lens, see, Nishida (2022), pp. 424–433 ("From this point of view, second-order cybernetics itself can be seen as the work 'observing observing systems', and when we take into account the fact that we ourselves are also observing systems, it will be realized that the work of second-order cybernetics is involved in the dazzling recursiveness of observing which takes the form of observing observing observing… " Ibid., 429).

[55] Brier (2019), pp. 81–92 ("In Peircean triadic semiotics, semiosis is a relational dynamics that defines the basic process of mind becoming matter as 'instantiations'. Our universe is produced by a type-token dynamism going far beyond the conceptual linguistic human sociocommunicative realm into the biological as well as physical-chemical aspects of realty" ibid., p. 86); Cobley (2010), pp. 2045–2066 ("the implications arising out of cybersemiotics' focus on qualia and 'languaging' while also suggesting that the latter, especially, might yet be re-figured in terms of modelling.", Ibid., 2046).

[56] Harste (2021), pp. 108–130.

language and simulated subject[57] for meaning-making and control—enables not just time travel through experimental analytics toward altered futures,[58] but also to reinforce the preconceptions through which the world is ordered.[59] This is the world of so-called Siren Servers,[60] that is of servers and their analytic metaverses that are constantly intertwined with the ideologies that shape them even as they shape their belief systems.[61]

And thus back to the problem of the model and the semiotics of analytics. Recall first, that the object of this exercise is not to signify the individual but rather to rationalize the sig that is the collective—as an object, as a symbol, and as a meaning-verse. The objectification of collectives—as a thing and as a system, like a human being (as a body and as a point of action)—is focused on its signification and interpretation. That is, its semiotics is grounded in the imperative to describe, to predict, and ultimately, to control. It is easy enough to apply a semiosis of description, prediction, and intervention (control) to the individual—human science, religion, and culture have been quite adept at this. The reason is simple—the entirety of a human is an object of practical study. But the semiosis of the human collective—as well as its offal (science, religion, politics, culture) by which it can be signified—becomes much more difficult. The difficulty lies in its multiplicity both latitudinally (there are lots of factors in a disaggregated collective at any one time) and longitudinally (these factors change—people die, constant iteration produces snowflakes). To signify the whole one has to grasp the whole, and over time. That is what makes it impractical. Semiosis, then, requires a Golem—a simulation of the collective, the description, prediction, and intervention (control) of which can then serve as the model for the modeling of the whole. The simulation stands in for the collective simulated because it is the only way in which the entirety of the object to be signified can be approached. Every model of a collective requires a simulation of the thing to be studied—and that simulation not merely stands in for the collective as a whole but in some respects becomes the whole. The simulation is signified, and thus signified instrumentalized as an object of action, becomes the thing itself in a semiotic sense.

[57]For an example of its use in descriptive and perhaps predictive terms, see, Newmark (1989), p. 56 (the author notes the premise: "How would you have run Teddy Roosevelt's 1912 Campaign? Here's your chance to find out—this hypertext-based program let's you be the campaign manager"). For an interesting discussion, see Myers and Beach (2002), pp. 538–546; Kinsey (2018), pp. 154–182.

[58]Crosby (1997).

[59]Deely (2012), pp. 325–363 ("Or will we see those errors without recognizing them as errors, and instead, beguiled by seeming truths (such as the sedimentation down to the level of common speech of the early modern usage of "objects" as synonym for "things" in awareness, for example), perpetuate the worst of the old ways into our own future?" Ibid., p. 336).

[60]Lanier (2013), pp. 53–57. "Siren Servers gather data from the network, often without having to pay for it. The data is analyzed using the most powerful available computers run by the very best available technical people. The results of the analysis are kept secret, but are used to manipulate the rest of the world to advantage." Ibid., p. 55. Here one has the Second Foundation, Asimov (1951).

[61]Lanier (2013), pp. 124–132 (ideologies and the nostalgic turn).

That is the reality of the simulated object is centered on its simulation.[62] What is signified within the simulation (because it is only in the simulated space that such efforts are practically possible) is that reality is constructed and exported to the 'real world' of the object of the simulation. What stands in the place of becomes the thing itself. And the thing itself becomes the space where the meaning made (description, prediction, and control) in simulation is then acted out in physical space.

2.2 The Reality of the Model and the Model of Reality—Modeling COVID in the US

Semiotics, then, in the context of the simulation of collectives, becomes the art of the technologically possible, and the conceptually quantifiable. Both are driven by technology. Technology, in turn, is then driven by the ideologies around which the possibilities of conceiving and applying technology are framed.

The effects can be quite significant on ordered political collectives. One example will suffice: the implications revealed by an ascendancy of data-driven Pandemic; likely the most important legacy of COVID-19. Its effects have touched virtually every aspect of collective life.[63] The COVID-19 pandemic exposed the insinuation of simulation into and as the discourse of politics. This represented a heightened application of a long trajectory of substituting intuition, now rationalized within quantified models of things (objects and processes) once intuited. That core ordering presumption, of course, generated an ecology of principles and approaches the elaboration of which we are only now beginning to see manifested in ordinary (political. economic, societal, and cultural) life.

In *The Measure of Reality*,[64] Alfred Crosby summarized the arc of 350 years of development of an Anglo-European trajectory the object of which was to replace or supplement text with images and numbers. Western thinkers increasingly sought to know something not through a textual description but visually and in ways that could be measured. "Then you posses a quantitative representation of your subject that is, however simplified, even in its errors and omissions, precise. You can think about it rigorously. You can manipulate it and experiment with it, as we do today with

[62] Ulmer (1991) (on the reflexivity of object and subject-simulacra).

[63] What follows is derived from two earlier essays: Larry Catá Backer, Data Driven Pandemic and the Ascendancy of Simulated Reality as the New Political Space: The Administration of Disease and the Disease of Administration in the Light of COVID-19, Law at the End of the Day (28 April 2020); available <https://lcbackerblog.blogspot.com/2020/04/data-driven-pandemic-and-ascendancy-of.html>; and Larry Catá Backer, Simulating Politics in the Shadow of COVID-19: 'like the school nurse trying to tell the principal how to run the school' Law at the End of the Day (4 May 2020); available <https://lcbackerblog.blogspot.com/2020/05/simulating-politics-in-shadow-of-covid.html#morel>.

[64] Crosby (1997).

computer models."[65] The trajectories of what Crosby called "The New Model" of perceiving the "mysteries of reality" and, thus perceived, of rationalizing these mysteries within them,[66] has continued in fits and starts through to the current age. It has marked, sporadically and unevenly to be sure, the entirety of the organization of human institutions as much as it has shaped the current forms of its perceptions of itself. Collectives no longer have to perceive themselves in the abstract as an aggregation of premises and principles. Instead, collectives can visualize themselves by their own quantifiable simulacra, especially through the art of modeling—of rendering reality in abstract space drawn from data.[67] In the process it has transformed time, space, and the way we mark them, and with that the world around us. The trajectories, however, have changed. What through the seventeenth century had been a means for rationalizing the world around us, by the twentieth century had now inverted the relationship between reality and perception. When what is perceived becomes real, reality is relevant only as a means of accountability, as a check on the viability of perception itself. That, of course, has produced a powerful philosophical reaction in the twentieth century from an engagement with the nature of phenomena,[68] and later to its political manifestation.[69] It was also bound up with the problem of mechanical reproduction and authenticity[70]—now applied in an entirely different context—not in the context of the replication of a work of art, but of the social collective itself and its sensory perception.[71]

COVID-19 exposed the extent to which those inversions have come fully to government at last. The pandemic has now exposed the way that quantitative representation has altered the lens through which politics and human organization is perceived. That shift then substantially affects the way that the reality of those perceptions is shaped, understood, and controlled. CVID-19 has now also exposed the extent to which, whatever the lingering elements of the post-1945 era *ancien regime* intelligentsia suggest otherwise, the reality of politics is being manifested as the product of a perception of data that produces a managed simulation of the world in which it seeks to control.[72] Modeling is the way we create these simulacra and

---

[65] Ibid., 227, 228–229.

[66] Ibid. 239.

[67] S.C., 'Building Better Models: Why Macroeconomics Needs to Ente4r,' The economist (3 August 2010); available <https://www.economist.com/free-exchange/2010/08/03/building-better-models>.

[68] Husserl (1970) (§9 Galileo's Mathematization of Nature).

[69] Habermas (1973); see also Kahn (1988), pp. 361–387.

[70] Benjamin (1969).

[71] Ibid. ("The artistic performance of a stage actor is definitely presented to the public by the actor in person; that of the screen actor, however, is presented by a camera, with a twofold consequence." Ibid., p. 9)

[72] For a fascinating discussion from the periphery, see, Dominguez and Fusco (2003), pp. 151–162 (on electronic disturbance theater nudging—"in other words, members of each group face a challenge to their identity: hackers used to secrecy have to "come out," activists committed to working in the street meet on-line, and actors and audiences accustomed to purely fictional

through that creation creates for itself a more prominent role in the political management of human affairs. The character of that role is not as a tool of politics but as politics itself. That, in *essence* (and we deal almost entirely now in a world that operates by reducing objects to their essence and then layering those reduced essences into models of reality), is what COVID-19 has revealed in 2020.

The COVID-19 pandemic exposed an ecology of simulation and modeling lying just below the surface of institutional decision-making. It reconstituted the world of the pandemic in abstracted space—reduced and essentialized to a useable form. Its utility spoke to three lenses that the simulation provided.

The first is the descriptive lens. The descriptive e simulation provided a complete imitation of the world-verse it reflects. It provides the lens through which the imitated object can be better observed from multiple angles ad at leisure. It can be stopped, or it can be set in motion. It can be rotated, disaggregated, and reconstituted to provide a better view. It reduces the environment to its essentials, at least for the purpose which the imitation is to serve. In the case of COVID-19, the descriptive model reproduced the pathways of the pandemic and the object of observation.

The second is the predictive lens. Having produced an imitation of the environment, it could then set that environment in motion. The model remains passive and reactive. In its predictive operation, it merely projects a descriptive environment forward (and backward) in time. It changes nothing other than the time at which a descriptive imitation is viewed. Yet prediction makes it possible to temporally split the object from its modeled imitation. That, in turn, makes it possible to consider reactive measures—and permits planning in anticipation of what may occur in the 'real' world. In the case of COVID-19, the predictive model makes it possible to consider the effects of a variety of mitigation and remedial measures—lockdowns, stimulus packages, and the ordering of stability.

The third is the intervention or altering lens. If description is the essence of imitation—the foundation of the environment that is the imitative simulacra—and prediction is that environment in motion, which can be observed and against which one can plan and react (but which one cannot change), then control moves one from outside to inside the simulacra itself. It is the form of simulation in which the object is to change the environment itself. This is the insertion of the observer into the simulation—the place where outside and inside collapse. It is the active engagement with one's environment but within the realities of its simulation. This is the simulation where an infinite number of simulated variations may be attempted—the realization of alternative realities projected forward by varying the present. This is a way of approaching the contemporary metaverse—as an infinite sense of technologically possible realities existing simultaneously and connected to the objects they imitate or from which they seek to escape.[73] In the case of COVID-19, one speaks

representations of reality with no social repercussions to their engagement find themselves in a simulation that does have a visible impact on the social." Ibid., 152).

[73]Eric Ravenscraft, 'What is the Metaverse, Exactly?,' Wired (25 April 2022); available https://www.wired.com/story/what-is-the-metaverse/.

here, for example, to the introduction of the disease, the creation of vaccines, or measures that profit from one or the other.

2.2.1 Constituting the COVID-19 Golem

One of the most interesting aspects of the COVID-19 pandemic has been the way in which it is exposing growing disjunctions—growing gaps—between the principles, customs, and traditions on which a political order is organized and the way it has been operated after January 2020. Those who have made it a point of protecting the conceptual basis of the old order have been especially sensitive to this disjunction and have, even early in the emerging era of the pandemic, sought to alert and correct (or better put, fill) the gaps that have existed for a while, but which are now inescapably apparent. These efforts are particularly notable in the context of the developing conceptual regimes of human rights.[74] As noted at the time by the Council of Europe:

> The major social, political and legal challenge facing our member states will be their ability to respond to this crisis effectively, whilst ensuring that the measures they take do not undermine our genuine long-term interest in safeguarding Europe's founding values of democracy, rule of law and human rights .... The virus is destroying many lives and much else of what is very dear to us. We should not let it destroy our core values and free societies.[75]

Most spectacularly, of course, has been the way in which states and other institutions were able to mobilize the masses in ways that substantially altered their lives, their freedoms of action and movement, and their access to collective activities (economic, religious, social, and political).[76] This ought not to be taken lightly. By 2022, China could effectively lock down one of the largest cities and most important on

[74] Amnesty International. Report: Europe at a Crossroads; Respecting democracy, rule of law and human rights in the framework of the COVID-19 sanitary crisis (2 April 2020); available <https://www.amnesty.org/en/documents/eur01/2079/2020/en/>.

[75] Council of Europe, Respecting democracy, rule of law and human rights in the framework of the COVID-19 sanitary crisis: A Toolkit for Member State, SG/Inf(2020)11 (7 April 2020), p. 2.

[76] See, Jiachuan Wu, Savannah Smith, Mansee Khurana, Corky Siemaszko and Brianna DeJesus-Banos, 'Stay-at-home orders across the country What each state is doing — or not doing — amid widespread coronavirus lockdowns,' NBC News (29 April 2020); available <https://www.nbcnews.com/health/health-news/here-are-stay-home-orders-across-country-n1168736>; Wuhan lockdown: A year of China's fight against the Covid pandemic,' BBC News (22 January 2021); available <https://www.bbc.com/news/world-asia-china-55628488>; 'Coronavirus: What are the lockdown measures across Europe?,' Deutsche Welle (2020); available <https://www.dw.com/en/coronavirus-what-are-the-lockdown-measures-across-europe/a-52905137>; Michael Cohen and Amogelang Mbatha, 'South Africa Orders Three-Week Lockdown to Curb Virus Spread,' Bloomberg; available <https://www.bloomberg.com/news/articles/2020-03-23/south-africa-orders-three-week-lockdown-to-curb-virus-spread#xj4y7vzkg>; Manveena Suri, Swati Gupta and Ivana Kottasová, 'India, population 1.3 billion, orders 'complete' coronavirus lockdown,' CNN (24 March 2020); available <https://www.cnn.com/2020/03/24/asia/india-lockdown-coronavirus-intl/index.html>.

earth.[77] Without much of a block, even the "freest" society deployed the language of war and national emergency to loosen the usual restraints on the exercise of power.[78] As notable has been the way in which traditional principles of macro-economic policy has been sidelined as the usual gatekeepers and regulators abandoned restraint in efforts to preserve at least short-term stability.[79]

The magnitude of these disjunctions has acquired a somewhat different character in the context of the pandemic. COVID-19 responses centered on the use of metrics and data-based analytics in managing responses to infection in a more comprehensive way. These metrics take two forms. The first is data-based surveillance. The second and more indicative of the future is simulation.

2.2.2 The Building Blocks of Imitation

Monitoring, surveillance, reporting, and data harvesting is well-worn territory—at least as measured by the span of a human life.[80] These are meant to serve both as tools and as the substance of regulation. As tools, these are the means by which accountability can be quantified and reduced to a value against which other values can be compared (or compared against triggers). They also serve (as a sort of performance of accountability) as proof of the value or "correctness" of political and policy choices made. At the same time, they also substitute for the regulations they are meant to make visible where the construction of the systems or premises of data gathering, surveillance, and the like, are left to those constructing or implementing them, and where their choices effectively have a normative effect.

---

[77] See, Patrick Jackson and Zubaidah Abdul Jalil, 'Shanghai lockdown: China eases Covid restrictions after two months,' BBC (1 June 2022); available <https://www.bbc.com/news/world-asia-china-61647687>.

[78] See, Ryan P. Burke, 'The 'war' on COVID-19 doesn't mean military lockdown,' The Hill (20 March 2020); available <https://thehill.com/opinion/national-security/488433-the-war-on-covid-19-doesnt-mean-military-lockdown/> (on likely limits to lockdown protocols).

[79] See, e.g., Daniel Villareal, 'Here's How U.S. Coronavirus Stimulus Package Compares to Other Countries Around the World,' Newsweek (10 April 2020); available <https://www.newsweek.com/heres-how-us-coronavirus-stimulus-package-compares-other-countries-around-world-1497360>; Council of the European Union, Report on the comprehensive economic policy response to the COVID-19 pandemic (9 April 2020); available <https://www.consilium.europa.eu/en/press/press-releases/2020/04/09/report-on-the-comprehensive-economic-policy-response-to-the-covid-19-pandemic/>; International Monetary Fund, 'Policy Responses to COVID-19; available <https://www.imf.org/en/Topics/imf-and-covid19/Policy-Responses-to-COVID-19>.

[80] See, Urs Gasser, Marcello Ienca, James Scheibner, Joanna Sleigh, and Effy Vayena, 'Digital tools against COVID-19: Framing the ethical challenges and how to address them,' arXiv:2004.10236 [cs.CY]; available <https://arxiv.org/abs/2004.10236>; Larry Catá Backer, Data Driven Management of COVID-19: The Case of Taiwan, Law at the End of the Day (6 March 2020); available <https://lcbackerblog.blogspot.com/2020/03/data-driven-management-of-covid-19-case.html>.

The way in which COVID-19 is counted is an example of where both functions merge. The counting is meant to be used to *accoun*t for the presence of the disease.[81] It is also meant to provide the measure against which political decisions might be made, for example, eliminating "stay at home" rules" or economic closures.[82] Yet the numbers, which appear so solid because of the unassailable solidity of a number as an object whose meaning cannot be varied (three always means three), exist only in themselves. When one tries to give them meaning in context, that becomes far.[83] Where the *counting* rules vary, then a comparative *accounting* becomes impossible—though politically valuable. The value comes in when public entities are tempted to use numbers strategically to support political decisions and then seek to suppress numbers that might undermine their choices in favor of data that supports it.[84] It is a temptation to use the unassailability of numbers to hide what or misdirect, or better put, to manage numbers the way that infections of COVID-19 are managed through policies of stay-in-place rules.[85]

Numbers do not lie, but numbers do not speak the truth either. They are objects and symbols of something that has meaning (three means three), but the significance of that meaning cannot be determined except within a specific context (three apples, three oranges in Spain, and thirty oranges in Italy). The understanding of a number as (a) sense or signification, (b) meaning or intention, and (c) significance or ideal worth)[86] is also dependent on the way in which the number is given meaning. In the

[81] Teri Schultz, 'Why Belgium's Death Rate Is So High: It Counts Lots Of Suspected COVID-19 Cases,' NPR (22 April 2020); available <https://www.npr.org/sections/coronavirus-live-updates/2020/04/22/841005901/why-belgiums-death-rate-is-so-high-it-counts-lots-of-suspected-covid-19-cases>.

[82] 'Wolf administration clarifies metrics used for reopening Pennsylvania,' Northcentral PA.com (26 April 2020); available <https://www.northcentralpa.com/life/covid-19_updates/wolf-administration-clarifies-metrics-used-for-reopening-pennsylvania/article_98cbf44a-8752-11ea-bf3f-ef71d66ee372.html>.

[83] Alan Reynolds, 'The Misleading Arithmetic of COVID-19 Death Rates,' Cato at Liberty (2 March 2020); available <https://www.cato.org/blog/misleading-arithmetic-covid-19-death-rates>.

[84] Kathleen McGrory and Rebecca Woolington, 'Florida medical examiners were releasing coronavirus death data: The State Made them Stop,' Tampa Bay Times (29 April 2020); available <https://www.tampabay.com/news/health/2020/04/29/florida-medical-examiners-were-releasing-coronavirus-death-data-the-state-made-them-stop/> ("The moves to withhold information comes at a sensitive moment for state leaders. Florida's coronavirus death toll is continuing to rise and state officials have begun talks about when and how to start reopening.").

[85] Soutik Biswas, 'India coronavirus: The 'mystery' of low Covid-19 death rates,' BBC News (28 April 2020); available <https://www.bbc.com/news/world-asia-india-52435463> ("Most affected countries have inadvertently under-reported deaths. Studying mortality data in 12 countries, The New York Times found that in March at least 36,000 more people died during the coronavirus pandemic than the official death counts... And a Financial Times analysis of overall fatalities during the pandemic in 14 countries found that the death toll from coronavirus may be almost 60% higher than reported in official counts.") Ibid.

[86] Lady Welby, "Significs," in Encyclopedia Britannica (1911).

case of COVID-19, that has proven hard to do.[87] It is in this context that numbers serve a critical role in triggering policy decisions, in providing the conditions necessary to justify governmental (or private) action, or in justifying political positions, especially in the context of the competition among states eager to prove that their systems were better suited to meeting the crisis (by reference to triumph measured by numbers).[88] Those decisions touch on pandemic responses, but also serve as a backdoor to justifying other system changes.[89]

COVID-19, of course, is not just about counting; it is also about keeping track. By 2020, some of it appeared to be less problematic when measured against the old constraints on the state.[90] But surveillance has a large, and for some troublesome element as well. First, tracking people's movements poses a challenge to old notions of privacy.[91] It is also undertaken by private enterprises. It is here, and for the most part only here, that there is a point of convergence between COVID-19 driven data based governance and the traditional discourse and human rights/constitutional principles. The European Union's efforts under its regulatory/rights framework provide a nice example of the engagement.[92] These focus on the relation of data to the individual; it does not focus as well on data and the transformation of governance and democratic ordering. That is to be expected under a framework in which the individual and individual rights are centered but in which the use of data by collective entities is understood as a species of techniques with little effect on key

[87] Cathy O'Neil, Opinion: '10 Reasons to Doubt the COVID-19 Data: The Pandemic's True Toll May Never Be Known,' Bloomberg (13 April 2020); available <https://www.bloomberg.com/opinion/articles/2020-04-13/ten-reasons-to-doubt-the-covid-19-data#xj4y7vzkg> (among others testing data does not reflect true rates of infection, tests aren't accurate, hospitalization rates are not comparable, underreporting of non-hospital deaths, officials in some countries have incentives to underreport in others to overreport, and the like).

[88] Mark Moore, 'China questions US handling of coronavirus amid global backlash,' New York Post (27 April 2020); available <https://nypost.com/2020/04/27/china-questions-us-handling-of-coronavirus-amid-global-backlash/>.

[89] See, Backer (2021); Joel Simon and Robert Mahoney, 'How China's Response to COVID-19 Set the Stage for a Worldwide Wave of Censorship: Authoritarian governments in eighty nations have enacted restrictions on free speech and political expression that were falsely described as public-health measures,' New Yorker (25 April 2022); available <https://www.newyorker.com/news/news-desk/how-chinas-response-to-covid-19-set-the-stage-for-a-worldwide-wave-of-censorship>.

[90] See, e.g., European Centre for Disease Prevention and Control, *Strategies for the surveillance of COVID-19* (April 2020); available <https://www.ecdc.europa.eu/sites/default/files/documents/COVID-19-surveillance-strategy-9-Apr-2020.pdf>.

[91] See, Larry Catá Backer, Automated Law and COVID-19: Data Driven Measures With National Characteristics In China and Israel and the Future of the Law-Governance Complex, Law at the End of the Day (24 March 2020); available <https://lcbackerblog.blogspot.com/2020/03/automated-law-and-covid-19-data-driven.html>.

[92] European Data Protection Board, Guidelines 04/2020 on the use of location data and contact tracing tools in the context of the COVID-19 outbreak Adopted on 21 April 2020; available <https://edpb.europa.eu/sites/default/files/files/file1/edpb_guidelines_20200420_contact_tracing_covid_with_annex_en.pdf>.

principles that support the character of the political model adopted in liberal democratic states.[93]

And, indeed, that partial convergence of the framework for the protection of individual liberties under constitutional and international frameworks suggests the limited utility of old conceptions of such rights systems in the face of a technology of government the measures of which tend to fall between the cracks of that framework. In this process of mediating between data collection and societal organizational principles, ideology substantially affects the way that a simulation imagines and imitates what it is supposed to model. What eventually winds up being modeled is an ideologically informed imitation—something between the ideal state and an ideal framework into which contemporary data points are inserted. That, then, is taken as the virtual object which when signified in virtual space, provides the descriptive, predictive, and control measures that then find their way back to the original.

2.2.3 The Simulation as the Modeled Collective

This brings us to a brief consideration of the second, and for our purposes, far more interesting form is the role of modeling. Modeling takes data, develops premises of relationships between them, and then constructs from this data and these presumed interactions a simulacrum of the reality they are meant to mimic. By so mimicking, the model can then be used to study the character of the reality thus simulated, and, if comprehensive enough, can also be used to predict and change the outcomes predicted. To simulate society is to reproduce it in ways that can be used to look back (for confirmation of the robustness of its characteristics) and to look forward (suggesting how the simulation will encounter and react to stimulus, for example, a COVID-19 pandemic). The modeling project makes visible the mathematical recreation of our world through a process of reduction and essentialization of chosen key factors (data and relationships), rationalizing these reduced and essentialized bits, and then developing a means of visualizing layers of essentialized responses in time.

> Newer, "agent-based models" are like the video game SimCity, but with a rampaging pathogen: using computing power unimagined even a decade ago, they simulate the interactions of millions of individuals as they work, play, travel, and otherwise go about their lives. Both of these approaches have often nailed projections of, for instance, U.S. cases of seasonal flu.[94]

[93]But see, Council of Europe, Respecting democracy, rule of law and human rights in the framework of the COVID-19 sanitary crisis: A toolkit for member states SG/Inf(2020)11 (7 April 2020) ("The major social, political and legal challenge facing our member states will be their ability to respond to this crisis effectively, whilst ensuring that the measures they take do not undermine our genuine long-term interest in safeguarding Europe's founding values of democracy, rule of law and human rights." Ibid., p. 2).

[94]Sharon Begley, 'Influential Covid-19 model uses flawed methods and shouldn't guide U.-S. policies, critics say,' Stat (17 April 2020); available <https://www.statnews.com/2020/04/17/influential-covid-19-model-uses-flawed-methods-shouldnt-guide-policies-critics-say/>.

Societies have moved from using big data-based games for entertainment to seeing in them the potential to re-create the entirety of human society, and on that basis extending the ability of those with the power to do so to intervene in the affairs of (simulated) humanity. In effect, data-driven pandemics now constitute a form of time travel in which models carry us forward to alternative futures that can be embraced or avoided by traveling back in time from the outer temporal space of the model and correcting the factors that produced a specific temporal outcome.[95] What was once the realm of politics (choices) is now the stuff of statistics. Indeed, modeling turns politics from the subject—the means by which decisions are made and authenticated (in accordance with current theories of popular participation, however, attenuated) to its object. In a political context dominated by models, politics and political decision-making become the thing that must be managed and directed in accordance with the genius of the model. Politics moves, therefore, from the act of decision-making to the acts of model making and application.

The trajectories of all this activity appear clear enough: the politics of COVID-19 responses and its structuring are now driven not by judgment based on data, but on the judgment of the models that are used to construct the alternative world scenarios whose reality is assumed and on that basis is used to make a determination of what ought to be imposed. There is a sense that at a minimum, these models are useful.[96]

> The epidemiological models of COVID-19's initial outbreak and spread have been useful. The Imperial College model, which predicted a terrifying 2.2 million deaths in the United States, agitated drowsy policymakers into action. The University of Washington's Institute of Health Metrics and Evaluation (IHME) model has provided a sense of the scale and timeline for peak hospitalization. Other models have estimated the effects of quarantine and of travel restrictions, or sought to find the pandemic's turning point. Despite some notable flaws, the epidemiological models have cumulatively had a beneficial effect on the national conversation.[97]

Where bad policy choices once called for better decision-making within the normative structures of politics (liberal democratic or Marxist Leninist); now bad choices call for better models that are better simulacra. "Existing models have been valuable, but they were not designed to support these types of critical decisions."[98] Political decisions are calculated and driven by the model; politics is undertaken in the choice

[95] See Sharon Brody and Derek J. Anderson, 'Mass. General Hospital Builds COVID-19 Simulator To Help Predict Impact of Policy Decisions,' WBUR (26 April 2020); available <https://www.wbur.org/news/2020/04/26/mass-general-hospital-covid-19-simulator>.

[96] Alex Engler, 'A call for a new generation of COVID-19 models,' Brookings (23 April 2020); available <https://www.brookings.edu/blog/techtank/2020/04/23/a-call-for-a-new-generation-of-covid-19-models/>.

[97] Ibid., links omitted ("Their ability to incorporate some epidemiological knowledge and the limited available data led to better—and harder to dismiss or deny—predictions of the near future than mere guesswork would have allowed.").

[98] Alex Engler, 'A call for a new generation of COVID-19 models,' supra ("Thousands of policymakers across the country, mostly at the state and local level, will need to decide where and when to re-open schools, ease business and social distancing restrictions, allow sports to resume, and make a myriad of other choices. * * *").

of the model, decisions about the way it is populated with data, and decisions about the relationships deemed critical in the process of reduction and essentialization that flattens lived reality to the simulation within which policy choices can be tested.[99] The political classes—in this model (here used with the irony it has come to deserve)—are reduced to the administrators of the systems whose decisions they are charged with implementing.

There is a certain irony here. Before 2020 and the COVID-19 pandemic, enthusiasm for simulation was blunted to some extent by the challenge of aligning the imitation to the idealized social values expressed in a collective's political and moral orders.[100] The object, at its heart, was to more closely align the new mechanics of governance and the new government it would birth, more closely with the normative values that appeared to still matter (or at least on the basis of which political collectives still officially adhered). But in the rush to meet the challenges of the pandemic, there was an equivalent rush to embrace the suzerainty of the model as the chief vehicle through which a politics of pandemic could be rationalized, and thus understood, and implemented.[101] The triumph of the simulation has shifted the center of politics where the insights of imitation are at their most influential to a politics of modeling—one that does not dispute the animating premise of the new governmentality.

The basic premise of a modeled society is this; the model must be obeyed. Politics becomes contests over the authority of competing models by the respective acolytes—and battles over control of the operation and maintenance of the model itself. Political power is a function of dominance in contests for championing first the "right model" and then the "correct application" of that model. As Nietzsche might suggest, our priestly class has broken the idols of our old gods and raised a new shiny, scientific, and data-driven god for the priests to serve as an intermediary and on whose alter human society will be offered.[102] These are battles fought through political figures but with the support of the researchers and technicians who now practice politics in their construction and tending of the models from which they derive their power and whose oracles are offered up to those with formal political power, who ignore than at their peril.

And the greatest irony—simulacra are as imperfect as the world it seeks to model. It reflects not just the flaws of the world simulated, but it may also amplify and distort those flaws in ways.[103] There is already an awareness of the ways in which models may reflect. "The essence of these arguments lies in an important, and perhaps counterintuitive observation: Using data and technology in a decision-making

[99] Begley, Influential COVID-19 Model, supra; Giordano et al. (2020), pp. 855–860.

[100] Discussed above text at notes 90–92, § 2.2.2.

[101] Criticized in Job McCloskey, 'Why No COVID-19 Models Have Been Accurate, And How To Fix That,' The Federalist (27 April 2020); available <https://thefederalist.com/2020/04/27/why-no-covid-19-models-have-been-accurate-and-how-to-fix-that/>.

[102] Nietzsche (1923), § 42.

[103] Discussed earlier at §2.1.

process doesn't make a decision automatically free of problematic (and possibly illegal) social discrimination."[104] But that produces a contradiction. A simulation is useful only to the extent that it reflects the world it models. But to model that world also reveals the disjunctions between its idealized view of itself, and the reality of the way that those ideals may have little or different connection with the actual behaviors of human actors. The model, as an accurate reductive mirror, reflects not merely the imperfections (the measurable spaces between social ideals and realities, and social tolerance of that gap, but also the changing landscape of the privileging of bias. All societies are biased in the sense that societal characteristics—and the ideal they represent—are the sum of choices about those forms of conduct, approaches, and ways of looking at the world that are to be privileged, and those that are to be suppressed. Good and evil—right and wrong—are in this sense little more than the semiotic expression of biased choices within collectives that give them their distinctive character and the fixed pole for assessing good from evil, imperfection from perfection, error from truth.[105]

---

[104] Emily Shaw, 'Avoiding prejudice in data-based decisions,' Sunlight Foundation (31 July 2015); available <https://sunlightfoundation.com/2015/07/31/avoiding-prejudice-in-data-based-decisions/>. See also Hannah-Moffat (2019), pp. 453–470 (reshaping risk and risk assessment).

[105] Compare Encyclical Letter Fides Et Ratio of The Supreme Pontiff John Paul II To The Bishops of The Catholic Church on The Relationship Between Faith and Reason (14 September 1998); available <https://www.vatican.va/content/john-paul-ii/en/encyclicals/documents/hf_jp-ii_enc_14091998_fides-et-ratio.html>.

> One of the most significant aspects of our current situation, it should be noted, is the "crisis of meaning". Perspectives on life and the world, often of a scientific temper, have so proliferated that we face an increasing fragmentation of knowledge... Indeed, still more dramatically, in this maelstrom of data and facts in which we live and which seem to comprise the very fabric of life, many people wonder whether it still makes sense to ask about meaning. The array of theories which vie to give an answer, and the different ways of viewing and of interpreting the world and human life, serve only to aggravate this radical doubt, which can easily lead to scepticism, indifference or to various forms of nihilism... A philosophy which no longer asks the question of the meaning of life would be in grave danger of reducing reason to merely accessory functions, with no real passion for the search for truth. To be consonant with the word of God, philosophy needs first of all to recover its sapiential dimension as a search for the ultimate and overarching meaning of life. (Fides et Ratio ¶81).

With Friedrich Nietzsche, Beyond Good and Evil (Helen Zimmern (trans), Complete Works of Friedrich Nietzsche 109-1913; Project Gutenberg EBook #4363 (7 December 2009).

> The falseness of an opinion is not for us any objection to it: it is here, perhaps, that our new language sounds most strangely. The question is, how far an opinion is life-furthering, life-preserving, species-preserving, perhaps species-rearing, and we are fundamentally inclined to maintain that the falsest opinions (to which the synthetic judgments a priori belong), are the most indispensable to us, that without a recognition of logical fictions, without a comparison of reality with the purely IMAGINED world of the absolute and immutable, without a constant counterfeiting of the world by means of numbers, man could not live—that the renunciation of false opinions would be a renunciation of life, a negation of life. TO RECOGNISE UNTRUTH AS A CONDITION OF LIFE; that is certainly to impugn the

Here one begins to see the way in which politics may insinuate itself in the production and use of models. One does not model a world merely to describe its imperfections (understood as the measurable distance between the ideal of itself in the aggregation of privileged biases) but to predict the future course of that gap between reality and ideal without intervention, and, more importantly, the effect of intervention on closing that gap. It is at the stage where one determines what world the model will simulate—the world as it exists or the ideal world as the modeler would like it to be. It follows that the creation of a simulation that reproduces an idealized reality is to further distort the simulation and reduce its utility. It also suggests that simulation cannot avoid the embedding of politics—only that the politics is hidden within the premises and modalities of simulation construction. That is, a simulation is used not merely to see how a specific set of factors have effects on communities or individuals, but at the same time how human and communal behavior relates to the ideal version of itself. As such, a simulation does not necessarily reflect reality but instead the reality of perfectibility.

But the politics of simulation is not evidenced merely by the way in which it relates to the tensions between the real and idealized version of the society it simulates. It also embeds politics in the way a simulation chooses to emphasize (amplify) certain human or individual characteristics and reduce others to a marginal space. In this sense, even without a goal of conscious prediction or intervention—the mere construction of a model can produce effects that change the future at the macro- and micro-levels of collective social organization.[106] This is not just a matter of data harvesting (the information that is used to build simulations and that which is ignored—a well-known issue), rather it is the way that this data is weighted and embedded within the mathematical relationships that together create a functioning simulation. Thus, politics, and prejudice, filter into the construction of the mathematical relationships through which a simulation is constructed and then manipulated to aid in the construction of conclusions. This is unavoidable—the essence of simulation is essentialization that is in turn the expression of the need to reduce the complexity of reality to a manageable level. Reductionism, then, produces an important site for politics. The way in which one decides how and why reality is reduced; the choice of who makes those decisions; the way that reduction is expressed; the expression of the essential; these are the spaces in which politics is practiced in a world in which human society is managed through models. But note the consequence—where politics is now embedded in the construction of models, it no longer is centered on those who are formally vested with political authority—

traditional ideas of value in a dangerous manner, and a philosophy which ventures to do so, has thereby alone placed itself beyond good and evil. (Ibid., ¶4).

[106] Shaw, 'Avoiding prejudice in data-based decisions,' supra ("Because data stemming from criminal-justice-related events are often legally used to prevent people from accessing social goods — such as the right to vote, certain kinds of employment, or places to live — the question of whether released individual-level data can systemically harm traditional subjects of discrimination looms particularly large").

whether that authority is exercised through a Marxist-Leninist or a liberal democratic model.

The same applied to the use of the model. Part of the value of simulation is predictive. But prediction assumes that nothing changes. The real value of simulation is to test policies and other interventions before they are actually put into effect. How one chooses those interventions, how those interventions may be constrained by higher order values; how those solutions may be guided by the political character of a society, and how those interventions reflect the customs and expectations of a society will make a great deal of difference. The way the range of choices is constructed and the importance of these meta-principles serve to mold the spectrum of choices deemed plausible points to yet another point of politics in simulated governance.[107] Where the power to develop a choice spectrum is delegated to technicians and modelers, those external constraints either disappear in the service of a "value-free" choice spectrum is constructed, or more likely, the choice spectrum will reflect the personal views of the modeler. One has yet to consider the rules for testing those choice processes—except at the level of the ideal. There is much talk that aspects of modeling (AI; surveillance, data use, etc.) must conform to the highest ideals of society, but there is very little in embedding those ideals into the practices of simulation as a substitute for engagement in the real world which it is meant to serve.[108] The ideological ruptures among the objectives toward which models are centered and the ideological foundations of social collectives were already much in evidence at the start of the pandemic.[109]

[107] Matissa Hollister, 'AI can help with the COVID-19 crisis - but the right human input is key,' World Economic Forum (30 March 2020); available <https://www.weforum.org/agenda/2020/03/covid-19-crisis-artificial-intelligence-creativity/> ("The COVID-19 crisis, therefore, will highlight something that has always been true about AI: it is a tool, and the value of its use in any situation is determined by the humans who design it and use it.").

[108] See, e.g., 'Ensuring that business respects human rights during the Covid-19 crisis and beyond: The relevance of the UN Guiding Principles on Business and Human Rights,' Statement by the UN Working Group on Business and Human Rights (27 April 2020); available <https://www.ohchr.org/en/statements/2020/04/ensuring-business-respects-human-rights-during-covid-19-crisis-and-beyond?LangID=E&NewsID=25837> ("To mention but a few illustrative examples, this responsibility also applies to tech companies developing applications to monitor the spread of the virus, who need to address the human rights risks of intrusive data collection and surveillance, including by thinking ahead for when the health crisis is over."); Independent High Level Expert Group on Artificial Intelligence, 'Ethics Guidelines for Trustworthy AI,' (Brussels, European Commission (8 April 2019); available <https://digital-strategy.ec.europa.eu/en/library/ethics-guidelines-trustworthy-ai> ("Trustworthy AI has three components: (1) it should be lawful, ensuring compliance with all applicable laws and regulations, (2) it should be ethical, ensuring adherence to ethical principles and values and (3) it should be robust, both from a technical and social perspective since to ensure that, even with good intentions, AI systems do not cause any unintentional harm." Ibid., p. 35).

[109] Astrid Prange, 'Will Germans trade privacy for coronavirus protection?,' Deutsche Welle (29 March 2020) available <https://www.dw.com/en/will-germans-trade-privacy-for-coronavirus-protection/a-52943225> ("In Taiwan and South Korea, it isn't illegal to leave your home, and shops and restaurants remain open. 'Big Data' is far more effective at fighting the virus than the

For all that, there is a certain comfort to this data-driven turn, one that might have raised hackles in almost any other context in which political decisions are being made. This is a culture well trained in the certainty of science and the power of quantification as inherently less ambiguous and deceptive than words. They provide our contemporary wizards with the power to "read the past, present, and future in accordance with numbers and computations" (Crosby, supra, p. 124) based on the faith that reality is mathematical (Ibid., p. 123). That is simulations can be used to create our world in a form in which it is possible to travel in time and in so doing to change predicted outcomes by changing present responses now makes those of us with power feel like we (they) might wield the power of the gods. That the power is flawed and imperfect is of little moment in terms of its utility for exercising power.

> So if epidemiological models don't give us certainty—and asking them to do so would be a big mistake—what good are they? Epidemiology gives us something more important: agency to identify and calibrate our actions with the goal of shaping our future. We can do this by pruning catastrophic branches of a tree of possibilities that lies before us.[110]

The model becomes the "Holy Spirit" of a magisterium of experts in whose hands decisions are now vested.[111] And these are useful gods indeed—even better than the gods of law and theory; for these gods are less intelligible; they are immanent within the algebraic formulations of mathematically driven reductionist relations, and they may be only interpreted, constructed, and applied by a priestly class whose power is now assured. These are the matters that ought to give us all pause, but not panic. That pause need not be directed toward a reactionary effort (and pursued ultimately in vain) for the return of the old order. It is far too late for that (and in a sense that effort also constitutes a sort of simulation of nostalgia). It ought to be directed toward the principles on which our new high priests of modeling, and their control of the political collective can be constrained and made responsive to whatever higher order set of principles we believe, as a collective, express our (and the ultimate irony here) essence.

While most political elites tend to be quite opaque about their engagements in this respect (especially those who most loudly claim to center transparency in governance—an irony which is both ordinary and profound in contemporary culture), the leading elements of American political culture now appear to embrace transparency. A recent story widely circulated provides a window on the way that the theoretical musings earlier elaborated are actually shaping the forms, discourse, and language of politics.[112]

absurd border closures in Europe." Ibid., quoting the German Korean philosopher Byung Chul Han writing an opinion essay for the Spanish daily newspaper El Pais).

[110] Zeynep Tufekci, 'Don't Believe the COVID-19 Models,' The Atlantic (2 April 2020); available <https://www.theatlantic.com/technology/archive/2020/04/coronavirus-models-arent-supposed-be-right/609271/>.

[111] For the analogy in contemporary religion, see, e.g., O'Gara and Vertin (1996), pp. 125–142.

[112] Francis Mulraney, 'Trump administration officials thought COVID-19 death toll would never reach 60,000 and that medical experts caused the president to overreact 'like the school nurse telling

2.2.4 Simulation as Politics and the Battle of the Models in the United States

"Policy makers must make trade-offs among competing values in a pandemic... they need to balance health and safety and economic development, individual freedom and collective interest . . . , transparency and privacy, rights and obligations, efficiency and equity, and free expression and preventing rumors and panic."[113] Simulation increasingly provides both the framework and the conceptual universe within which that balancing may be authoritatively undertaken. This post considers the way that the reporting illustrates the ubiquity of the simulation as the vehicle for politics, and the way that this has produced its own simulated politics.

This was highlighted in the intense conflicts within the Trump Administration in the first weeks of the pandemic in the United States in 2020.[114] As reported by the Washington Post:

> The epidemiological models ... showed the novel coronavirus was likely to kill between 100,000 and 240,000 Americans. President Trump was apprehensive about so much carnage on his watch, yet also impatient to reopen the economy—and he wanted data to justify doing so. So the White House considered its own analysis. A small team led by Kevin Hassett—a former chairman of Trump's Council of Economic Advisers with no background in infectious diseases—quietly built an econometric model to guide response operations.

The Washington Post had not been well disposed to the Trump Administration generally, and the well-publicized feuding between its owner and Mr., Trump, provided a challenge.[115] But the critical reporting[116] also reflected the unstated embrace by the writers (and the editors approving the story for publication in the way it was written) of a set of political assumptions and choices quite irreconcilable with those of senior Trump Administration officials centered on the core principle that aggregate human death prevention must be advanced over aggregate economic difficulties producing its own set of tragedies; and that simulation that de-centers this

---

the principal how to run the school,' Daily Mail (3 May 2020); available <https://www.dailymail.co.uk/news/article-8281555/Trump-administration-officials-thought-COVID-19-death-toll-never-reach-60-000.html>.

[113] Yang (2020), p. 658.

[114] Philip Rucker, Josh Dawsey, Yasmeen Abutaleb, Robert Costa, and Lena H. Sun, '34 days of pandemic: Inside Trump's desperate attempts to reopen America: Though Trump remained fixated on reopening the economy, he and his administration fell far short of making that a reality,' Washington Post (2 May 2020).

[115] See, e.g., Roger Yu, 'Trump Tweet Blasts Bezos, Amazon,' USA Today (17 August 2017) ("Trump's blistering tweet, his first of the day, was issued hours after The Washington Post -- the newspaper owned by Amazon chairman Jeff Bezos -- ran an editorial with the headline, 'Mr. Trump gives comfort to racists.'" Ibid).

[116] For reporting from a different perspective, see, Francis Mulraney, 'Trump administration officials thought COVID-19 death toll would never reach 60,000 and that medical experts caused the president to overreact 'like the school nurse telling the principal how to run the school', Daily Mail (3 May 2020); available <https://www.dailymail.co.uk/news/article-8281555/Trump-administration-officials-thought-COVID-19-death-toll-never-reach-60-000.html>.

core premise ought to be approached with suspicion as to intent and robustness .... And the politics of liberal democracy.[117] "'They're all about science, science, science, which is good, but sometimes there's a little bit less of a consideration of politics when maybe there should be.' ... More recent conflicts between the science-led and politics-led parts of the administration have come as a pathway to reopening has been announced that will rely heavily on widespread testing."[118]

Whatever the critical analytics of the politics of COVID-19 undertaken by the Trump Administration, those politics were driven by and through models. The simulation of politics and political choices determined both the valuation and the range of plausible alternatives. The models offered simulated realities that valued different objectives and did so differently—human versus economic mortality. And the debates about policy centered on the viability of the model, the robustness of their data and analytics, and their underlying assumptions. Predictive analytics—grounded on the assumption of the 'truth' of its descriptive simulation projected forward became the reality from out of which decisions about the future course of the modeled subject would be taken.[119] And, in its more advanced stage, both descriptive and predictive simulations provided the basis for the assessment of the risk of alternative futures in the face of conscious intervention. were current actions altered. These can be grouped into eight related points.

First, there is still a tenancy to personalize simulation. The usual seraglio politics of spaces that are effectively hermetically sealed (e.g., a Standing Committee of a Political Bureau, or an Office of a President) appear to shift their focus but not their target in a context where decisions are made around or through simulation. There is a tendency, then, to align, to *create an identity, between the simulation and the simulator.* It follows that the effective essence of this essentializing tool is the personal politics and ambitions of the simulator. In effect, the simulation is an extension of the simulator as much as it is the modeling of the slice of reality from out of which a policy decision must be made. Simulations, then, are the masks worn by those who wish to hide personal agendas in the more neutral language of quantified reality.

Second, simulations are understood as the way that values are now expressed. To choose a particular form of simulation is to choose a set of values that are to be advanced by the simulation. But more than that, choosing a particular form of simulation is meant to foreclose any debate on the premises on which that simulation

[117] Philip Rucker, Josh Dawsey, Yasmeen Abutaleb, Robert Costa, and Lena H. Sun, '34 days of pandemic,' supra (discussing the actions of the group of officials led by the Vice President's chief of staff who discounted the mortality projections and viewed as much more damaging the economic projections of more comprehensive health measures).

[118] Ibid. (quoting a senior administration official about the medical and health expert team at the White House and drawn from an interview reported by the Washington story, Philip Rucker, Josh Dawsey, Yasmeen Abutaleb, Robert Costa, and Lena H. Sun, '34 days of pandemic,' supra).

[119] Cf., Thapa (2019) ("data-based political evidence resonates with the popular "rationalist model of politics", 43 which implicitly promises to supplant messy democratic deliberation with clean scientific decisions.." Ibid., p. 29).

was chosen. *Choosing simulations is a form of choosing sides in a political contest.* In the case of COVID-19, that necessary fragmentation was understood as separating out those who placed a greater value on economic simulation against those who would value health more. Both of course are after the same ultimate result—the maximization of the welfare of the American people—but each of their conceptual universes produces highly different pathways to that goal—and with those pathways quite different effects on individuals.[120] There is an analogy in international law—the fracture of the human rights listed in the Universal Declaration of Human Rights among two International Covenants. One was modeled on the principle that all economic, social, and cultural rights could only be realized through the primary protection of civil and political rights. The other is that human rights could only be modeled on the basis that civil and political rights were merely the fruit of the attainment of robust economic, social, and cultural rights.

Third, the authority of simulations remains a function of class. I do not mean class in the simplistic (though valuable for the time) way that it is understood by Marxist-Leninism, or as societal rankings in the West. Rather I mean prestige and authority classes as those are formulated within a societal ordering. There is not a soul on Earth who is not trained in assessing these in accordance with the ranking rules of the society she inhabits. One's simulation is only as authoritative as one's standing within these prestige classes. Even the writers of the article understood this, placing that referent in the headline of the story. It was nicely distilled in the reporting: "One former senior administration official told the Post that the bloc looked at the health experts 'like the school nurse trying to tell the principal how to run the school'."[121] This quote effectively tells one all one needs to know about simulation within a vertically structured social, political, and economic order. It is both refreshingly candid and quite rigid about what it suggests as the connection between simulation and authority.

Fourth, simulation shifts the locus of politics. Where politics once occurred around simulation (that is politics was exogenous to simulation), now politics occurs within the simulation (that is it is now endogenous). One does fight about the use of politics—as a tool, as a measure of reality, as anything, really. Instead, one fights about its assumptions, its constructions, and the evaluation of its predictive qualities as one shifts contingent factors that move the model in any direction. That shifting of

---

[120] Larry Catá Backer, Ruminations 90: Sacrificing the Most Humble on the Altar of Leadership-- May Day 2020 in the Shadow of Pandemic, Law at the End of the Day (1 May 2020); available <https://lcbackerblog.blogspot.com/2020/05/ruminations-90-sacrificing-most-humble.html> ("That debate has not been undertaken in the usual manner of a bottom up representative republic; that is by and for the electorate. Rather that debate has been performed for the electorate as audience and for their consumption. The value of that performance is meant to harvested and consumed, in turn, as polling data to feed electoral simulations. Those simulations (on the value of simulations here) in turn are meant to provide the mechanism through which what is said and what is debated might be most usefully constructed in ways that manage popular opinion." Ibid.)

[121] Frances Mulraney, 'Trump administration officials thought COVID-19 death toll would never reach 60,000,' supra.

politics one about to one within predictive analytics becomes impossible in the face of techno-expert capture in a modeling universe of hyper-silos. When that happens, as it did in the Trump Administration faced with the unprecedented predictive and intervention its demands of early COVID, then that politics is undertaken through the construction of an alternative model. In this case, it was based on the availability of a health versus an economics-centered model. These two models, like *condottieri* in fifteenth century Italy, then march around endlessly in battles of attrition in which total victory is impossible and unwelcome, but the marginal advantage decides the fate of all. This, then, is what the chronicles of the intrigues within the White House might be reduced to—and always the simulation in the background, and the foreground.

Fifth, simulation substitutes quantified for qualitative moral authority or principle. Quantification and the simulations it produces have the great virtue of providing the authority that is necessary to advance projects. This virtue is especially important in the absence of either personal, moral, or principled authority. In a sense, then, the rise of simulation is the strongest point of the decay of politics. Politics can only be expressed with the reassurance of quantified and simulated reality in a context in which the old political institutions and structures, along with those eager to serve within them, no longer enjoy the level of trust necessary to buttress a political and societal system entirely on its own.

Sixth, the more effective tools of politics are now quantifiable and predictive. Politics has lost its moorings in values and principles. Instead, it is now moored in outcomes. And outcomes are themselves the managed product of simulation. This is neither new nor transformative: it is instead an intensification and deepening of tendencies already quite visible in politics globally. Nonetheless, it is particularly appealing for an administrative apparatus to which politically charged discretionary decision-making is delegated. "In the risk-averse environment of public administration, the incentive structures are clear: If caseworkers follow the algorithmic recommendations and they turn out to be wrong, they can shift the blame to the ADM system."[122] The predictive quality of simulation inevitably moves analysis from mere prediction to intervention. That movement has a further and important effect—it shifts the character of risk and risk-taking from one that might have been risk neutral or risk-seeking to a risk-averse anticipatory model. Indeed, that reshaping of risk marks much of the reliance on simulation—prevention, mitigation, and remedial principles have reshaped the premises of economic and administrative approaches to the management of social collectives.[123] One enters here the world of predictive policing.[124]

Seventh, simulation reduces the populace (individuals and collectives) to silence. Simulation ultimately realigns democratic authority. Democratic input is generated

---

[122] Thapa (2019), p. 31.

[123] van den Homberg et al. (2020), pp. 456–467 (human rights centering risk prevention respecting the simulation and modeling of administrative and economic activity).

[124] See, e.g., Seele (2017), pp. 675–676.

from the harvesting of data identified as valuable and its admixture through descriptive analytcs that then serve as the foundation for predictive modeling. Politics *within the model* is expressed thorugh data choices and analytics; but its object is now to perfect the model. Politics though the model is expressed through simulation; it is simulated in the way that the dissociated aggregated democratic populace is represented (and animated) through the model. The ultimate outcome of a simulated politics is the intensification of the construction of the electorate (or the masses elsewhere) as passive stakeholders. But more than passive, simulation reduces the people to silence, the silence of an onlooker unable to understand the reality around her without the aid of those who can interpret the simulacra of reality and thus guide them toward an alignment of simulated and experienced reality. Principles are easy to engage—anyone can do it. Predictive analytics makes it harder for just anyone to participate.

Eighth, simulation ultimately reduces the power of the leadership core. Simulation indicates the rise of the machine (AI) and its techno-expert priests and the diminution of the populace as an effective political actor (even when measured from the cynical baselines of the end of the twentieth century). But it has a more pernicious effect—it can reduce the core leadership to a similar state. Core leaders exercise decision-making power in a world of simulation, but it is the simulation (and their simulators) who actually wield the power to order (and manage) the reality within which decisions may be plausibly made. One enters the world of the coder and the modeler who have the power to translate the normative decisions of traditional political centers into the model from which decisions will be extracted. At the same time, it opens a new venue for corruption—the reverse engineering of predictive simulation in the service of a decision seeking justification. In either case, the authority of the core leadership can be diminished, and with it another supporting pillar in the foundations of a political system.

3 In Search of Semiotic 'Trantors': The Modeling of Predictive Universes

Technology has made it possible again to de-center the individual from their humanness, even as it focuses more intensely on the individual eccentricities that collectively define the human.[125] And it has enabled the relocation of the subjective from the individual to the collective and from their outward into inter-collective subjectivity and back inward into the dialogical challenges of the human being as a data point against the leveling power of the algorithm. Simulation merges system and lifeworld in an interactive metasystem of mutual reflection—the simulated world is

[125] Ingersoll et al. (1987), ("I deliberately and specifically dealt with what we might call political science or the science of history, and developed a technology for" Ibid., 75).

objectified and reproduced as an autonomous lifeworld that impacts the simulated world even as that impact changes the simulated reflection.[126]

Nonetheless, technology cannot absorb all data everywhere across space and time and species. An initial reduction is necessary. That was the lesson of Trantor at the core of the human galactic empire and the caution of the Genesis recounting of the danger of the Tree of Kowledge. That reduction requires the creation of a simulation that will reproduce in a manageable way (given the limits of technology) the universe of data that is to be (1) identified; (2) analyzed; and (3) used to see the effects of policy and other political choices in virtual reductionist and essential human simulated spaces. We are now what we measure.[127] System and lifeworld collapse in and as its simulation; one in which each is the simulation of the other, a mutual objectification that moves toward the *dissipation* of the boundaries between the imagined and the concrete. But we cannot measure everything—that would be necessary for a complete model.[128] Instead, we have metastasized our crude first effort at simulating simulation—the focus group—into a comprehensive but working reduction from out of which it might be possible to simulate a model of what is to be observed.

One can see how this operates in real space in the context of a pandemic—a situation in a portion of the world that is technologically possible to model on these terms.

And thus back to Asimov and his *Prelude to Foundation* and as well to the Tree of the Knowledge of Good and Evil. Technology brings one back to a mechanization of signs and an instrumentalization of signification. And so Emperor Cleon—ruler of thousands of worlds within a galaxy so large that even planets are granular eccentricities—is moved to ask: "*I am given to understand that you believe it is possible to predict the future*."[129] The question itself was nudged by a simulation of the individual—the Emperor's robot advisor who represented the initial effort to incarnate the singularity of humanity within the singularity of its mechanical expression. The robot R. Daneel Olivaw nudges key individual behavior at critical junctures to increase the probability of a desired future outcome.[130] The simulation would do the same but by aggregating the individual into a collective, and by nudging the collective, and ensure aggregate movement. In the process, one substitutes mathematics (data-based quantification) for intuition (language and communication). That, in turn, requires methods of the incarnation of collectives; these then structure the necessity and challenge of modeling—of modeling humanity, one that is in its

[126] Cf., Krispin (2019), pp. 869–887.

[127] Dan Ariely, Column: You Are What You Measure, Harvard Business Review, June 2010; available [http://hbr.org/2010/06/column-you-are-what-you-measure/ar/1]; Sam Luce, "We are What We Measure," Sam Luce.com (26 May 2011); available [https://samluce.com/2010/05/you-are-what-you-measure/].

[128] This transforms the old debates about objectification, freedom, system and lifeworld by shifting both its language and locus. Cf., Cook (2005), pp. 55–78.

[129] Asimov (1988), p. 10.

[130] Ibid.

essence comprised of a problem of identification ad of the management of humanity toward "good" ends.[131] To that end, it is necessary to construct a model of humanity from the aggregation of models of individual human beings—of the aggregation of collective eccentricities that then produce both the norm and its range of deviation. In effect—the simulation of humanity is built on the simulation of the human individual. The robot, who names himself ironically enough as the robot that for its own purpose named himself Hummin (as the incarnated simulation of humanity), represents that foundational simulacra of the individual, one which was necessary but not sufficient to model humanity. One might ask, however, whether in that reconstitution one also seeks to eat of the Tree of Life and through machine learning medeling seek to become God ("Behold, the man is become one of us, to know good and evil; and now, lest he put forth his hand and take also of the tree of life, and eat, and live for ever" (Gen 3:22).

3.1 The Construction and Operation of Contemporary Trantors—The New Semiotics of Regulations and Social Relations Trantor

The twenty-first century has now witnessed the birth of a large community of Hari Seldons, each seeking to find their own Trantor into which to project the predictive powers of a model that can be used not merely to predict—but to experiment with alternative versions of the future by manipulating in hypothetical space, the present. Humanity now constructs robot incarnations of itself at the micro level. Like Robots, simulations encapsulate a specific portion of the greater construct that is humanity, the simulation of which is the great ambition of a collective that seeks to reproduce an autonomous but identical representation of itself. To that end, the Robot is necessary—the way that Trantor is necessary for the larger project—as a simulation of the object to be a simulation, through which simulation is possible. One cannot simulate the humanity reproducing it but only by constructing a model of it for the end. For humanity a planet was necessary. The perfect simulation is always seeking its own simulation—its Trantor on which to model a descriptive, predictive and controllable version of itself from out of which it can observe and experiment on itself but in the body of its image constructed from an essentialized model of itself.

[131] Thus R Daneel Olivaw explains to Hari Seldon:

> But what is humanity? To what can we point when we speak of humanity And how can we define harm to humanity ? . . . When I heard your speech to the Decennial Convention, I realized at once that in psychohistory there was a tool that might make it possible to identify what was good and bad for humanity. With it, the decisions we would make would be less blind [that is less reliant on individual intuition]. I would even trust to human beings to make these decisions. . .

Ibid., pp. 426–427.

The power of this insight had not escaped the global community—and certainly, political sociologists—from a time well before the possibility of simulation and predictive-control analytics was nothing more than science fiction. At the beginning of the twentieth century, the focus was on eugenics and the simulation of human hybridity. Academics and commentators in Argentina, for example, sought to qualitatively model the new Argentine hybrid by conceptually simulating the appropriate intermixing of the component peoples of Argentina drawn, like cooking ingredients, from its indigenous and migrant populations.[132] But it was in the United States that its leading social forces especially after 1945 sought to transform the United States into the Earth's Trantor. That simulation was the gateway to embracing the idea of the United States as the simulation of the world; and so simulated, it served both as the world's laboratory but also as its leading forces. The idea, ultimately, was to produce a merger between the simulation (the United States) and its object under the guidance of the simulation.[133]

> Thus with the 44th President, the symbolic evolution of the United States from ethnos to universal community comes one step closer to realization. The United States is more than a state, it is instead the symbolic amalgamation of all of the people's of the world. Its vision is not merely national, but global, and on account of its makeup and history, and the realization of the truth of that history, it can stand legitimately for the world... No other state can claim this representative legitimacy. But religion has... It follows, that within the United States, the global laboratory now operates to generate a valid new truth for the world, a new global governance covenant. Within this forged new community, a new framework, a new truth—the fulfillment of the old covenant—can now be revealed and advanced for the betterment of the United States and the world. "What the cynics fail to understand is that the ground has shifted beneath them -- that the stale political arguments that have consumed us for so long no longer apply."[134]

But the quantification and measurability of simulation—its more scientific rationalization, has produced a transformation in the search for Trantor, for that space from which it is possible to simulate the object of simulation. Sometimes that production

---

[132] Ingenieros (1988, 1918).

[133] Larry Catá Backer, Democracy Part XIV: "For Now We See Through A Glass, Darkly; But Then Face to Face"; On President Obama's Inauguration Speech, Law at the End of the Day (21 January 2009); available <https://lcbackerblog.blogspot.com/2009/01/democracy-part-xiv-for-now-we-see.html>.

[134] Ibid., citing Barack H. Obama, 'For Now We See Through A Glass, Darkly; But Then Face to Face', Speech Delivered on his Inauguration as President of the United States (21 January 2009); available <https://obamawhitehouse.archives.gov/blog/2009/01/21/president-Barack-obamas-inaugural-address>. Here the critical language form the speech:

> For we know that our patchwork heritage is a strength, not a weakness. We are a nation of Christians and Muslims, Jews and Hindus -- and nonbelievers. We are shaped by every language and culture, drawn from every end of this Earth; and because we have tasted the bitter swill of civil war and segregation, and emerged from that dark chapter stronger and more united, we cannot help but believe that the old hatreds shall someday pass; that the lines of tribe shall soon dissolve; that as the world grows smaller, our common humanity shall reveal itself; and that America must play its role in ushering in a new era of peace. Ibid.

of Trantor—in virtual communities, produces a virtual world of linguistic control (suppressing sensitive terms that refer to sensitive realities in the simulated community). That appears to be nicely evidenced on the Chinese platform community and its social media where analytics of control has produced what appears to be an endless game of changing vocabulary—to vest the naming of a prohibited object with another word—and over and over within a sub-community receptive to the changing meanings of words.[135]

Education serves as its own Trantor, with its own simulations, descriptive, predictive, and control analytics. Education, it has been noted, "is increasingly treated as a 'computational' project."[136] , characterized by simulation recursivity—object and simulation mirror and change each other with each intervention.[137] And now with the growing risk of school violence, predictive analytics and interventions have expanded their universe through the techniques of scenario planning.[138] Central here is the strong convergence between the object and its simulation in the form of active shooter simulations.[139] These focus on so-called wicked problems marked by information gaps, conflicting values, and confusion.[140] These can also be simulated for better study and adaptation.[141] For this purpose, the universe of schools can be simulated through exercises in representative institutions and thus a simulated model. Scenario planning and active shooter drills serve as distinctive applications of

[135] See Stella Chan, 'Don't You Dar Say "WeChat",' China Media Project (27 July 2022); available <https://chinamediaproject.org/2022/07/27/dont-you-dare-say-wechat/> ("'No wonder all of these program hosts say these really strange words,' wrote one user in a comment that received more than 30,000 likes. For others, the word restrictions exposed what seemed entirely futile policies that went against human nature... Could such online language obstacles, which forced users into constant creative detours such as the use of homonyms and intentional misspellings, have a real impact on language development?" Ibid.)

[136] Williamson (2016), pp. 128–131. Quoting Selwyn (2015), pp. 64–82 Williamson notes the cyclidity of control simulation:

> algorithmically driven 'systems thinking' – where complex (and unsolvable) social problems associated with education can be seen as complex (but solvable) statistical problems. ... This leads to a recursive state where data analysis begins to produce educational settings, as much as educational settings producing data. (Selwyn 2015, p. 72).

[137] Williamson (2016), p. 124.

[138] Jay Ogilvy, 'Scenario Planning and Strategic Forecasting,' Forbes (8 January 2015); available <https://www.forbes.com/sites/stratfor/2015/01/08/scenario-planning-and-strategic-forecasting/?sh=24e2d38f411a> ("Scenarios are alternate futures in which today's decisions may play out. They are stories with beginnings, middles and ends. Good scenarios have twists and turns that show how the environment might change over time." Ibid.).

[139] See, e.g., Jonson et al. (2020), pp. 154–166 ("first study to compare the two competing paradigms informing active shooter drills (traditional lockdown versus multi-option responses) to determine which could potentially end the event more quickly and result in fewer injuries and casualties." Ibid., 162).

[140] Wright et al. (2019), pp. 12–15.

[141] Phadnis (2019), pp. 1–15.

the theory of Trantor—as a simulation of the more complex environment of all schools exposed to active shooters.[142]

And yet, the greatest Trantors are all around us. And they are useful to a variety of actors, One speaks here of the great vats of data that are the social media platforms. Twitter appears irresistible to state security apparatus.[143] Its possibilities have the ambition of Sheldon's psychohistory.[144] It can be used to help reshape the world that it mirrors—in a representative and essentialized form.[145] These all suggest the essential role of Trantors—of data sets, of platforms, of a self-reflexive and contained simulation of the object of study that replicates it in a simpler but essential form. It is the hunt for Trantor that serves as the foundation for the complexities that are emerging in a semiotics of imitation. That hunt has now produced its own models and off-the-shelf objects, the purpose of which is to create Trantor when it is otherwise unavailable.[146] What follows is now inescapable—our modernity, our contemporary space, is built on the mutual stimulation of an object and its simulation.

3.2 Reading the Runes: The Semiotics of Modelling and the Modelling of Semiotics

Modeling and simulation remind us that signification is not identical to self-actualization. It marks a triumph of digitalization and its quantification, as the abstracted signification of the thing modeled. And it permits an intersubjectivity of models, of simulations, through which simulated realities may themselves be combined in simulated space to produce a larger and larger simulation of realities that may be experimented with, and from which it may be possible to adjust behaviors. It is rather the externalization of creation. It is the recognition of a repeating pattern of opposition that in their naming might then be objectified for higher order interactions and the careful management of the granular realities of the individual whose own relationship with themselves can be nudged through the application of stimulus from outside the quantum and trajectories of which are provided by and in the model, and through the model it is possible to move forward in time to predict the effects of the nudging of individuals and collectives. And thus, Hari Seldon's answer to Emperor

[142] Asimov (1988), pp. 412–414 (the representative reduction and essentialized standing for thew whole). See the excellent discussion in Abrajan (2007), pp. 105–127.

[143] Weinburger (2011), p. 301.

[144] Ibid. ("There is already plenty of published literature on predicting stock market volatility based on open sources, says Kalev Leetaru, a computer scientist at the University of Illinois at Urbana-Champaign. But that's a long way from being able to predict a riot next Wednesday.").

[145] For example, Leili et al. (2017), pp. S4343–S4356.

[146] See, e.g., Butterworth et al. (2014), p. 288 ("open-source simulation analysis platform, freely downloadable, running on Linux, Macintosh, and Windows, providing tools for the steps in the modeling analysis of data").

Cleon's question is redolent with subtle potential: "In studying human society, it is possible to choose a starting point and to make appropriate assumptions that will suppress chaos. That will make it possible to . . . calculate probabilities."[147]

What Seldon expresses is the signification of the incarnation of an object, humanity, as an object that may be molded—modeled, and animated, through the study of its own simulation. He is not predicting the future, but he is offering a means of shaping the future—of imposing meaning projected forward through the application of "appropriate assumptions." That effectively is the new face of meaning-making. Moreover, it is also democratic: Seldon concedes the leveling effect of modeling—"With proper mathematics, anyone would be able to assess the probabilities. It wouldn't take the rare human being who is successful because of a remarkably intuitive sense."[148]

In the process, the semiotics of the human shifts as well. And that is the object of this contribution. It considers the phenomenon of simulation, of modeling, on which reality is now dependent for its understanding of itself. This is the ironic fulfillment of one expression of Nietzsche's phenomenology; and also the rise of Broekman's Self-E.[149] But more than that, simulation now does not merely model reality, it is made to predict; it is a system of divination that speaks to the future by considering the sum of the past. The object of this examination is to suggest the beginnings of a simulated semiotics for a simulated reality. Simulation represents here both a reduction and modeling of the world which both represents and is the reality is models, and at the same time it provides the platform through which that model may be bent, adjusted, and refined at the instance of those in command of the levers of meaning. It gives form to the technologies of power over aggregated populations that Foucault would predict (in a cruder form) as the notion of biopolitics.[150] Those levers, now reduced to a symbol, themselves reshape the real by shaping its simulacra. It is in this context that meaning, narrativity, and the real develops not

---

[147] Asimov (1988), p. 10.

[148] Ibid., pp. 10–11.

[149] Broekman (2023) ("What is suggested here? It is like a description and at the same time a construction of the semiosphere which should unfold in a continuously changing, floating, formatting, knowing and knowledgeable Self! For that reason we introduced the Self-E." Ibid., p. 180. Also Nietzsche (1909) where he declares:

> That which we now call the world is the result of a mass of errors and fantasies which arose gradually in the general development of organic being, which are inter-grown with each other, and are now inherited by us as the accumulated treasure of all the past,—as a treasure, for the value of our humanity depends upon it. From this world of representation strict science is really only able to liberate us to a very slight extent—as it is also not at all desirable—inasmuch as it cannot essentially break the power of primitive habits of feeling; but it can gradually elucidate the history of the rise of that world as representation,—and lift us, at least for moments, above and beyond the whole process. Perhaps we shall then recognise that the thing in itself is worth a Homeric laugh; that it seemed so much, indeed everything, and is really empty, namely, empty of meaning. (Ibid., ¶ 16).

[150] Foucault (2004).

just a new language vessel through which meaning is conveyed but also the triumph of a subjectivity that can be rationalized, and thus rationalized invested with the attributes of an idealized objectivity. Semiotics now enters the world of the simulation of sign, and simulation is reified as the ultimate objective subjectivity; *dixitque Deus fiat lux et facta est lux.*[151]

4 Conclusion: Interpreting Pharoah's Dream in Trantor

The decisive move toward the objectification of reality and its meaning through its simulation (present) and its modeling (future)—that is the quantification, and digitalization of humanity—has brought humanity to a great transformative moment. Now comprehended only as and by its own simulation, the modalities of objectification, of signification, and ultimately of the encounters with meaning and its making, has now (again) removed itself from an immanent to a transcendent condition. This contribution considered the challenges for semiotics, for the understanding of the conditions of meaning in relation to the human, that is posed by a global obsession with the attainment of reality and its instrumentalization through the mechanics of simulation. If humanity is reducing itself to its own essence and from that grasping at the essence of its own meaning and its plasticity, to the reduction of meaning to that essence contextually contingent, then semiotics can either embrace that reconstitution of the human or content itself to a decreasingly relevant footnote in the history of humanity's self-obsessions with its self-objectification.

Simulation is founded on its (static) descriptive power. The autonomous simulation describes its object by the very act of simulation. It represents and reproduces the environment and thus detaches it from the environment so that it might be better observed. Human collectives model themselves and everything that they hold dear—their mirror and their window into themselves. Perhaps it has become an autonomous object against which what is modeled may be judged; that is the essence of modeling and simulation in the construction of ratings and assessment systems and in the great 21st project of accountability.

It is made more desirable by its (dynamic) predictive qualities. That prediction is passive and becomes powerful precisely because of the completeness of the descriptive power of the simulation. It is the simulation in motion going forward. The value of this motion is to peer into the future to mitigate or remedy its pathways—the way one moves away from a low-lying coastal area where a simulation predicts that the area lies in the path of a hurricane. If this was all there was, if the entirety of the simulation was descriptive and predictive then its semiotics would be interesting but unremarkable.

---

[151] Gen. 1:1 (Vulgate).

But simulations also acquire a life of their own—they do so when they become the reality within which it is possible to actively intervene in both the construction of the present and the alteration of the future. One does this in simulation by experimenting with the effects of changing present variables, that is by changing the environment and thus changing the simulation itself. One can do this over and over precisely because the simulation exists in abstract space. It is here that metaverses can be operated in infinite variation.[152]

The essay examined the implications of this movement from the conventional signification of objects to the objectification of signification in the context of the initial responses to the COVID-19 pandemic in 2020. The analysis suggested the implication of this movement for social organization and governance and its conundrums for the signification of human collectives and the rationalization of their managerial apparatus (social, economic, cultural, and political). Into that conundrum, Jan Broekman has pointed a way forward for semiotics, or at least that branch of its study that embraces not just simulation but its ultimate condition—the understanding of the objectification of subjectivity and the instrumentalization of the "Human, All-Too-Human" collective now made abstracted flesh but incarnated all the same.

References

Abrajan MG (2007) Trantor: la ciudad-mundo. Polis 3(2):105–127

Asimov I (1951) Foundation and empire. In: Asimov I (ed) The foundation trilogy. Doubleday & Co.

Asimov I (1988) Prelude to foundation. Doubleday, NY

Backer LC (2021) Hong Kong between 'one country' and 'two systems'. Little Sir Press

Baudrillard J (1994) Simulacra and simulation (trans: Glaser SF). University of Michigan Press, p 6

Benjamin W (1969) The work of art in the age of mechanical reproduction. In: Arendt H (ed) Illuminations (trans: Zohn H). Schocken Books, NY (1935)

Bird KA, Castleman BL, Mabel Z, Song Y (2021) Bringing transparency to predictive analytics: a systematic comparison of predictive modeling methods in higher education. AERA Open 7(1): 1–19

Brier S (2019) Cybersemiotic systemic and semiotical based transdisciplinarity. Transdiscip J Eng Sci 10:81–92

Broekman JM (2016) Meaning, narrativity, and the real. Springer

Broekman JM (2017) Legal signs fascinate: Kevelson's research on semiotics. Springer, Dordrecht

Broekman JM (2020) Like your emoji — a philosophical context. Soc Semiot 30(3):415–429

Broekman J (2023) Rearguards of subjectivity. In: Fleerackers F (ed) Rearguards of subjectivity. Springer, Dordrecht, forthcoming

Broekman JM (2023) Knowledge in change the semiotics of cognition and conversion. Springer Nature, Cham

Butterworth E, Jardine BE, Raymond GM, Neal ML, Bassingthwaighte JB (2014) JSim, an open-source modeling system for data analysis. F100 Res 2:288

Buttimer A (1976) Grasping the dynamism of lifeworld. Ann Assoc Am Geogr 66(2):277–292

[152] Mystakidis (2022), pp. 486–497.

Ciula A, Øyvind E (2017) Modelling in digital humanities: signs in context. Digit Scholarsh Humanit 32(1):i33–i46

Cobley P (2010) Cybersemiotics and human modeling. Entropy 12:2045–2066

Cook D (2005) The sundered totality of system and lifeworld. Hist Mater 13(4):55–78

Crosby AW (1997) The measure of reality: quantification and western society, 1250-1600. Cambridge University Press

Cullenwood D, Sudarshan A (2011) Psychohistory revisited: fundamental issues in forecasting climate futures. Climate Change 104:457–472

Deely J (2012) Analytic philosophy and the doctrine of signs. Am J Semiot 28(3/4):325–363

Dekel E, Gurley DG (2017) Kafka's Gloem. Jew Q Rev 107(4):531–556

DeLeon AP (2008) Are we simulating the status quo? Ideology and social studies simulations. Theory Res Soc Educ 36(3):256–277

Dominguez R, Fusco C (2003) On-line simulations/real-life politics: a discussion with Ricardo Dominguez on staging virtual theatre. Drama Rev 47(2):151–162

Eigen M, Schuster P (1978) The hypercycle: a principle of natural self-organization Part B. The abstract hypercycle. Naturwissenschaften 65:7–41

Foucault M (2004) Security, territory, population: lectures at the Collège de France, 1977-1978 (trans: Birchall G). Picador, New York

Giordano G, Blanchini F, Bruno R, Colaneri P, Di Filippo A, Di Matteo A, Colaneri M (2020) Modelling the COVID-19 epidemic and implementation of population-wide interventions in Italy. Nature (Medicine) 26:855–860. Available <https://www.nature.com/articles/s41591-020-0883-7.pdf>

Guiguzi G (2016) China's First Treatise on rhetoric: a critical translation and commentary (trans: Wu H). Southern Illinois University Press, Carbondale, p 156

Habermas J (1973) Legitimation crisis (trans: McCarthy T). Heinemann, London

Hannah-Moffat K (2019) Algorithmic risk governance: big data analytics, race and information activism in criminal justice debates. Theor Criminol 23(4):453–470

Harste G (2021) The Habermas-Luhmann Debate. Columbia University Press, pp 108–130

Husserl E (1970) The crisis of European sciences and transcendental phenomenology (trans: Car D). Northwestern University Press. (1952)

Ingenieros J (1988 edition; 1918) Sociología Argentina. Hyspamérica editiones Argentinas

Ingersoll EG, Asimov I, Gerald GF, Wolf J, Duberman J, Philmus R (1987) A conversation with Isaac Asimov. Sci Fict Stud 14(1):68–77

Jonson CL, Moon MM, Hendry JA (2020) One size does not fit all: traditional lockdown versus multioption responses to school shootings. J Sch Violence 19(2):154–166

Kahn RP (1988) The problem of power in Habermas. Hum Stud 11(4):361–387

Kinsey C (2018) Blind windows. Hist Hum Sci 31(5):154–182

Kralemann B, Lattmann C (2013) Models as icons: modeling models in the semiotic framework of Peirce's theory of signs. Synthese 190:3397–3420

Krispin J (2019) Culturo-behavioral hypercycles and the metacontingency: incorporating self-organizing dynamics into an expanded model of cultural change. Perspect Behav Sci 42:869–887

Lanier J (2013) Who owns the future. Simon & Schuster, pp 53–57

Lawrence CR III (1987) The Id, the ego, and equal protection: reckoning with unconscious racism. Stanford Law Rev 39:317–388

Leili MA, Chang WT, Chao C (2017) Driverless governance. designing narratives toward democratic technology. Des J 20(sup1):S4343–S4356. https://doi.org/10.1080/14606925.2017.1352931

Lupyan G, Clark A (2015) Words and the world: predictive coding and the language-perception-cognition interface. Curr Dir Psychol Sci 24(4):279–284

Matsuda MJ (1990) Pragmatism modified and the false consciousness. South Calif Law Rev 63: 1763

Myers J, Beach R (2002) Hypermedia authoring as critical literacy. J Adolesc Adult Lit 44(6): 538–546
Mystakidis S (2022) Metaverse. Encyclopedia 2:486–497. https://doi.org/10.3390/encyclopedia2010031
Newmark A (1989) The election of 1912: a hypertext simulation. New York Mag 8(5):54
Nietzsche F (1908) Human, all too human (trans: Harvey A). Charles H. Kerr & Co., Chicago
Nietzsche F (1909) Human, all-too-human: a book for free spirits (trans: Zimmern H). TN Foulis, London; Project Gutenberg May 2, 2016 [EBook #51935]
Nietzsche F (1923) The antichrist (trans: Menken HL). Alfred A Knopf, NY
Nishida Y (2022) The relationship between autopoiesis theory and biosemiotics: on philosophical suppositions as bases for a new information theory. TripleC 9(2):424–433
O'Gara M, Vertin M (1996) The holy spirit's assistance to the magisterium in teaching: theological and philosophical issues. CTSA Proc 51:125–142
Olteanu A, Rabitz F, Nalivaikė A (2021) A semiotic comparison of mass media representations of the swine flu and Covid-19 pandemics: observing Narcissus Narcosis. Punctum 7(1):45–68
Palumbo D (1996) Psychohistory and chaos theory: the "foundation trilogy" and the fractal structure of Asimov's Robot/Empire/Foundation Metaseries. J Fantast Arts 7(1):23–50
Phadnis SS (2019) Effectiveness of Delphi- and scenario planning-like processes in enabling organizational adaptation: a simulation-based comparison. Futures Foresight 1(2):1–15
Plessner H (1928) Die Stufen des Organischen und der Mensch [The steps of the organic and the human]. W. de Gruyter & Co, Berlin/Leipzig, p 289 f
Portmann A (1956) Zoologie und das Neue Bild des Menschen [Zoology and the new image of man]. B. Schwabe & Co, Basel 1951, Rowohlt, Hamburg
Salleh A (2014) Emoticon language is "shaping the brain". ABC Science Online. Australian Broadcasting Corporation, Ultimo (Feb 6, 2014)
Sante L (1998) The factory of facts. Pantheon Books, NY
Seele P (2017) Predictive sustainability control: a review assessing the potential to transfer big data driven 'predictive policing' to corporate sustainability management. J Clean Prod 153:673–686
Selwyn N (2015) Data entry: towards the critical study of digital data and education. Learn Media Technol 40(1):64–82
Tanaka-Ishii K (2008) Narcissus in language: a semiotic contrast of natural and computer language through self-reference. Semiotica 172(1/4):299–311
Thapa BEP (2019) Predictive analytics and AI in governance: data-driven government in a free society – artificial intelligence, big data and algorithmic decision-making in government from a liberal perspective. European Liberal Forum
Theunissen M (1965) Der Andere, Studien zur Sozialontologie der Gegenwart [The other. Studies on the actual social ontology]. W. de Gruyter & Co., p 156 f
Ulmer G (1991) Grammatology hypermedia. Postmodern Culture Project MUSE 1(2). https://doi.org/10.1353/pmc.1991.0012
Unger RM (1983) The critical legal studies movement. Harv Law Rev 96(3):561–675
van den Homberg MJC, Gevaert CM, Georgiadou Y (2020) The changing face of accountability in humanitarianism: using artificial intelligence for anticipatory action. Polit Gov 8(4):456–467
Wagner P (2002) Identity and selfhood as Problemmatique. In: Friese H (ed) Identities: time, difference and boundaries. Berghahn Books, NY, pp 32–55
Warfield JN, Perino GH (1999) The Problematique: evolution of an idea. Syst Res 16(3):221–226
Weinburger S (2011) Spies to use twitter as a crystal ball. Nature 478:301
Weissman D (2021) Are we trapped in Plato's Cave? Metaphilosophy 52(5):650–654
Williamson B (2016) Digital education governance: data visualization, predictive analytics, and 'real-time' policy instruments. J Educ Policy 31(2):123–141
Wright G, Cairns G, O'Brien FA, Goodwin P (2019) Scenario analysis to support decision making in addressing wicked problems: pitfalls and potential. Eur J Oper Res 278:3–19
Yang K (2020) Unprecedented challenges, familiar paradoxes: COVID-19 and governance in a new normal state of risks. Public Adm Rev 80(4):657–664

Students Making Meaning: Teaching Legal Semiotics in the Context of International Law

Clara Chapdelaine-Feliciati

> *We no longer travel to our oracles; we create schools to which we pose the great questions of the day and receive the oracular responses of the current age. (Broekman and Catà Backer 2015, pp. 4–5)*

Abstract This chapter considers the challenge of teaching legal semiotics to students from distinct legal traditions, civil law, Common Law, as well as hybrid and mixed systems, and in a bilingual—French and English—Canadian academic setting. Following the tradition established by Jan M. Broekman's *Roberta Kevelson Seminars on Law and Semiotics*, and building on his publications on the semiotics of law in legal education (2009, 2010, 2011, 2013, 2015, 2016, 2018), this chapter explores the significance of applying semiotics as a methodology to examine the content of international treaties, and the international legal framework, more broadly. It shares the meaning behind adding publications such as 'Student Positions and Opinions' (IJSL 2010) and 'Reading Semiotics' (Broekman and Catá Backer, *Signs in Law* 2015) as compulsory readings in an international law course. This chapter describes students' feedback when asked to discuss the role of semiotics in several legal contexts, including in the courtroom, and how this translates in their final papers and presentations that simulate UN meetings in which they act as government officials presenting the State Report to UN treaty-bodies, such as the UN Committee on the Rights of the Child. It notes Kevelson's concern that legal education usually focuses on the black letter law and in training 'superb legal technicians with deficiencies in humanity and the humanities' (1987, 13). The chapter concludes by underscoring the importance of providing students with the necessary tools to evaluate legisigns, understand the meaning behind icons, and deconstruct the master discourse. Finally, it considers the role of law teachers as 'semioethicians' (Petrilli and Ponzio 2010).

C. Chapdelaine-Feliciati (✉)
Xi'an Jiaotong-Liverpool University, Suzhou, China
e-mail: clara.chapdelaine@xjtlu.edu.cn

F. Fleerackers (ed.), *The Rearguard of Subjectivity*, Law and Visual Jurisprudence 9,
https://doi.org/10.1007/978-3-031-26855-7_4

1 Introduction

The *Roberta Kevelson Seminar on Law and Semiotics,* established by Jan M. Broekman, Distinguished Visiting Professor of Law at Penn State University's Dickinson School of Law in 2008, constitutes a milestone in the history of legal semiotics, and legal education more broadly. The Kevelson Seminar was the very first fully incorporated seminar, with corresponding credits, in the regular program in a United States Law School (Broekman and Pencak 2009a, 1–2). Indeed, while semiotics as a science and doctrine has been embraced by several disciplines and their corresponding faculties and departments, including linguistics, translation and to some extent, architecture, law schools appear to remain unchanged. Legal education usually focuses on the black letter law and in training 'superb legal technicians with deficiencies in humanity and the humanities'(Kevelson 1987, p. 13). One only needs to consider the law school curriculum to witness the prominence of mandatory six credit courses such as torts, contractual obligations, property law and business law in the first and second years, and the many specializations in upper years, for example advanced torts, restitution, remedies, equity and trusts, wills and estates, successions, sale, loan and deposit, limited interests in land, protection and enforcement of creditors' rights, taxation, real estate transactions, bankruptcy and insolvency, corporate finance, corporate taxation, insurance, estate planning, securities, regulation, and compare it to the limited offerings in the field of legal philosophy. Additionally, very few law schools explore the socio-political and philosophical underpinnings of law making. Among those that do, legal semiotics is virtually absent. A notable example is the present writer's alma mater, McGill University, that offers a bilingual (English-French) trans-systemic law program in the Civil Law and Common Law traditions (B.C.L./J.D.). This program encompasses broader options, such as legal theory, jurisprudence, advanced jurisprudence, theories of justice, comparative legal institutions, comparative modern legal history, and linguistic and literary approaches to the law, and its mandatory courses also explore the theory behind the law. And yet, this combined program still fails to consider legal semiotics as a method of legal inquiry.

Another notable feature of the *Seminar on Law and Semiotics* is that Jan M. Broekman brought with him an interdisciplinary training in law, philosophy, psychiatry and education, and moreover, an expertise in the Civil Law tradition in terms of legal reasoning, jurisprudence and doctrine, thereby enriching Penn State's students' education, which normally focused on the US Common Law. Legal semiotics was thus taught by an expert in diverse legal traditions, evidencing very different ways of approaching the law and its many symbols, in an interdisciplinary perspective. As noted by Broekman, Mootz III and Pencak: 'The world map of legal systems is continuously at the background of the seminar, whereas the diversity of legal systems around the globe fortifies the unity of semiotic approaches towards law' (2011, xii). Accordingly, this approach consolidated both the teaching of 'law' in the broader sense, and that of legal semiotics. More so, Jan M. Broekman's pedagogical inquiry was deeply interactive: students were encouraged to participate actively in this seminar, and thereafter publish their own views on the contributions of semiotics of law in the classroom (Broekman and Pencak 2010; Broekman and Mootz III 2011).

Most importantly, not only did Jan M. Broekman bring semiotics to the Law school, but he also examined the outcomes of this enterprise in several publications (Broekman and Fleerackers 2018; Broekman 2016; Broekman and Catà Backer 2013, 2015; Broekman and Mootz III 2011; Broekman and Pencak 2010; 2009b), which in turn inspired others to follow him in this fascinating, and at times challenging, adventure. It is thus a great honour for me to contribute to this volume and discuss the impact that Professor Broekman's *Roberta Kevelson Seminars on Law and Semiotics* in a US Law School has had on my own international law courses in a neighbouring country, Canada, more specifically at York University in Toronto. This chapter stems from the International Roundtable for the Semiotics of Law 2021 celebrating Jan M. Broekman's important contributions to the field of semiotics, held virtually at KU Leuven, Belgium, and organized by Frank Fleerackers and Anne Wagner. It is noteworthy that also in attendance at this Roundtable were Larry Catà Backer and Francis J. Mootz III, co-authors with Jan M. Broekman of several central publications on semiotics in legal education. While most authors and scholars whose work I had the pleasure of reading, such as Lady Welby, belong to other centuries, it was quite a unique experience to meet and discuss legal semiotics with experts in actual life, albeit virtually.

2 Method and Students

Before beginning this examination, it is important to point out that my approach differs from Professor Broekman's seminar in that I do not offer a seminar *on* the semiotics of law, but rather international law courses in which legal semiotics is incorporated as a method to explore the meaning behind the law, and its ultimate significance. In this context, publications on semiotics in legal education are called upon to familiarize students with the method *and* methods of legal semiotics, the latter defined as 'the scientific approach that regards law as a system of signs and meanings' (Broekman and Pencak 2011, p. v).

Also, while I have employed semiotics in my teaching at prior institutions, including at the University of Toronto Law Faculty and its Ethics, Society and Law and Margaret MacMillan Trinity One programs based at Trinity College, as well as the Toronto Metropolitan University Law and Business Department, the present chapter will focus on experiences encountered while at York University, Glendon College. One of the unique features of Glendon College is that it is bilingual (English-French). I therefore taught some international law courses in French, others in English, and in each case, some class readings were in the other official language. Students are bilingual, and close to half of them are international students who came to Canada for their university degree: many are francophones from West African countries, for example from the Ivory Coast, the Democratic

Republic of the Congo, Guinea and Benin; North Africa, notably Morocco and Algeria; and others from Switzerland and France, especially since we have exchanges with Sciences Po Paris and Sciences Po Strasbourg. Among the anglophones, many come from India, China, Latin-America, Nigeria, Russia, some from the US, and some are English Canadian francophile students, mainly second generation Canadians whose families were raised in other continents. In a single class, students speak up to 40 languages, and come from various legal systems: civil law, Common Law, many hybrid or mixed systems, including with customary law, Sharia and Talmudic law. This reality arguably facilitates the teaching of legal semiotics as many students are aware that there can be different legal structures, practices and procedures, rather than a single rule. Still, we live in times of simple solutions and absolute truths, which makes teaching semiotics all the more important. International law courses are electives with small class sizes of around 20 students at the undergraduate level, and even smaller class sizes at the graduate level, around 10 students, thus allowing for seminar presentations and dynamic discussions as well as debates. Students are invited to actively participate and thereby contribute to shaping course content. While the syllabus and assignments are clearly delineated and shared at the beginning of the term, each course unfolds differently, in line with Kevelson's view that 'the way we interact is through an idea, which is something you hold on to at both ends' (Broekman and Fleerackers 2018, p. 43). Indeed, as noted by Broekman, Mootz III and Pencak, seminars allow for an exploration of legal semiotics and 'ideas on signs, signification, meaning or naming' which is difficult to reproduce in the classical ex-cathedra teaching (2011, pp. viii–xii).

3 Reading Semiotics

The first question with teaching semiotics is best formulated by Broekman and Pencak: 'What should be offered to law students in a first confrontation with semiotics? (2009a, 2). A significant challenge is students' initial belief that semiotics is an abstract concept that can solely be understood by a select few. Based on this assumption, some consider that semiotics has nothing to do with the law, since the latter is viewed as practical or concrete; and that it might further complicate this already complex subject. While readings vary between courses, two central texts have been very useful for an introduction to legal semiotics: 'Reading Semiotics'(Broekman and Catà Backer 2015) and 'Student Positions and Opinions' (Broekman and Pencak 2010). In 'Student Positions and Opinions', the texts 'Visual Semiotics: A Means to Manage Legal Discourse' by Meghann Garrett, and 'Understanding and Using Gender Signs in the Culture of the Courtroom' by Amber Sizemore, and their respective explanations of gender signs in the courtroom, visual semiotics and jury selection, resonate with students for they demonstrate that semiotics does not solely bear on the textual meaning of the law. For example, in a course on feminist legal theory and international law, Sizemore's following interrogation: 'can an attorney be female, or feminine, and also authoritative within the culture of the courtroom'? (Broekman and Pencak 2010, p. 35) generates interesting debates. Moreover, Garrett's observation that visual semiotics are essential in criminal trials: 'I will turn my semiotic attention to the defendant, telling my client to come to court dressed in a suit, cleanly shaved with his hair brushed (...) to cover any tatoos or remove piercings (...) to sit still at trial, not to slouch or lean on his elbows, and to look attentive and remorseful' (Broekman and Pencak 2010, p. 38), allows for a discussion on the *meaning-intention* behind each sign or symbol (Welby 1903, pp. 1–11; 1911, pp. 8–10): the intention of the creators of this sign, be it the attorney preparing her client for the trial, or the drafters of an international treaty. Anidra Amoh summarizes students' initial concerns, and the importance of underscoring the role of semiotics in everyday life: 'Semiotics may seem hard to understand at first but applying it in our communities and in the activities of our daily lives provides a deeper understanding of the concept' (Student Opinions, York University, June 2021, on file with the author, hereinafter SOYU 2021). The objective is firstly to ensure that students understand the role of semiotics, and notably that it allows for a thoughtful analysis of the meaning(s) of signs and symbols, as explained by Carlos Rojas:

> I took part in an International Law class where the theory behind semiotics was constantly present throughout the texts we analysed. Semiotics grants the student an opportunity to inquire on the nature of a sign or symbol in order to grasp the deeper meaning behind it. (SOYU 2021)

We usually begin with an essential concept, explained very clearly in *Reading Semiotics*, that a text does not have '*one forever fixated* meaning' (Broekman and Catà Backer 2015, p. 7). The role of interpretation is thus underlined. Welby's discussion on the Plain Meaning myth (Welby 1893, pp. 512–513) and Peirce's final interpretant (Peirce 1931–1958 CP 8.184) are explored in this context. The notion that signs constitute guideposts for semioticians is also helpful as an introductory approach. As noted by Eranga Wikramanayake:

> these rules can be understood through signs, which, as Jan Broekman and Larry Backer in 'Reading Semiotics' indicate, are guideposts that provide us with hints, directions and meanings about the past, present and future which are then utilized to manage our lives (...) In the legal context, these signs are also not presented plainly and thus, legal scholars must examine documents from beyond their face value. (SOYU 2021)

Before delving into the international legal framework, we discuss the differences between legal systems, notably civil law and Common Law, bearing in mind that legal signs exist in a network of contexts.[1] This leads us to a discussion on Catà Backer's definition of *global law* as concerns fracture, fluidity and permeability (Broekman and Catà Backer 2015, p. 16). We then turn to the different implementation mechanisms in monist and dualist states, the latter adopting the

[1] An interesting reading is Cyran's comparative analysis of the civil law and Common Law systems, and his discussion on which legal tradition is more 'just', which always appeals to students (Cyran 2011).

'transformative' model. Another important notion in *Reading Semiotics* is that 'texts are (. . .) never independent from their confrères; each text lives a life of context for another' (Broekman and Catà Backer 2015, p. 6). This is especially pertinent in the international legal framework, where each provision of a treaty must be read in light of the latter's object and purpose, and in relation to other provisions of the same treaty, and to a certain extent, its *travaux préparatoires* as well as general principles of international law, as stipulated in the Vienna Convention on the Law of Treaties (United Nations 1969 articles 31–33).

4 Semiotics and Interpretation

After an introduction to legal semiotics, we turn to specific international human rights treaties, such as the UN Convention on the Rights of the Child ("Convention on the Rights of the Child" 1989), and employ semiotics as a method to analyse, or more specifically, deconstruct, their content. As observed by Carlos Rojas:

> It became apparent to me that interpretation is what allows the student to discover the codes needed to understand the meaning behind the texts in international law. Thus, interpretation is a key component within the field due to the ambiguity of codes and their symbolization of reality through the exchange of language. As this became clearer in my studies, I understood the significance interpretation had in legal semiotics. (SOYU 2021)

In this context, reference is made to the *travaux préparatoires* of the treaty examined in order to explore the *meaning-intention* (Welby 1903, 1911) behind the formulation of those rights and fundamental freedoms. The *travaux* also allow for an investigation of the context in which the treaty was drafted, and potential power relations between various nations at the time. Discussions on the *travaux* also underscore that the meaning given to the provisions examined, when adopted, might have differed among delegates, and moreover, that it might not be the same today. This notion is related to Broekman and Catà Backer's explanation that 'a text is never the text we read, and the text we read today is not the same as the text that was read a century ago' (2015, p. 9). As noted by Eranga Wikramanayake:

> The study of semiotics provides us with the necessary linguistic tools to comprehend not only the words on the document but also the intentions of the person who wrote the document. Therefore, without semiotics, there is no understanding of the why behind international law decisions and without knowing the why, can we truly comprehend any international legal document in its entirety? (SOYU 2021)

When examining treaty provisions, we also discuss relevant treaty body general comments and general recommendations that clarify States parties' obligations. We explore Welby's Threefold Laws of Meaning (1903; 1911) as a framework to decode signs and symbols in international law, for instance with regards to the International Covenants (Chapdelaine-Feliciati 2013), the issue of gendercide (Chapdelaine-Feliciati 2018) and reservations to treaties (Chapdelaine-Feliciati 2022). The Socratic method is employed. Questions are varied, and include the following: are

State party obligations, and notably States' duty of due diligence, formulated in strong or weak terms? Who does this provision protect? Who was it originally meant to protect? These discussions often lead to debates, as students can have different views on the matter – the objective is not to impose a viewpoint to the class, but rather to encourage the unfolding of legal reasoning and semiotic thinking. Students are required to support their opinions with arguments: why do you consider that this right or fundamental freedom is formulated in weak terms? Can you compare it to other provisions in the same treaty, or another treaty? And when you contrast it to domestic legislation? I also encourage students to see the relationship between the rights as described in international law, and their concrete application in our lives. We consider the role of terminology to phrase treaty provisions, as well as its significance for the final interpretant (Peirce 1931–1958). As observed by Eranga Wikramanayake:

> Studying international law has emphasized the importance of word usage and how in many circumstances, certain words must be utilized to prevent international documents from providing too much leeway for countries to freely interpret the words to fit their narratives (...) their specific phrases or words are an example of semiotics in play because whether it's the treaty itself or the committees, the word choice is beyond just their basic meaning. They must also consider how these words or phrases can be interpreted by a country (...). (SOYU 2021)

Students are thereafter encouraged to apply semiotics as a method to evaluate the implementation of a treaty in a country of their choosing. Ayla Slijvar examined the following as concerns the rights of persons with disabilities in Bosnia and Herzegovina, in light of the UN Convention on the rights of persons with disabilities ("Convention on the Rights of Persons with Disabilities" 2006):

> A more disappointing instance is that some treaties and conventions remain ambiguous, allowing states to be vague regarding human rights issues. This vicious cycle of ambiguity and 'silence' results in the 'silencing' of voices that require attention and aid. I encountered this issue during the research stages of the research essay for Dr. Chapdelaine-Feliciati, where the paper required to focus on a state party's report in conjunction with a treaty. I focused on Bosnia and Herzegovina (BiH) as having failed to ensure that persons with disabilities (PWDs) have an adequate standard of living according to Article 25 (Health) of the Convention on the Rights of Persons with Disabilities (CRPD). There are inconsistencies between what BiH had signed and ratified and what they have done in practice to protect the rights and entitlements of PWDs. The Constitution of BiH, for example, upholds that both Entities of BiH (the Federation of Bosnia and Herzegovina and the Republika Srpska) "shall ensure the highest level of internationally recognized human rights and fundamental freedoms" (Bosnia and Herzegovina Constitution, art. 2, para. 1). Upon closer examination, however, the rights and freedoms listed do not include any specific rights and entitlements for those who have "long-term physical, mental, intellectual or sensory impairments" which the CRPD lists as forms of disabilities that could "hinder [one's] full and effective participation in society on an equal basis with others" under article 1 (Convention on the Rights of Persons with Disabilities, adopted 13 Dec 2006, entered into force 3 May 2008, 2512 UNTS 3). The omission of rights and entitlements designated to protect PWDs speaks volumes regarding BiH's interests in such matters. (SOYU 2021)

Another example is Serge Kacou's analysis of States parties' obligation to protect individuals against torture under the International Covenant on Civil and Political rights ("International Covenant on Civil and Political Rights" 1966). Article 7 of the ICCPR reads: 'No one shall be subjected to torture or to cruel, inhuman or degrading treatment or punishment. In particular, no one shall be subjected without his free consent to medical or scientific experimentation', and Serge Kacou made the following observation as concerns the implementation of this right in Cameroon:

> In book II of the criminal procedures of Cameroon, it is mentioned under section 122 that: 'The suspect shall not be subjected to any physical or mental constraints, or to torture, violence, threats or any pressure whatsoever, or to deceit, insidious manoeuvres, false proposals, prolonged questioning, hypnosis, the administration of drugs or to any other method which is likely to compromise or limit his freedom of action or decision, or his memory or sense of judgment'. It is noteworthy to acknowledge that this code goes beyond the provision given in article 7 of the ICCPR by providing more information on the effects of torture, namely the psychological effects on the individual concerned. Moreover, they give more indication of the types of methods that are considered to be 'torturing or causing harm' whilst in custody. However, chapter one of the third part of Cameroon's criminal code stipulates that 'Whoever involuntarily causes death by torture shall be punished with life imprisonment.' The phenotext in the previous sentence can be very misleading in terms of its genotext, because the word 'involuntary' can imply that the code only and strictly applies to "involuntary' acts of torture. Furthermore, the fact that in order for the infraction to be punished, the 'involuntary' act of torture has to cause death is also worrisome. (Student Papers, York University, December 2019, on file with the author, hereinafter SPYU 2019)

5 Silence as a Sign in International Law

I also explore the concept of silence in international law, based on Welby's Significs of Silence (Welby 1911, 40) as well as Susan Petrilli's Signs of Silence (Petrilli 2014, pp. 111–120). It is noteworthy that this topic constitutes one of the most popular seminars. We begin with a discussion on the power of silence in everyday life; from relationships, to politics. Silence is considered in terms of textual silence, notably as concerns the content of treaties and treaty-body documents, as well as silence by action and inaction, silence in speech, and the issue of acquiescence or objection.[2] We then move to international law and the importance of 'listening to the silence of international law' (Waring 1992). In this context, Ayla Slijvar notes:

> the study of semiotics as a whole played a significant role in helping students examine international law. Through reading publications in semiotics (the science that studies signs and symbols in various fields of study), the argument for 'silence' as the act of 'suspending the word' (Susan Petrilli, *Sign Studies and Semioethics: Communication, Translation and Values*, De Gruyer Mouton 2014, p. 110) came to the forefront of my mind. To provide further context, Petrilli's work 'deals with the problem of silence understood as the absence of words' (p. 111). While the 'absence of words' can differ in various contexts, it can speak volumes on the meaning behind it. (SOYU 2021)

[2]The author wishes to thank the participants of the International Roundtable 2021 held at KU Leuven for feedback, and most notably Larry Catà Backer for his exploration of the various forms of silence unveiled by legal semiotics.

A striking example for students is the absence of any reference to violence against women in the main international treaty promoting women's rights, the CEDAW ("Convention on the Elimination of All Forms of Discrimination Against Women" 1979). In this regard, Ayla Slijvar notes:

> An issue that I have come across as a student when examining treaties in international law, for example, was the omission of certain words that would change the interpretation of the treaty. A prominent example that comes to mind is the omission of the word 'violence' in the Convention on the Elimination of all Forms of Discrimination against Women (CEDAW). The CEDAW's silence on the matter of violence against women and girl children is deafening since women and girl children encounter various forms of violence, in varying degrees, from microaggressions to life-threatening instances, daily. (SOYU 2021)

In this context, students are encouraged to consider the significance of this silence. Ayla Slijvar argues that this silence could be interpreted as indicating that the CEDAW, or even the United Nations, does not consider that violence constitutes a form of discrimination against women:

> Now, had I completely foregone the opportunity to learn about semiotics or the 'Signs of Silence' before delving into conventions and treaties, I would have overlooked the significance of omitting certain words and terms. By refusing to include an eight-letter word ('violence') in a treaty that acknowledges that 'extensive discrimination against women continues to exist' (CEDAW, Preamble), the reader would assume that the United Nations does not view the term 'violence' as being a form of discrimination against women and girl children. (SOYU 2021)

Anidra Amoh contends that this silence allows States parties to ignore, or at least disregard, the issue of violence against women:

> The silence or in this case, the elimination of that word, may give leeway to some States parties that have ratified the convention, and give them the ability to perform violent acts against women. The justification to these acts may be the fact that the convention does not specifically define what exactly constitutes violence against women. (SOYU 2021)

We also discuss the silence present in other treaties, such as the Marriage Convention ("Convention on Consent to Marriage, Minimum Age for Marriage and Registration of Marriages" 1962) which, in spite of its very name, fails to offer a minimum age for children to get married. Anidra Amoh discusses the significance of this sign:

> Similarly, the Convention on Consent to Marriage, Minimum Age for Marriage and Registration of Marriages, specifically in Article 2, states that State Parties should take legislative action to specify a minimum age for marriage. The convention does not mention a specific age which is acceptable for marriage which ultimately fails to prevent child marriages. (SOYU 2021)

Another observation is that the silence regarding several human rights violations in State party reports and Concluding Observations constitutes a sign in itself. Indeed, it allows one to infer States' and Committees' *rapport* and respective intentions. In this regard, Eranga Wikramanayake notes:

> Silence in international law can come in the form of completely avoiding the acknowledgement of an issue or avoiding recognizing specific issues, thus silence acts as a way for treaty signatories to make a stance without a single word. Studying semiotics and specifically, the signs of silence, have allowed me to recognize issues in international legal documents where

> instead of questioning why specific events or issues are not identified in these documents, I understand that in almost every instance, this silence represents a position that can only be understood by looking beyond the face value of the document. (SOYU 2021)

As concerns State party reports, he argues that States parties are deliberately silent on certain matters and thereby communicate their unwillingness to tackle them:

> Another example of why understanding semiotics and the sign of silence is important can be seen through the examination of state reports for international treaties. In many circumstances, countries will provide reports that purposely avoid mentioning issues that are blatant in their nation thus they practice silence as a sign by notifying the treaty bodies and international legal scholars that they wish to ignore the issue in its entirety. (SOYU 2021)

Another example is the absence of any reference to 'sexual orientation' as forms of discrimination in several treaties as well as State party reports. Eranga Wikramanayake observes that:

> Throughout my analysis of international legal documents, silence acts as a way for international organizations to take a stance by taking no stance, which means they are choosing to either not mention specific issues in their agenda or purposefully neglect to comment on circumstances that may put the international organization in a position where their perspective may be rejected by a good portion of the treaty signatories. This can be seen through the topic of sexual orientation, which in most treaty bodies is either neglected entirely or the concept is mentioned but there are no specific binding protections to expand upon how the minority group is protected under the international treaties. (SOYU 2021)

As noted in the examples above, legal semiotics can be applied as a method to teach students how to identify the signs of silence in international treaties as well as in the treaty-body general comments, general recommendations, State reports and concluding observations. Another effective exercise, from a semiotics perspective, is that of reading States Parties' reservations as well as State objections to other States' reservations (United Nations 1969 articles 19–23), and discuss the signs and symbols identified in the wording of these official statements. What do they say about reserving States parties' intention to fulfil their duties under the treaty? Why do some States object to other States' reservations? And why do they fail to object to certain States parties' reservations, even when the latter are incompatible with the object and purpose of the treaty in question? In this context, what is the meaning of their silence with regards to others' reservations?

6 Simulating UN Treaty-Body Meetings

Another interesting exercise is that students simulate UN meetings in which they act as government officials presenting the State report to UN treaty-bodies, such as the UN Committee on the Rights of the Child, or as members of the Committee that evaluate the State report in their 'concluding observations'. Students are asked to be 'in character' during their presentations, and encouraged to dress professionally for this purpose. The student acting as the government representative underscores the measures implemented in the country in question, in other words, its accomplishments. The Committee member, instead, must remain very diplomatic and polite, regardless of the serious human rights violations taking place in the country examined. In this context, I re-create the UN State reporting meetings that I attended at the Palais Wilson in Geneva while working as Child Rights Project Officer at the UNICEF Office of Research in Florence, Italy. These presentations are followed by a panel discussion during which the students are no longer 'in character' and can share their own views of the State's record of implementation. This is an excellent opportunity for students to learn about the UN process while developing their presentation skills. Moreover, this exercise combines visual and textual semiotics. As concerns textual semiotics: the student representing the government is required to read 1) the State report thoroughly to present its strengths to the Committee and 2) the concluding observations of the Committee to be able to answer any questions on the matter. The same goes for the student acting as a Committee member. Students thus examine the wording used by both institutions. This enables them to explore the respective positions of the State and the Committee. In this regard, Ayla Slijvar observes:

> A memorable experience in learning and applying semiotics in Dr. Chapdelaine-Feliciati's course was the recreation of UN treaty-body meetings where students would act as Committee Members or State Representatives. This exercise would allow for students to understand the positions of Committee Members and State Representatives on various treaties and conventions, including the specific issues at hand, whether it is concerning the health, safety and rights of women, children, people with disabilities, people of advanced age, people belonging to racialized groups. (SOYU 2021)

Some students were struck by the weak wording employed by the treaty bodies when commenting on State parties' implementation of human rights and fundamental freedoms, and notably, by their 'congratulatory' approach. Combined with Welby's semiotic notion of the *meaning-intention* (Welby 1903, 1911), some students, such as Eranga Wikramanayake, extrapolated the following:

> Another example of understanding semiotics being crucial in the context of word choice can be seen through the treaty committees who, when presenting their recommendations for state reports, utilize the most formal and passive words to provide countries with recommendations for meeting treaty obligations. Therefore, rather than being direct or utilizing blunt terms to push them to meet the requirements of the treaty, they resort to first applauding the country for their progress and working around their solution before presenting it in the most passive terms. The committees' approach highlights their understanding that they do not have the power to compel countries to make the necessary changes to their legislation to meet the requirements of the treaty, thus they decide to take an approach that appreciates the membership of the country and passively pushes them to respect the responsibilities of being a treaty signatory without forcing them to adopt all the responsibilities. (SOYU 2021)

Additionally, students were able to establish links between 'Reading Semiotics' and their observations on State reports. For example, students referred to Broekman and Pencak's exploration of traffic signs as significant symbols for the general public, and their meaning(s) at the international and domestic levels - which may not coincide - as well as their legal implications, including court decisions: 'their function, the essence of a sign represented in public (...) the striving for international consensus on those signs and the many differences in various nations (...)

their relation to legal rules and court decisions' (Broekman and Pencak 2009a, p. 3). In this regard, Carlos Rojas notes:

> I became aware of how states can interpret and employ the meaning behind international laws through the use of symbols during a simulation of UN Treaty Body Meetings. In this scenario, I was the state representative of the Republic of Panama and I analysed how the government employed the rights of children with disabilities under the Convention on the Rights of Persons with Disabilities (CRPD) through the use of symbols. As defined by Charles Hardwick, a symbol is 'a sign which is determined by its dynamic object only in the sense that it will be so interpreted. It thus depends either on a convention, a habitat, or a natural disposition of its interpretant, or of the field of its interpretant' (Charles Hardwick and James Cook, *Semiotics and Significs. The Correspondence between Charles S. Peirce and Victoria Lady Welby,* Indiana University Press, 1977, 33). With this knowledge, it became evident that the language of law, interpreted as a symbol, indicates how individuals should conduct themselves regularly. For instance, as in many states, Panamanian law makes use of handicap parking slot symbols to illustrate what the requirements are for any individual who seeks to park in those areas. Through this, the population becomes subject to the parking symbol and must therefore interpret the meaning behind it in accordance with the law. (SOYU 2021)

Another interesting result of this simulation is that students use visual semiotics. They dress professionally, and even during the covid-19 pandemic and thus online classes on the zoom software, a student representing the Bhutan wore a suit and a tie and used a landscape of Bhutan as a 'zoom background'. Content nevertheless precedes format, and a student once even wore a Maple Leafs (famous hockey Toronto team) hat cap during his presentation, which made for an entertaining event. A fascinating outcome of this exercise is that students are so engaged in the process that one begins to think that students acting as 'government representatives' are sincerely enthusiastic about their State's successes, or even, that the State party in question has adopted best practices that should be emulated worldwide, only to realize, during the panel discussion, that they were simply playing a role and that the State has failed to adopt the most basic measures of law reform, awareness-raising, or education.

7 Law Teachers as Semioethicians

Finally, a concept that can initially seem alien to many is that reading texts is a supreme form of action, or more specifically that '[t]ext and action are (. . .) soul mates in the case of legal texts' (Broekman and Catà Backer 2015, p. 8). Many students originally view the content of international law as an immutable foreign entity, and themselves, as passive observers. Semiotics enables them to go beyond the 'how to manual' or 'utilitarian approach' to international law, and to become active participants in its analysis; critically examining its content; analyzing the reason behind its framework; and conceiving alternate possibilities. In this regard, law teachers act as legal semioethicians that employ legal semiotics to assist students in identifying avenues to address problematic signs and symbols in the law. The theory of semioethics, devised by Augusto Ponzio and Susan Petrilli, underscores the ethical role of semioticians as they analyse signs and their significance (Ponzio and Petrilli 2010). In the context of legal semiotics in the classroom, law teachers who adopt a semioethic approach will not solely ask students to consider the meaning of legislation or caselaw, but also to critically examine them, and to explore potential alternatives. For instance, when examining the content of treaty provisions, and whether rights and fundamental freedoms are formulated in strong terms, the semioethician law teacher will take the additional step of asking: 'Could this provision be worded differently to strengthen the right in question? How so? And why?'. The discussion can thereafter lead to examining how such modifications could be put forward. For example, in the case of international treaties, whether it could be clarified by the relevant treaty-body in its general comment, or even, by amending or revising the provision in question. The desire to question legal signs, be it at the domestic or international level, can be paralleled to Broekman's notion of re-engineering:

a third possibility to assess semiotics in legal discourse is in *reengineering* legal institutions and legal discourse. It means that not unlike the redesign of an organization and its social processes, one should redesign law's organizational and communicative processes (...) approaches such as exploring the reverse of law's top-down approach, introducing new criteria for appreciating the law's communicative skills, re-interpreting the legal subject's position (Broekman and Pencak 2009a, p. 7).

For example, Vincenzo Sansone, in his final paper on Tunisia, referred to legal semiotics as a means to propose replacing problematic signs to increase the protection of LGBTQ+ rights:

> Concerning the issues presented and discussed in this paper, I advance two recommendations. First and foremost, article 230 of the Tunisian Penal Code currently in force must be repealed immediately. As stated by the Committee in their Concluding Observations on Chile, "legislation that criminalizes homosexual relations between consenting adults [...] may reinforce attitudes of discrimination between persons based on sexual orientation" (Chile Concluding Observations (1999), UN Doc CCPR/C/79/Add.104, para. 20). Such a statement unfolds the performative nature of legal texts that, in semiotic terms, participate in a process of knowledge construction influencing social reality. It follows that if the decriminalization of homosexual relationships is legitimized by law, discriminatory social attitudes and practices will progressively change. In other terms, the legal discourse can play a remarkable role in creating knowledge that is relevant to society and ultimately contributes to the transformation of its structures and promotes non-discriminatory attitudes (Jan M. Broekman and Larry Catà Backer, "Reading Semiotics" 3-20, in *Signs in Law – A Source Book: The Semiotics of Law in Legal Education III* (Cham Heidelberg New York, Springer 2015), 18). (SPYU 2019)

8 Conclusion

In conclusion, Jan M. Broekman's pedagogical approach is inspirational, and can be applied not only in seminars dedicated to legal semiotics, but also in law courses, and arguably, in all legal traditions. One must nevertheless bear in mind that each professor, each class, and each semiotic encounter is unique. As Broekman and Fleerackers aptly noted regarding legal texts, one can argue that seminars in legal semiotics constitute an anchor place in space: 'always elsewhere, always on the move, always in the mode of encounter' (2018, p. 35). Legal semiotics offers several advantages for students and professors alike. Students acquire the ability to look beyond the surface and examine the meaning behind legal symbols. They learn to question the meaning of law and attempt to identify possible alternatives to problematic signs. Carlos Rojas notes:

> Many students are unaware of the need for a semiotic form of learning in their study of international law. Students often try to understand the law in the quickest way possible to limit the time and energy that is used in doing so. Nevertheless, students are encouraged to engage in semiotic analysis because it guides them to a deeper understanding of the law. While a simple read through of text in international law is important, an analysis of the signs and symbols will unveil the true meaning and purpose behind the laws themselves. Without the help from semiotics, I would not have been able to understand the bigger picture that is international law. (SOYU 2021)

Eranga Wikramanayake adds:

> the study of semiotics in international law is integral to understanding underlying issues behind international legal documents (. . .) Whether it is the usage of specific words or phrases or the use of silence to present a position, without studying semiotics, we, as students of international law, would only understand half of the picture. (SOYU 2021)

An interesting outcome of this exercise is that students have different opinions on the impact of international norms. Some leave the course enthusiastic about the international legal framework and aspire to actively contribute to its development. Others are critical of some weaknesses, and wish to employ legal semiotics to address them. And finally, others are completely disenchanted and consider a paradigm shift in the relationship between states and international institutions. Ayla Slijvar observes:

> By applying the study of semiotics to international law, we open up a new 'world' of the human language that powerful states, governmental agencies and non-governmental agencies speak to forward a specific plan concerning the rights and freedoms of certain groups of people. (SOYU 2021)

For law teachers, each course becomes a truly unpredictable encounter. Through the application of legal semiotics, we can observe students' reasonings as they uncover signs and the varying and sometimes opposite interpretations of the textual meaning of treaties and State reports. Furthermore, we realize that the unfolding of legal reasoning is a unique matter. Lastly, an interesting outcome of teaching legal semiotics is that many students report that they begin to employ semiotics in their lives. For example, Anidra Amoh notes that:

> learning about semiotics has allowed me to analyze texts on a deeper level in terms of paying attention to the specific words used and words omitted. Semiotics has taught me that silence truly does have many meanings and must not be ignored. Having this knowledge has made me conscious in the words and phrases I use when writing and has impacted my daily life by allowing me to be more aware of statements and conversations as a whole. Signs and symbols behind a text, treaty and others, are important in international law and policy making because it shows that there is almost always more than one meaning behind a text. (SOYU 2021)

Moreover, some students note that they also apply visual legal semiotics to uncover the meaning of signs and symbols in their professional and personal lives. In some instances, they report that legal semiotics enabled them to pay attention to certain details that they would otherwise have failed to notice, and thereby, to uncover clues that have in turn acted as warnings to avoid life-threatening situations.

References

Broekman, Jan M., Francis J. Mootz III, and William A. Pencak. 2011. Preface - semiotics in the seminar. In The semiotics of law in legal education, Jan M. Broekman and Francis J. Mootz III, v–xiv. Dordrecht: Springer.

Broekman JM (2016) Meaning, narrativity, and the real: the semiotics of law in legal education IV. Springer, Dordrecht

Broekman JM, Catà Backer L (2013) Lawyers making meaning: the semiotics of law in legal education II. Springer, Dordrecht

Broekman JM, Catà Backer L (2015) Reading semiotics. In: Signs in Law - A Source Book: The Semiotics of Law in Legal Education III. Springer, Dordrecht, pp 3–20

Broekman JM, Fleerackers F (2018) Legal signs fascinate: Kevelson's research on semiotics. Springer

Broekman JM, Mootz FJ III (eds) (2011) The semiotics of law in legal education. Springer, Dordrecht

Broekman, Jan M., and William A. Pencak. 2009a. "Introduction: lawyers making meaning: the Roberta Kevelson seminar on law and semiotics." Jan M. Broekman and William A. Pencak. International Journal for the Semiotics of Law 22 (1): 1–10.

Broekman JM, Pencak WA (eds) (2009b) Lawyers making meaning: the Roberta Kevelson seminar on law and semiotics at Penn State University's Dickinson School of Law. Int J Semiot Law 22(1)

Broekman JM, Pencak WA (eds) (2010) Signs of law. The Roberta Kevelson seminar on law and semiotics at Penn State University's Dickinson School of Law. Int J Semiot Law 23(1)

Chapdelaine-Feliciati C (2013) "The Sense, Meaning and Significance of the Twin International Covenants on Political and Economic Rights." *Semiotica*, Special Issue: On and Beyond Significs: Centennial Issue for Victoria Lady Welby (1837-1912) 196(1):325–352

Chapdelaine-Feliciati C (2018) Deconstructing the convention on the rights of the child: semiotics, significs and semioethics of gendercide. Cambridge Int Law J 7:29–50

Chapdelaine-Feliciati C (2022) Les réserves en droit international ont-elles des limites? Étude sémioéthique du droit à l'éducation de la Convention relative aux droits de l'enfant. Int J Semiot Law 35(1):309–338

"Convention on Consent to Marriage, Minimum Age for Marriage and Registration of Marriages" (1962) 7 November 1962, Entered into Force 9 December 1964) 521 UNTS 231

"Convention on the Elimination of All Forms of Discrimination Against Women" (1979) (Adopted 18 December 1979, Entered into Force 3 September 1981) 1249 UNTS 13

"Convention on the Rights of Persons with Disabilities" (2006) (Adopted 13 December 2006, Entered into Force 3 May 2008) 2515 UNTS 3
"Convention on the Rights of the Child" (1989) (Adopted 20 November 1989, Entered into Force 2 September 1990) 1577 UNTS 3
Cyran EJ (2011) Common law lawyers should mind their trial practices: understanding, identifying, and correcting a semiotic imbalance. In: Broekman JM, Mootz FJ III (eds) The semiotics of law in legal education. Springer, Dordrecht, pp 115–128
"International Covenant on Civil and Political Rights" (1966) (Adopted 16 December 1966, Entered into Force 23 March 1976) 999 UNTS 171
Kevelson R (1987) Introduction to the first round table on law and semiotics. In: Kevelson R (ed) Law and semiotics: Volume 1. Plenum Press, New York, p 354
Peirce CS (1931–1958) In: Burks A (ed) The collected papers of Charles Sanders Peirce, vol. 7–8. Harvard University Press, Cambridge
Petrilli S (2014) Sign studies and semioethics: communication, translation and values. De Gruyter Mouton, Berlin
Ponzio A, Petrilli S (2010) In: Cobley P (ed) The Routledge companion to semiotics. Routledge, London
SOYU (2021) Student Opinions York University
SPYU (2019) Student Papers York University
United Nations (1969) Vienna Convention on the Law of Treaties. (Adopted 22 May 1969, Entered into Force 27 January 1980) 1155 UNTS 331
Waring M (1992) Gender and international law: women and the right to development. Aust Yearb Int Law 12(1):177–189
Welby V (1893) Meaning and metaphor. The Monist 3(4):510–525
Welby V (1903) What is meaning? Studies in the development of significance. Leopold Classic Library, Victoria
Welby V (1911) Significs and language: the articulate form of our expressive and interpretative resources. MacMillan, London

Clara Chapdelaine-Feliciati is a licensed Lawyer (Barrister and Solicitor) with the Law Society of Upper Canada and Associate Professor at Xi'an Jiaotong-Liverpool University, Suzhou, China. She holds a Ph.D. in Law from Oxford University, a Juris Doctor and Bachelor of Civil Law (J.D. and B.C.L.), McGill University, and a Master of Laws in Human Rights (LL.M.) from King's College London. She has a forthcoming book *The Status of the Girl Child under International Law: A Semioethic Analysis* with Cambridge University Press and is the author of *Feminicides of Girl Children: An International Human Rights Law Approach* (Brill 2018). She published articles in several law journals, including the *International Journal of Legal Discourse*, *Cambridge International Law Journal*, *Semiotica* and the *International Journal for the Semiotics of Law*. She is conducting a bilingual study on girl performers from a legal semiotics perspective, with the support of the Social Sciences and Humanities Research Council Insight Development Grant. Email: clara.chapdelaine@xjtlu.edu.cn; **ORCID:** 0000-0002-6654-1630

On Language and Power

Lieven De Cauter

Abstract In this concise synthetic little essay the author tries to overlook the problem of the link between language and power from antiquity to the present. From the Greek belief in rhetoric as the basis of power, via Foucault's concept of 'the order of discourse' as the control of who can say what and the concept of hegemony of Gramsci, he casts his gaze on neoliberalism, alt right and woke as power battles based on language.

Language is one of Man's "media," according to Marshall McLuhan. But upon closer inspection language is not just another medium, alongside money, roads, printing, and media in the more common sense, such as television or radio. Language is perhaps our most important, highest, and first technology, even a technology of power in the sense of Foucault. Language is not a "medium of man", it is *the* medium of the human species: not a means but a 'middle', a milieu, in the sense of environment. Humans live and move before anything else within language. Even more than in architecture, because there you can still be outside it. There is no outside to language, oracled Derrida.

The invention of Language is a miraculous, almost inexplicable leap, even more amazing than the mastery of fire. It must have been a gift from the gods. Or were the gods cosmonauts? In all theology, language is god-given, almost God himself: 'In the beginning was the word and the word was God.' The *logos*. And there is some truth in it. God is perhaps just the name for the miracle of language. For the power of language. Being able to name things is immediately a power grab—right from Adam in Paradise onwards. Knowledge is power, language is knowledge. No knowledge and certainly no transfer of knowledge without language. So: language is power.

All right, granted, language is common, it bubbles up from the throat of the people—not only Rabelais, but also Shakespeare is a brilliant example of this. Language belongs to everyone. But not speaking, not discourse: not everyone has

L. De Cauter (✉)
Erasmus University College, RITCS, Brussels, Belgium
e-mail: lieven.decauter@kuleuven.be

F. Fleerackers (ed.), *The Rearguard of Subjectivity*, Law and Visual Jurisprudence 9,
https://doi.org/10.1007/978-3-031-26855-7_5

the same access to discourse, not everyone has the same right to speak. Children are "infantile," it cannot be repeated enough: *infans* means non-speaking.

And since women did not have the right to vote until recently (1948 in Belgium, that is yesterday), one could consider them in political terms as children: infants, speechless creatures. The person who has no right to speak is impotent. Who wants power must speak well, must be eloquent. The Sophists already knew it: politics rests on eloquence, not truth. The rhetoric of power is a pleonasm. Rhetoric is the exercise of power. The exercise of power always also relies on rhetoric.

No one understood this power over discourse better than Michel Foucault, and exposed it in his classic, exemplary inaugural address at the Collège de France: *l'ordre du discours*. The "discipline," in the sense of the profession with its methods and its jargon, the author as a body with the right to speak, the institutions and the channels of speech, all "power technologies" are there to order discourse, to control and limit the right to speak. Not only of who speaks but also of *what* can be said and thought.

It is this power over discourse that is the foundation of what Gramsci called "hegemony. Hegemony is the domination of an ideology. Gramsci was thus trying to explain why the working class chooses a bourgeois, liberal ideology against its own interests: because of the hegemony, namely, of that bourgeois ideology. One of the best examples of hegemony in the present is neoliberalism and its accompanying management jargon.

I, along with two intellectual buddies, have devoted an entire book to it (*Small lexicon of management jargon. A critique of the new Newspeak—only in Dutch though*). So here I can be brief. Neoliberalism has been able to *mainstream* itself through all kinds of think tanks, such as the Mont Pellerin Society or the writings of Ayn Rand, Von Hayek and Milton Friedman, so much so that Reagan and Tatcher implemented it as adepts, and spread it around the world, so that eventually even Third Way socialists embraced it. The management jargon that has permeated everywhere, really everywhere, is the linguistic lubricant to get the neoliberal worldview and conception of human nature (as egotist and competitive) into the smallest cells of our brains. We speak and think neoliberally: everything is a business, everything is a market, because everything is economy and the economy everything. So you have to give way to the market and businesses: liberalize, privatize, deregulate. We're all thinking 'market-based,' we're all meeting 'targets,' thinking in terms of 'career planning,' 'competitive advantage,' 'spin offs,' and whatnot... 'return on investment,' especially. We are all sworn neoliberals, and all too often willingly and knowingly. Until burn out follows. Even the omikron virus now has "market share", as one newspaper has put it at some point. Picture this. On twitter, a friend of mine rightly made fun of it: the omikron variety is a neoliberal virus. We can no longer describe the world in any other terms than as a market, it seems. That's not neutral, this is not wordiness, no, this is symptomatic: we are caught up in a language that dictates a worldview to us.

There is a new candidate for this hegemony on the horizon: the global *alt right* network, which is fully *mainstreaming* its language. The fact that terms like "repopulation" or the "great replacement" and "cultural Marxists" are becoming mainstream is a sweeping sign. *Mainstreaming* is another word for the pursuit of hegemony. And it is also in and through its "language war" on social media and elsewhere, its culture war, that Vlaams Belang, our local Flemish extreme right party, scores so high in the polls, and may become the largest party in Flanders at the next election (in 2024).

This is an ominous example of the power of language. The mainstreaming of conspiracy theories, through words like "repopulation" and "cultural Marxists," is not innocent: more and more people actually believe that we are victims of a deliberate forced migration of non western, non white, Muslim aliens organized by cultural Marxists (the left say) to destroy Western, Christian white culture. Renaud Camus, Eric Zemmour, Thierry Baudet. But also Anders Berhring Breivik, Brenton Tarrant are believing in this theory. And there was also our own Jürgen Conings, a Belgian soldier gone beserk who stole weapons, wanted to kill an arch cultural Marxist, attack a mosque but instead killed himself. Even in distinguished journals, such as *Doorbraak,* (*Breaktrough,* a nationalist magazine and website) texts appear that take repopulation (*omvolking*) as an established fact. This conspiracy discourse is "performative": it leads not only to polarization but also to terrorism, like almost in the case of Jürgen Conings. But very dramatically in the case of Tarrant and Breivik.

Also from the other side, unfortunately or hurrah, I haven't figured it out yet, there is a language battle going on. Audre Lorde, one of the great inspirers of the ongoing decolonization movement, said, in a now famous slogan, "*the master's tools will never dismantle the master's house*". And there is, of course, much truth in that. What she says is a retelling of Gramsci's counterhegemony. Language matters, concepts matter. But the literalization of that decolonization discourse can lead to absurd situations. Let me make that clear with an anecdote.

A colleague friend of mine recently gave a brilliant introduction to the film "I am not your Negro" about the life and work of James Baldwin in an art school, where we both teach. Wonderful introduction, almost better than the film I thought, I happened to be there. During that anti-racist introduction to an anti-racist film about the black American civil rights movement, he quoted Baldwin twice with quotes from the film that included the word Negro. When I went for a smoke after the movie, a student told me that there had been a commotion about it: my colleague had used the N-word! I looked incredulous. It's in the title of the movie! I AM NOT YOUR NEGRO! They are quotes from Baldwin. The great Frantz Fanon, constantly uses the word "*nègre*" in his classic *Peau noir, masques blancs*. Censor it away? An anti-racist, decolonizing introduction to an anti-racist, decolonizing film? Where are we headed? The spirit and the letter. Argued I briefly. But *lo and behold*. It went all the way to the confidential mediator of the school.

Surely the colleague was momentarily stricken. What I called in an email to that colleague "the literalization of decolonization discourse" is ... really not a good idea. It could well be the death knell of Woke. Language policing with self-proclaimed decolonizing mollahs who want to (de?)colonize our language will only fuel polarization. Fighting the power of colonial, racist "white" language can indeed lead—the anecdote of my colleague (well versed in decolonization discourse) proves it—lead to puritanical idiocy, and even iconoclastic *cancel culture*.

We must liberate language from hegemonies rather than fight it with censorship and *cancel culture*—however well-intentioned. After all, the power of language is also the power to stand up to power. *To speak the truth to power*, is the title of a chapter from Edward Said'*s Representations of the intellectual*, about the role of the public intellectual, which is very dear to me: to put power on guard by throwing uncomfortable truths in its face, that is one of the public intellectual's most important tasks. Fighting power with the weapon of the language of truth. As all dictatorships and also many democracies prove: the powerful do not like that. Hence so many intellectuals have been censored, persecuted, imprisoned, murdered, from burning at the stake to simply going missing. Language is not only on the side of power but is essentially subversive of power, which is why the right to speak must be contained in *the first place*. In this sense, it is perhaps no coincidence that the main dissident, one might say the only one, in America, Noam Chomsky, is a linguist.

That one can hurl truth in the face of power has been proven once again by the catchy words of little Greta Thunberg, when she addressed the Greats of Earth in Davos: 'I don't want your hope .... I want you to panic... Our house is on fire.' It is. Perhaps the liberating power of language can wake us up. Because even the ecological crisis is not just a "natural process" (or a conspiracy theory) but also a "language problem". The Anthropocene, the geological epoch that expresses the crushing footprint of the human species, invites us to a different attitude, different stories, a different way of speaking about and dealing with the non-human environment, so-called nature. It is urgent that we better understand, value and treat the world of nonhumans. This is not a matter of green sentimentality but a matter of survival. A little more every day.

The corona pandemic as a zoonosis (a disease that crosses from animal to human) is a sign in this regard, but also no more than a sign: a foretaste of catastrophes to come. In the face of this "permanent catastrophe," as I called it back in 2001 in an essay of the same name, language is powerless. Hence many choose the negation of the common world, a world where there is no global warming, no sixth mass extinction and no migration, an *hors sol,* as Latour called it: away from the world. We will need all the world's language power to figth the climate negationists and conspiracy theorists. But besides this the permanent catastrophe we are facing, should make us humble: thinking has become an exercise in speechlessness.

Even for that "spleen of the Anthropocene" (which I chant and invoke in all kinds of texts, including poems) we need to find words, and defend the commons of language not only against hegemonies and counter-hegenomies, as those described above. A language for describing and making a common world, that is what we need more than ever.

Rethinking Legal Thinking

Frank Fleerackers

Abstract Can one reduce legal thinking to mere juridical or normative thought? Such conclusion may be derived from the categorical way of thinking, broadly used in legal reasoning: a form of fixated and fixating thought, grounded in an understandable but mostly fallible quest for (legal) certainty. This thinking of what is understood as 'law' mirrors the certainty that truth, reality, even law and justice, are to be 'found' through instruments taught in Law Schools and administered in legal practice. But the insight that legal thinking proceeds in- and through interactivity requires a leap of thought. Until today, magistrates experience little impetus in their professional interactivity and common interaction that influence their adjudicative processes caused by changes in society and patterns. Perhaps a collegial decision that causes any interaction may be found in the shadows of a courthouse. Yet diverse forms of deliberative consultation allow magistrates to ascertain their own prejudices and open their thoughts in favour of change and transformation. That is the conversion they witness when they analyze a 'case': the myriad determining factors (or 'affectors') as such never reduced or reducible to categorically identified elements of 'law'. This Article aims to point out the importance of such a conversion for practicing jurists and anyone focusing on 'reading law'.

1 Law, Lawyer and Judicial Thoughts

1.1 Case and Law

Laws are rules and rules embrace, in every aspect, norms. They crystallize principal values and patterns of behaviour. Rules often conflict, but their application is

Originally published in: Jan M. Broekman and Frank Fleerackers (2020), Legal Thoughts Convert: Rethinking Legal Thinking, Springer, p. 7–20, republished here in a slightly revised version.

F. Fleerackers (✉)
Faculty of Law, KU Leuven, Leuven, Belgium
e-mail: frank.fleerackers@kuleuven.be

F. Fleerackers (ed.), *The Rearguard of Subjectivity*, Law and Visual Jurisprudence 9,
https://doi.org/10.1007/978-3-031-26855-7_6

formalized in a case. Law as such is non-existent without precedents and cases as its juridical realization. Law is realized in and through cases—even though 'realization' may sound awkward in context. Actual legal thinking is not merely formalized in a case but encompasses the case in its uniqueness. Thinking the law in and through cases is as differential and dynamic as the case itself. Evidently, such a type of thinking requires an approach that differs from a generic understanding of human through processes. Any such approach will adapt to an ongoing reality. In each case, reality shows itself to the jurist, because values and norms are realized in- and through cases. Not a single case adheres to existing legislation: each case is factually new, different and essentially variable. A judge's thinking is a thought *process* that bridges the divide between rules and cases. This bridging will always depart from the case, not the rule. As such, one should refrain from simply categorizing European continental law as *codified* and Anglo-Saxon law as *casuistic*. Both legal systems thrive on legalism and application thinking, no matter whether this application involves statutes or precedents.

Law finds its realization only in cases. The latter leave legislation to be implemented by the judge. This influences the dynamics of conversion, which determines the generation of meaning. Still, the act of speaking (and language in general) remains essential in legal thinking. Law is speaking from the case: it is a two-way process during which legal norms are verified in casuistry and cases realize law. Dynamics are ideally optimized as long as a judge is not reaching a decision in a case. This also means that judges, when eventually deciding a case, effectuate a shutdown of dynamics. What happens with the case (and its dynamics) when judgment is reached? This is an important aspect of conversion, as it continues the dynamics of legal practice. Even opting for any specific legal procedure invokes qualification and categorization. The latter are fed by a jurist's thinking in general rather than by his or her understanding of the case at hand. Procedural justice does for that reason not lead to effective justice, because no single procedure is intrinsically neutral. Any such suggestion will indeed reflect a particular policy.

The fundamental position of casuistry in law is a consequence of the human quest for certainty and the need for predictability, i.e.: similar cases will be decided similarly, whoever the judge may be. O.W. Holmes Jr's warning fiercely resonates here: "Who constitutes the law? You will find some text writers telling you that it is something different from what is decided by the courts . . ., that it is a system of reason, that it is a deduction of principles or ethics or admitted axioms or what not, which may or may not coincide with the decisions. But if we take the view of our friend the bad man, we shall find that he does not care two straws for the axioms or deductions, but that he does want to know what the . . . courts are likely to do in fact. I am much of this mind. The prophecies of what the courts will do in fact, and nothing more pretentious, are what I mean by the law."[1]

[1]Holmes (1897, 457f.).

1.2 Legal Argumentation

No classic research on legal argumentation may therefore suffice to understand the casuistic dynamics of performing judgments in law. The way a judging magistrate thinks becomes only visible in his actions, that is: when he is prepared to bare his thought process via and as interaction. Even though the judge may limit himself at first to a static apprehension of presented determining factors, social interactivity will allow him to find the case's underlying dynamic affectors. When confronting the latter with his prima facie reading of the case, he will be able to map possible solutions against a hierarchy of "affective factors".

One should not lose sight of the dynamic forces active in his thoughts and actions through the conversion of meaning. Affective legal thinking provides a clarifying view of these forces, notwithstanding a judge's personal leanings or juridical intuition. Experienced jurists will offset their own train of thought with the legal affective analysis at hand. This is why interactivity coincides with legal affectors as a case's determining factors, functioning as an instrument to approach the case's changeability as closely a possible.

The term "affect" refers in this context to Gilles Deleuze and Félix Guattari's *Mille Plateaux*. These authors do not limit the concept to personal sentiment or mere emotion. On the contrary, affect is defined, not unlike Spinoza's affectus, as the human capacity of affecting and being affected by one another. Deleuze even posits it as an essential human capacity. Each theoretical and static analysis will remain enclosed in its rationalizing stance, while every case is indeed affective in its essence. As such, cases are witnessed as obstacles to and in any rationalizing analysis, which is evidently not so in its affective alternative.

This affect, understood as a human capacity, is even more essential for law than the purported governing capacity of human reason. The latter is static, while an affective analysis mirrors a case's interactivity and dynamics. Legal thinking thus requires more than a mere juxtaposition of arguments, because the latter may only function as instrumental aids and even cloud the actual affectors. It is therefore not the human capacity of reason, but the capability in- and through interactivity to understand the differential and dynamic aspects of cases as well as their essential changeability. At the same time, jurists will have to see themselves as participating actors with similar affectors (γνῶθι σεαυτόν). The latter will only lead to a clear profile if the inherent dynamics of conversion are exposed. Unveiling the continuing conversion of meanings and their conceptual content as well as language typology (analogue and digital) will enhance such understanding among the legal profession and the public.

1.3 Interactivity

Legal procedures are dynamic processes enhanced by interactive practice to optimize an understanding of reality require not only interactive education of jurists, but also a continuing refinement of judicial codes and conduct. Magistrates could develop provisional decisions, requiring parties' response, while facts are being scrutinized and interpreted. But ultimately and evidently, collegial decision-making should prevail. This is not to say that interactive meaning generation would always hold sway in all forms of collegial decision-making. Even collegial processes involving three or more magistrates illustrate many examples of non-interactivity. The same is observable when cases are simply divided among judges or when certain magistrates weigh in too heavily (or too little). But such faults are easily circumvented since codes of procedural conduct will clearly state how collegial decision-making is to be organized. Legal processes are directed by a court president who, not unlike a theatre-director, will instigate their effectiveness. This involves a trespassing on the institutional force of law, which strictly posits speakers and actors into seemingly innocent positions. The same can be said of prosecuting magistrates. Whoever does not function optimally (together) will be replaced, albeit because of functioning badly or too effectively.

Ideally, diversity is a key and interactivity needs to be upheld. If members of a collegial decision-making process think too identical, then their unity and uniformity in qualification would reduce reality to a lethargic substrate. Their effective legal practice would become futile at the expense of vanishing cases. This is how juridical interactivity evolves into a form of encounter, allowing for jurists to somewhat liberate themselves from particular convictions or thought patterns. Interaction provides them with a means to distance themselves and shift their static positions to processes of changeability. At the same time, juridical interaction allows for a juxtaposition of opposing insights, at a distance of fixating rationalization. Only by dynamically exploring and recognizing differing insights, legal thinking will adopt and pervade them, leading to the eventual judgment. Even when concerning truth in a seemingly objective sense, true insight still demands interactive guidance in order to transfer and transmit the meaning of said truth. Juridical interaction prevails when such processes are at stake.

In this context, interaction is understood as crucial in the generation of meaning. Magistrates should accept interaction as the most essential capability for decision-making, which allows them to confront their own case analysis with those surrendered by their colleagues or by parties and their lawyers. A threefold conclusion results here. First, this shows how one's own analysis only divulged a (limited) part of the case, notwithstanding one's conviction to the contrary. Second, this leads to a critical understanding of the way one's analysis is marred by often-unknown prejudices. Third, this points out how one's own analysis unwillingly and often unconsciously resulted in static categorization. Conversely, the interactive confrontation with other magistrates provides for three remedies: enhancement and deepening of one's own analysis; mutual verification of one's prejudices; and an interactive, dynamic understanding of the case's evolving and changing reality. In this sense, interactivity is the central mode of law and legal thinking. The classic Socratic syndrome suggests that mankind is keen on jumping to conclusions and accordingly sticking to its guns, as our thinking presupposes that we, i.e. jurists, have a reasonable capability to understand the world and reality in accordance to categorical and comparable entities.

At the heart of this syndrome resides a dual denial of two core paradigms in human existence, as difference and dynamics constitute essential traits of every real life case, obviously contradicting the inherently static identification of classic legal thinking. Magistrates should therefore adhere to collegial decision-making as a form of mutual confrontation and interactive analysis, encompassing as well as dynamic and differential, optimally approaching a case's reality. Such an interactivity, however, requires individual development of one's own capacity to think, by way of summoning a scale of changeability, generating dynamics from within while appropriately reflecting the specificity of each case and allowing for an authentic, above all effective (legal) decision.

2 Formative Social Forces in Law

Social forces at play in the legal world regard adherence to past decisions as well as to stipulated (general) rules. Simply put, two strands of legal structure enclose both forces: precedent based law on one hand, statute law on the other. Their titles already indicate how social interests may play their roles without insurgencies or other forms of revolt.

2.1 Precedents and Statutes

It is interesting to see how Anglo-Saxon precedent-based law and European-continental statute law similarly undervalue the importance of day-to-day casuistry. Precedent-based legal systems, as much as their continental counterparts, focus on qualification and categorization techniques that underplay the case's changeability, bearing in mind their fixation on legal certainty. As statute law views cases as objects of legal norms to be applied whereas precedent-based law prioritizes comparative categorization and similitude to divergence. Both types of law do not allow for the differential and dynamic components of legal thinking to flourish. Both types reduce reality to a static substrate of what ever was, or could ever become. Both systems hold limited space for a case's differential and dynamic attributes, or for a case-driven analysis and implementation. This touches the social foundations of law, even though often unnoticed, when they surface as social forces in particular forms of protest, revolt, or anarchism, thus unveiling how such forces even dissemble in theoretical construct and (legal) traditions, as recent schools of thought like legalism, realism, proceduralism, textualism and pragmatism may show.

2.2 Legalism

Legalism has been accurately defined by Judith Shklar as a form of application thinking, which is not that much limited to the legal realm, but omnipresent among human beings. This apprehension of reality presupposes an understanding or real life as a collection of comparable occurrences. Within a legal framework, such apprehension requires a judge to remain bouche de la loi, where a government of laws, not men established the rule of law. Legislators legislate and judges adjudicate as if the relation between law and society would straightforwardly be one-on-one, and as if reality is at a standstill, petrified. This juridical apprehension contends reality to be inclined towards similarity and regulation, at the same time undervaluing a magistrate's inherent humanity. Assertions of mistrust towards judges and a gouvernement des juges are rationalized by way of compulsive legalism, in order to preclude personal or political excesses. Such distrust often has adverse consequences, whenever judges are (blatantly) politically appointed. Yet there's no effective theory on how to adjudicate when the law remains silent. Theory mostly remains circumscribed to modes of interpretation, where text outranks factual goals and legal certainty remains stuck in a (juridical) quagmire.

2.3 Realism

Realism originated as a reaction to legal positivism gone legalism, even though the latter allowed for moral independence, i.e. morality loosening its grip on law. If it hadn't been for legalism, procedural law would never have substantiated the way it did. Nevertheless, the inherently artificial confinement gave way to unacceptable excesses in the course of the twentieth century, epitomized by references to "Befehl is Befehl" during the Nuremberg Trials: as long as correct procedure was observed, actions were deemed legal: they were regarded morally reprehensible, yet juridically legal. Evidently, this is narrow legal thinking at its best, and linked to strong foundational references to (internationally) shared values as formulated in the European Convention on Human Rights or the Universal Declaration. Nevertheless, such references resuscitate the topic and influence of morality within and above the legal domain. Consequently one wonders how morality in its manifold forms can be kept at bay, while still upholding an intrinsic morality of law, at least related to its democratic origins. Legal realist scholars like O.W. Holmes Jr., Karl Llewellyn and Jerome Frank showed, early on in the twentieth century, how law and politics are intertwined.[2] Their casuistic and result driven approach, building on philosophical pragmatism by John Dewey, William James and Charles Sanders Peirce, was rejuvenated at the end of that very same century in the Critical Legal Studies Movement of jurists like Roberto Mangabeira Unger and Duncan Kennedy.

[2]Holmes (1897), Llewellyn (1930, 1960), Frank (1930).

2.4 *Legal Process*

The focus on the Legal Process school was a clear reaction to legal realism, even though scholars like Henry Hart and Lon Fuller suggested a middle way between a politically inspired legal realism and the juridical formalism of legal positivism.[3] Their pursuit for neutral, impartial, procedural principles and a specific legal morality failed, as well as a reconciliation among both strands of thought. On one hand, Hart rightly characterized Fullers inner morality of law as a mere deontology.[4] On the other, the legal process school still treated cases as objects of categorical thinking, embedded in categorizing procedures. Finally, the school was viewed as yet another strand of classic legalism, i.e. "thin proceduralism".[5] Nevertheless, criticism of legal realism expanded even further.

2.5 *Originalism*

Textualism or originalism can be seen as the most successful antithesis to legal realism and the *Critical Legal Studies Movement*. As the intersection between law and politics is publicly debated, it is interesting to focus on particular criticism by Alex Kozinski, the then president of the United States Court of Appeals for the Ninth Circuit: "Just to prove that even the silliest idea can be pursued to its illogical conclusion, Legal Realism spawned Critical Legal Studies. ... I am here to tell you that this is all horse manure. ... judges exercise their powers subject to very significant constraints.... The first, and to my mind the most significant, is internal: the judge's own self-respect. ... The second important constraint comes from your colleagues. If you're a district judge, your decisions are subject to review by three judges of the court of appeals. If you are a circuit judge, you have to persuade at least one other colleague, preferably two, to join your opinion. ... (But) what you absolutely cannot get away with is abandoning legal principles in favour of results on a consistent basis. A judge who tries to do this cuts deeply into his credibility...".[6] After rejecting legal realism and the more recent *Critical Legal Studies Movement*, he then forwarded his predilection for textualism or originalism as forms of a reclaimed legalism: "Now, there is an unspoken premise to what I have said, namely that there are more or less objective principles by which the law operates, principles that dictate the reasoning and often the result in most cases. I know you are taught to doubt this in law school, as I was; it is nevertheless true.... one principle I think is extremely important: Language has meaning. ... language used in statutes, regulations, contracts and the Constitution place an objective

[3] Fuller (1964).

[4] Hart (1958, 593f.), Fuller (1958, 630f.).

[5] Posner (2008).

[6] Kozinski (1993), O'Brien (2012).

constraint on our conduct. ... lawyers complain, with good reason, that within the same circuit there will be two lines of authority on the very same subject. The two lines go off in different directions without acknowledging each other's existence, like ships passing in the night. In such circumstances lawyers have much difficulty in advising clients how to conduct their affairs, the rule of law depending on who the judges in their case happen to be." And yet, it is that very same Kozinski who consequently admits: "We all view reality from our own peculiar perspective, we all have biases, interests, leanings, instincts. ... It is important to follow those instincts, because they can lead to a crucial issue that turns out to make a difference. But it is even more important to doubt your own leanings, to be skeptical of your instincts. My prescription is ... to fight them. ... Is (the) result justified by the law, fairly and honestly applied to the facts? Or is it merely a bit of self-indulgence?" Within the US Supreme Court, the late Antonin Scalia was viewed as a crucial proponent of textualism or constitutional originalism,[7] as he would coin the phrase. Such originalism would lend priority to the actual text or meaning of the Constitution. Still, the same Scalia called himself a faint-hearted originalist and allowed for a certain amount of pragmatism when plain textualism would apparently hinder an effective application of the law. Scholars like Ronald Dworkin would argue for reconciliation, construing law as a specific mode of political morality, yet epitomized by historical, often textual, readings,[8] unless not compatible with a deeper constitutional objective.

2.6 Pragmatism

Posner describes judging, as performed by his fellow magistrates, as a form of pragmatism. Beyond his criticism of legalism as well as legal realism, for their fixation on procedure or on political ideology, he portrays a highly personal, experience-based view of legal thinking, focusing on the consequences of adjudication: "pragmatic adjudication by judicial concern for consequences ... rather than conceptualisms or generalities." In line with philosophical pragmatism, he concentrates on human intuition, or more specifically, on the way magistrates develop a uniquely legal intuition over the years of their profession.[9] While canvassing the classic tension between principle and pragma, between foundation and praxis, he adamantly embraces the pragmatist school, as he joins O.W. Holmes Jr. in rejecting the simplicity of logical deduction in law, as well as John Dewey, in thinking forward instead of backward, positing empiricism above mere deduction.[10] Criticizing principled thinking in a legal context is understandable, whereas the absence of a

[7] Scalia (1984), Tribe (1985, 45).

[8] Dworkin (2011, 413).

[9] Posner (2008, 107).

[10] Posner (2008, 232), Holmes (1897, 457), Dewey (1924).

morally-neutral position underscores the importance of casuistry, and the weighing of principles. But on the other hand, pragmatism holds a risk of slippery slope or stepping stone reasoning, causing principles to gradually wither away.

Posner is the pragmatist who focuses on what effectively works, denouncing formalism and legalism, yet only when their application clearly falters: "(they) cannot resolve tough cases". But he also criticizes legal realism, when "vulgarly political" or "lacking in content".[11] In the heart of his narrative, Posner elaborates on how legal pragmatism may offer solutions at the crossroads of law and morality, of principle and praxis: "what counts as an acceptably pragmatic resolution of a dispute is relative to the prevailing norms of particular societies: pragmatism provides local rather than universal guidance to judicial action".[12] He bases this pragmatism in the context of a legal system where judges "must play by the rules of the judicial game". Even the rigorously procedural thought process of the legal process school, though focusing on impartial and analytical judges, pales in comparison with how legal pragmatism focuses on a case's consequences, thus resulting in yet another articulation of legalism. Proceduralism is the formalist mode of principled thought, where (neutrally) procedural principles endure the same thin and empty treatment as substantive principles. For Posner, proceduralism and legalism are schools of the past, while pragmatism epitomizes present and future.[13] He concludes that: "the good pragmatist judge is not a shortsighted pragmatist. He is not a philosophical pragmatist. But he is a constrained pragmatist": constrained, yet also self-composed, and as such restrained, abiding by the rules at hand: "the pragmatic judge must play by the rules of the judicial game, just like other judges. The rules permit the consideration of certain types of consequences but forbid the consideration of other types. They limit the judge to being . . . a 'rule pragmatist'".[14]

Interestingly, Scalia's "faint-hearted originalist" and Posner's "constrained pragmatist" seem to find each other in a similar quest for effective law.

According to Posner, judges hide behind application directed thinking: their legalism serves as a pretext to cover up intrinsic constraints, heralding a prototype of legal thought as a merely technical application of rules or norms, even though each and every magistrate is exposed to personal, strategic as well as institutional factors or affectors. Self-knowledge is evidently of the essence.

Posner argues that most judges, even when formally adhering to legalism, de facto succumb to legal pragmatism. In that sense, the need for self-examination is indisputable, not only focused on one's own predispositions, but above all with regard to any and all determining affectors at play: education, background, culture, experience, temperament, identification, preference, ideology, political views, convictions, or even strategic positioning amidst colleagues (e.g. reversal aversion or disproportional respect for higher instances). Hence, he directly links legal or

[11] Posner (2008, 238).

[12] Posner (2008, 241).

[13] Posner (2008, 247).

[14] Posner (2008, 254).

judicial intuition to self-examination (γνῶθι σεαυτόν) as a form of affective analysis. Intuition is in that case defined as a "capability of reaching down into a subconscious respository of knowledge". It is at the same time understood as a form of recognition as well as a plan of action, pointing to experience as a more essential affector (or determining effector) than juridical or procedural reasoning, particularly when the law is "open". In this sense, classic legal reasoning or procedural arguments are mostly ex-post rationalizations as well as justifications of said intuition.

Evidently, human interpretation as a capability is rooted in that very same intuition: "interpretation is an innate, universal and quintessentially human faculty." As such, Posner considers intuition to be more effective than technical analysis.

3 Law, Case and Concept

Let us return to the foundational question, which determines not only the behaviour of jurists and citizens, but also the social processes in which their lives unfold. How is legal thinking to be conceived? As if caught amidst a broader identity crisis, coinciding with a heightened sense of urgency against the backdrop of terrorism, a number of interesting monographs have been published[15] on the subject.

In essence, analysis evolved from mere legal interpretation and interpretive techniques or legal reasoning. As such, contemporary analysis should necessarily focus on how legal thinking upholds a particular relation between law and reality by converting juridically posited fields of meaning. Insight into this conversion directly relates to a jurist's self-interpretation and his institutional role.

3.1 Foundational Structures

Rules and results determine the foundational structures of legal thoughts. Yet the same rule may lead to different results at the hand of jurists, since their thinking emanates from a particular perspective. This personal perspective is more consequential for law than the mere existence of competing rules and their contradictory implementation. A total sublimation of man from law would evidently be useless—not because adjudication by artificial intelligence is unfeasible, but because it would be literally inhuman. The crux of judicial judgment is directed towards human action in all its aspects. Jurists (and judges foremost) will accordingly and ex officio prioritize cases over norms.[16]

[15] Sunstein (2001), Dworkin (2008, 2011), Posner (2008), Schauer (2009).

[16] Fleerackers (2000, 52–55).

Schauer offers a familiar comparison, where a younger child argues to have a 'right' to do something his older sibling was allowed to do at a similar age. He describes forms of reasoning his parents may use, and adds: "For however much these various forms of reasoning do exist throughout our decision-making lives, it is important not to forget that they are odd, and odd in a special way. And this special oddness is that every one of the dominant characteristics of legal reasoning and legal argument can be seen as a route toward reaching a decision other than the best all-things-considered decision for the matter at hand."[17] He thus describes legal thinking as counterintuitive in its focus on cases, and indeed, as both analogy and authority exude a certain institutional effect, they curb as well as restrain a self-evident implementation of doing the right thing.

3.2 *Case Driven*

Jurists are institutionally trained to forgo their initial impulse to instantly opt for a best case-driven solution and abide by generalizing as well as formalist rules (of authority), since human beings, hence also jurists, evidently embrace different opinions with regard to what may constitute a best solution. In other words, such solutions do not automatically, or naturally, follow from the case at hand, yet different people almost automatically, or naturally, adhere to different perspectives on what might be best in casu. To surpass this seemingly irreducible conundrum, which involves rule*s* of men, one may comprehend how the rule of law surfaced as a workable alternative in order to achieve legal certainty in a world confounded with particularisms. Accordingly, as cases incorporate antinomy, they will yield in front of decisions based on rules, analogy or authority. Such definition of judicial thought is understandable and even somewhat defendable. Yet this evidently categorical cure is worse than the disease, as even Schauer concedes. On one hand, we prefer to restrict the obvious perils of fallacious adjudication with an absolute Rule of Law. On the other hand, we would like to bolster good and wise decisions by providing for necessary space and headroom, though this would expose the Rule of Law to imperfection and fallibility.

So where does this leave us? Is it 'case against rule', 'man against institution', 'reality against law'?

3.3 *Case by Case*

This is where Cass Sunstein's adage comes in: one case at a time. Yet for Sunstein, prioritization of cases in law is even more important than the singularity of each and

[17] Schauer (2009, 7).

every occurrence, or each and every instance of human action. When judges apparently adjudicate with similar future cases in mind, legal thinking itself is at risk. Indeed, and even more so than legislators, judges wield a very limited view of the way future cases may develop. Such criticism evidently strikes at the heart of precedent-based law. Yet the same danger resides in the heart of any adjudication, as courts and tribunals aren't organized and structured to produce such juridically proactive decisions. Caution is indeed advised. Meanwhile, the cautionary essence of one case at a time is certainly at play in effective legal thinking. Rules have a general as well as formal constellation. Yet, underneath such generality and formality, a ratio legis resides. Understanding the effectivity of law and its thought patterns requires an insight in human actions, in rule-governed as well as adjudicative situations, which are susceptible to cognitive illusions. This does not mean that such situations belong to the domain of psychology. Indeed, psychology, philosophy, sociology, economics, as well as law are scientific domains related to human conduct, of which the legal field is primarily concerned with its normative aspects. Hence, rules and rule following are central themes of legal theory and questions regarding the underlying rationale of a rule are at the forefront of legal scholarship and legal education.

A legal rule's formalist as well as generalizing character is foundational to the Rule of Law, in order to uphold legal certainty, i.e. predictability and uniformity of legal decisions, yet also to curtail the decisive powers of individuals, such as policy makers, legislators and magistrates. With regard to its formality, legal rules boast a necessary textual, verbatim and literal character, upholding its weight amongst its non-juridical siblings, illustrating why the letter of the law often prevails and why a judge is somewhat mockingly characterized as "bouche de la loi". As such, both generalizing and formalist aspects of a legal rule adhere to its essence. Aristotle may have put it most clearly, arguing legislation to be universal, general as well as generalizing, while the nature of any case, and of reality for that matter, should be seen as singular and unique. Legal rules require case-by-case adjustment, not because they are inept or inconclusive, but because of their generalizing character. The notion of aequitas[18] (ἐπιείκεια) or equity would soften its harshest consequences. As Aristotle argues in his Ethica, not the rule is at fault but its generalizing stance is at odds with reality. In fact, two worlds collide, the generalizing world of rules and the innate particularity of a reality of occurrences or cases. Hence, these worlds are in need of bridging, which, for Aristotle and Cicero, aequitas would provide. In this Article, focus resides on who realizes such aequitas: the jurist as man of law, epitomizing man and law in crucial conversion.

[18] Waelkens (2015, 326).

References

Dewey J (1924) Logical method and law. Cornell Law Q 10(1) USA
Dworkin R (2008) Justice in robes. Harvard University Press, Cambridge, USA
Dworkin R (2011) Justice for Hedgehogs. Harvard University Press, Cambridge, USA
Fleerackers F (2000) Affective legal analysis. Duncker & Humblot, BRD, Berlin
Frank J (1930) Law and the modern mind. New York: Brentano, (2009^2) Oxfordshire, UK: Transaction/Routledge.
Fuller L (1958) Positivism and fidelity to law—A reply to professor Hart. Harv Law Rev 71. Harvard, USA
Fuller L (ed) (1964) The morality of law (revised ed. 1965). Yale University Press, New Haven, USA
Hart HLA (1958) Positivism and the separation of law and morals. Harv Law Rev 71. Harvard, USA
Holmes OW Jr (1897) The path of law. Harv Law Rev 10(8) Harvard, USA
Kozinski A (1993) What I ate for breakfast and other mysteries of judicial decision making. Loyola Los Angeles Law Rev 26:993. Los Angeles, USA
Llewellyn K (1930) The bramble bush: on our law and its study, (2009^2). Oxford University Press, Oxford, UK
Llewellyn K (1960) The common law tradition: deciding appeals. Brown, Hachette Book Group. Little, New York, USA
O'Brien D (2012) Judges on judging: views from the bench, 4th edn. Sage, London, UK
Posner R (2008) How judges think. Harvard University Press, Cambridge, USA
Scalia A (1984) Originalism: the lesser evil. Cincinnati Law Rev 57:849. USA
Schauer F (2009) Thinking like a lawyer. Harvard University Press, Cambridge, USA
Sunstein C (2001) One case at a time. Harvard University Press, Cambridge, USA
Tribe L (1985) God save this honorable court. Random House, New York, USA
Waelkens L (2015) Amne Adverso: Roman legal heritage in European culture. Leuven University Press

Reflecting on Law and Language

Jan M. Broekman's *Rethinking Law and Language: The Flagship 'Speech'*

Philip T. Grier

Abstract A summary overview of Professor Broekman's work on law and language, focused on its most distinctive theses and claims. The language in which any system of law must be expressed is to some extent an artificial one, with fairly rigid, pre-defined verbal formulae and an enforced precision in the use of terms that is not characteristic of any natural language in use. And yet every such specially-purposed legal language must be expressed using the resources of some existing natural language. This inevitable divergence between legal language and natural language does not arise as an issue *within* law, but raises a series of questions that arise from a variety of extra-legal (in this case mainly philosophical) viewpoints. One such viewpoint is what he terms the dominant "speaker-hearer" model of linguistic discourse, firmly embedded in our thinking by Hobbes, among others. Much of the argument of the book is aimed at demolishing this model of speech in natural language as inadequate to capture the special features of legal language. He aims to supplant this model with a much different one, rooted in what he terms a "*neo*-structuralist" analysis of language use. The argument culminates in a discussion of "digital" versus "analog" languages, and the complications engendered by "conversions" of one to the other, a conclusion from which I dissented in certain respects.

Originally published in *The Journal of Comparative Law*, vol. 15, no. 1, pp. 293–303, as a review/essay on *Rethinking Law and Language: The Flagship 'Speech'* by Jan M. Broekman (Cheltenham, UK; Northhampton, MA, USA: Edward Elgar Publishing, 2019) *xii* + 328 pp. It is republished here, with permission, in a slightly revised and expanded version.

P. T. Grier (✉)
Thomas Bowman Professor of Philosophy and Religion, Emeritus, Dickinson College, Carlisle, PA, USA
e-mail: grier@dickinson.edu

F. Fleerackers (ed.), *The Rearguard of Subjectivity*, Law and Visual Jurisprudence 9,
https://doi.org/10.1007/978-3-031-26855-7_7

1 Introduction

As the main title suggests, in this recent monograph Professor Broekman intends to provoke a wide-ranging re-examination of the relation between law and language. He does not begin by pointing to any single, specific, widely-acknowledged problem of law and language that must be addressed, beyond the inescapable starting-point that any system of law must be articulated in some appropriate natural language. Instead he proceeds to raise a succession of potentially deep worries and puzzles involving law and language (*any* legal system, *any* natural language) that can be seen to arise from several distinct philosophical perspectives.

Those various perspectives are loosely ranged around his own intriguing historical reconstruction of what he views as the dominant "Speaker-Hearer" model of language use as it has shaped the typical attitude toward language prevailing in most occidental theories of law. The "flagship 'speech'" referred to in the sub-title is in essence that same Speaker-Hearer model that conceives language use as a succession of rule-governed "speech-acts" performed by an individual speaker addressed to a designated hearer or hearers. Among the goals of the monograph is the final destruction ("wreckage") of that model.

Broekman's historical reconstruction of the dominant view of language in modern European history focuses upon Hobbes as one of the first theorists of language, one who powerfully influenced our thinking about both law and language. Rather than scrutinizing the text of the *Leviathan*, however, Broekman is able to deduce what matters most in Hobbes' thinking about law and language from an intriguing discussion of the famous frontispiece, the etching of *Homo Magnus* created by Hobbes' friend, the French-English artist Abraham Bosse. That etching was the product of a close and extensive collaboration between Hobbes and Bosse. Beyond its obviously intended purpose of illustrating Hobbes' conception of absolute sovereignty, Broekman claims that it also entrenched the Speaker-Hearer model of language among the presuppositions of modern legal theory so effectively that its dominance has largely persisted up to the present.

The remainder of Broekman's monograph could be described as a protracted campaign of guerilla warfare aimed first at exposing various largely unrecognized presuppositions of the standard Speaker-Hearer model and, second, calling into question their appropriateness as elements of an acceptable theory of law and language. At the center of this campaign, to some extent forming its ultimate basis, there is to be found a "neo-structuralist" contestation of the speaker-hearer model that Broekman develops in several directions, to be discussed below.

2 On Languages, Artificial and Natural, and the Construction of Socio-Political Orders

Broekman points out that law and language are necessarily intertwined in complex fashion. Law, which is to some extent an artificial language, can only be articulated within some natural language. However, legal language often includes fairly rigid, pre-defined verbal formulae, depends upon a prescribed vocabulary applying to specific sets of circumstances, and in general places great stress upon exactitude in the use of language, all to a degree that would be considered odd if practiced in ordinary non-legal conversation in a natural language. And yet law can only be articulated within the resources of a natural language. Broekman observes that this "gap" between legal language and natural language can be explored from a number of disciplinary perspectives, but is seldom if ever an explicit concern raised *within* the law.

His discussion of the problem is framed in terms of a contrast between two different models of the law-language relation: the "law-language model" and the "law-language-law model." He refers to these two models in the opening paragraph of the book, but unfortunately does not immediately reveal what he conceives to be the salient differences between them. The reader is obliged to sort that out gradually while working through the text; the contrast gains significance mainly as the critique of the Speaker-Hearer model unfolds.

Chapter 2 contains a highly original and interesting exploration of the significance of the frontispiece of Hobbes' *Leviathan*—the image of *Homo Magnus*—which he treats as equivalent in some respects to an extended text. Indeed, he asserts that the borderline between image and text was in Hobbes' time less strict [Broekman (2019), p. 28]; images no less than words were evidently treated as capable of presenting arguments. Broekman then proceeds to "read" the image at some length, stressing that it presents a theory of language as well as a theory of power, and that the two are essentially intertwined in Hobbes' conception of law:

The theme of power emerges as the possibility for a single man (the Sovereign) to hold both military and ecclesiastical power in his hands, hands belonging to a single identifiable subject, a human self, capable of speaking the words (laws) ordering the form of life to which all must submit [Broekman (2019), p. 30]. The source of that power is manifest in the image: the countless individuals ("particles") composing the torso of *Homo Magnus*. They are the "other" to whom the Leviathan speaks.

> the Magnus Homo is a portrait of the *Speaker* and it is also immediately clear how the citizens, participants of the *pactum unionis*, are made *Hearers*, so that a strong identity of linguistic and social structure is guaranteed [Broekman (2019), p. 63].

But in the image there is no basis for supposing that they speak to one another, or indeed to the Leviathan, prior to the formation of the new order of things dictated by him. And *after* the new order has been formed, they speak only as "actors," enacting the language "authored" by the Sovereign [Broekman (2019), p. 33]. Otherwise, silence would appear to be the necessary fate of the individual citizen. In this sense

Hobbes' frontispiece can be read as an extreme example of a Speaker-Hearer model of speech: the primary model of language use involves One speaking while the Others must listen in silence.

The main mechanism whereby individuals were brought into social union was the *contract*. Such an account of the formation of society presupposes three conditions: a shared understanding of the institution of contracts, a widespread grasp of the basic institutions of law and legal practice, and finally, some knowledge of the fundamentals of a natural language within which law can be articulated and accepted by the relevant population as "their" law [Broekman (2019), p. 43]. This understanding of the formation of contracts leads inevitably to the conception of a *legal subject* both as the author of the contractual language, and also as a way of designating each of the parties to the contract.

> Once they enter the realm of legal language, pluralities such as institutionalized groups of persons, capitals, corporations, political parties, and the like are expressed in the singular mode.... The *legal person* functions in law, legal theory, and legal practice as a singularity [Broekman (2019), p. 45].

The legal person (singularity) gives effect to his/her *will* as a *speaker* of a legal language embedded in the context of a natural language. As a coda to his observations on Hobbes' role as "father of the Speaker-Hearer model" [Broekman (2019), p. 64]. Broekman adds that Hobbes should also be honored within linguistic theory or philosophy of language as an important example of the "law-language-law" theme being explored in the present work, but up to now has not received any such recognition.

In Chapter 3, Broekman reminds us that the Napoleonic Code of 1804, like the frontispiece of Hobbes' *Leviathan*, was instrumental in "picturing the individual citizen in his or her sociopolitical context" [Broekman (2019), p. 70]. More specifically, the thirty-six original laws of Napoleon's Code formulated the legal (and implicitly socio-political) identities open to a "Citoyen" or a "Français," and were aimed at forming a French nation. Though the ostensible author, Napoleon, was the "Speaker," the "Hearers" were implicitly being invited to imagine for themselves the wealth of possible actions opened up to them by the Code. Thus those technically being addressed as "you," were in effect being encouraged to conceive of the roles made available for legal persons as pertaining to them in the first person: "*I* am empowered (or forbidden) to do such and such." The *socially effective* law is thus the awareness of the legal possibilities and the boundaries of which the population is *conscious*.

The *legal consciousness* of the society or the *Volk* therefore constitutes the actuality of law in one crucial sense. That consciousness is of course historically formed, and it is distinct for each culturally distinct society. Thus did von Savigny argue, ten years after the publication of Napoleon's Code, that it would *not* constitute an adequate basis for the codification of *German* law. Nor would the far older codification of Roman Law serve any such purpose. The only acceptable codification of German law would necessarily be one based on *German legal consciousness*, i.e., on the results of distinctively German historical experience.

Broekman stresses, however, that both Napoleon and von Savigny were aware that it is the impact of symbolic legal actions and enactments on the formation of the consciousness of the citizenry that ultimately matters. He points out that there is an unmistakably poetic quality in the articulation of the original Napoleonic Code, intended to evoke an emotional response in the population. The language of the original Code is quite different from the much more dry and technical subordinate codes issued over the following years: the 1807 Trade Code, the 1808 Criminal Procedure, and the 1810 Penal Code, as well as the alterations eventually made to the primary Code. In each case there was a movement from poetic inspiration toward greater technical perfection [Broekman (2019), pp. 72–73].

3 Language and the Formation of Legal Consciousness

Probing the thesis that language is the essence of law, Broekman argues that the vast field of possible meanings afforded by the natural language in which a legal system is couched is a necessary presupposition of the much narrower and more rigid formulations of legal discourse derived from that natural language. The process of forming a specific legal discourse requires a single "powerful type of dynamics: recognition" [Broekman (2019), pp. 84, 86]. Among the many dimensions of the phenomenon of recognition, two are important for the present theme: (1) a notion of the *other* (accompanied by the possibility of identification with that other), and (2) a notion of *agreement* between oneself and the other. These are the two essential bases for *legal consciousness*, a concept put into circulation originally by von Savigny, and destined to spread throughout the legal theories of most western, central and eastern European countries through the latter half of the nineteenth century, and into the early twentieth, (It has persisted for perhaps the most extended period in Russian legal thought, especially in the work of the early 20th century Russian philosopher of law I. A. Il'in, though mainly in the form of a Soviet version of "legal consciousness" that significantly distorted the meaning of von Savigny's original concept. However, since the collapse of the Soviet state, the meaning of the term has begun to reassume its original contours in some instances).[1]

Evaluative attitudes articulated in the prevailing natural language (i.e., prevailing social attitudes) can be absorbed by the legal system, and sometimes amplified by it, both in terms of written legal codes and in terms of the decision-making of judges and other legal officials. For example, the law tends to accord great respect to the powers of the first person subject (i.e., the "legal subject"), enlarging and defending the subject's field of action, while at the same time respecting the comparable rights of the other. It is this complex of inter-related rights and duties, as tacitly recognized by the general population, that composes the "legal consciousness" of a given society. The content of such a legal consciousness is not permanently fixed, but

[1] See Il'in (2014), esp. pp. 15–50.

always open to evolution through novel historical experiences and junctures, which changes should be generally progressive.

Von Savigny's 'legal consciousness,' the *Rechtsbewusstsein* of the *Volk* was also, among other things, a search for a special sense of the plural as it operates within legal discourse:

> His search for the plural reaches beyond the singularity of any grammatical or wider lingual position. The Volk is not a plurality of first person forms, of "I"s, nor of any other form like "You," "He," "We," or "They." The term Volk is a new plural which von Savigny explored, a plural that integrates language and law, first person singular and first person plural, second and third person positions included [Broekman (2019), p. 98].

This particular theme, the 'dissolving' as it were of the grammatical first person singular into a less determinate plurality of possible legal positions, becomes increasingly prominent in Broekman's discussion through the remaining chapters.

Certain patterns of speech in natural language (a society's normal mode of communication) may be set, or influenced, by the development of law. However, it is equally true (and perhaps more significant) that the evolution of a natural language (and our understanding of its sources and resources, i.e., linguistic theory) may shape the development of legal thought as well as the law itself. "One could venture to say that von Savigny's concept of '*Rechtswissenschaft*,' which he introduced almost globally, is in essence a matter of '*Sprachwissenschaft*'" [Broekman (2019), p.100].

4 Semiotics, Law, Subjectivity

Chapter Four surveys a specific episode in the emergence of just such a *Sprachwissenschaft*, the beginnings of Semiotics as an established field of research. One of the earliest forms of it emerged in the work of several Dutch theorists in the early 20th century, under the designation 'Significs.' That development, however, was preceded by the extensive and original contributions of the American C. S. Peirce to the study of signs, as well as the work of the English Lady Welby who corresponded not only with Peirce but also with the Dutch theorists of the day. Broekman has written extensively elsewhere on this development, focusing especially on the writings of the Dutch linguist and legal theorist J. I. de Haan, whose work lies at the intersection of law and significs. According to Broekman,

> The major theme of his work is the precarious relation between everyday language and legal language. He more than any other legal theoretician was fascinated by that relationship, because the architecture of all legal discourse follows from the many ways in which the two are linked by layman and lawyer alike. [Broekman (2019), p. 115]

It was de Haan's hope that a deeper understanding of natural language might lead to raising the 'spiritual' level of communication in natural language, and in turn, that might lead to a betterment of legal discourse and the law. This would be an early and especially pertinent example of what Broekman terms the "law-language-law" theme. Exploring the details of this complicated bit of intellectual history would lead us beyond the bounds appropriate for this essay, however. Broekman has himself explored it in more than one published work.

Insofar as one can identify an overall philosophical perspective from which Broekman conducts his examination of language and law, that perspective emerges in Chapter Five as a version of structuralism, or more accurately, *neo*-structuralism, because (especially in anglophone literature) the original structuralist movement is generally considered to have expired as an intellectual force sometime in the 1970s, and never to have occupied a dominant intellectual position in the US or UK, as contrasted with its importance on the continent.

Broekman attributes that difference in reception of the movement partly to failures of translation between the French and German of its original founders into English. For example, *décentrement* (the *de-centering* of the Cartesian subject, or individual subjectivity) was sometimes misunderstood in English language translations and discussions.

> These words are often misunderstood: they do not provoke an annihilation of the subject's being, but want to *uncover the fact and its consequences* of the *subject's central position in language*—as expressed in grammar, syntax, and other linguistic disciplines.
>
> . . . All those [structuralist] thinkers distanced themselves in particular from the central positioning of *first person singular* which Descartes had provoked with his slogan "cogito ergo sum" [Broekman (2019), p. 149].

Such a central positioning of the first person singular created "a specific form of the world which will change with the world," i.e., when the subject is successfully de-centered [Broekman (2019), p. 150]. According to Broekman the correct question should not have been understood as "what is a human being without subjectivity?," but rather, "what is a human being without the power to position itself in the role of subject, and name that role 'subjectivity'?" [Broekman (2019), p. 150].

In Broekman's view, structuralism should be understood, first, as an attempt, initially based upon the study of language, to develop a conception of methodology for the human sciences that would affect a variety of disciplines. Second, it aspired to formulate its own conception of philosophical procedure, rejecting the usual divisions among schools of philosophical thought (e.g., positivism, pragmatism, empiricism, existentialism) as not well founded, and further, rejecting the standard distinctions among logic, hermeneutics, and analysis, "in order to further an interdisciplinary approach" [Broekman (2019), p. 137]. Third, "structuralism wanted thus to display a new, independent, strong interest in elucidating *the deep structures of reality*," basing that pursuit of deep structure in significant measure on the study of language [Broekman (2019), p. 138].

It would not be an exaggeration to say that Broekman's entire discussion of law and language here is rooted primarily in such a neo-structuralist ambition, and therefore a reader expecting to find some of the most familiar, traditional philosophical touchstones framing his study will likely be disappointed.

> Structuralism's thought patterns have, more than semiotics or significs ever could, challenged traditional thought patterns. Structuralism's incorporated relativism regards *forms* of

> life and thought formation rather than statements concerning *any* being [Broekman (2019), p. 150].

In this chapter Broekman surveys a variety of developments in the history of philosophy over the last fifty years, attempting to show that a number of them intersect in what amounts to the central insight of structuralism, though that label is now widely regarded as passé. He includes in this survey references to phenomenology, deconstructionism, hermeneutics, and discourse theory.

That insight can be formulated as the claim that the first-person subject is not, *pace* Descartes, the ultimate arbiter of what is real. The subject is rather the *product* of deeper cultural structures that pre-exist the individual. In the case of language, one can say that individual speakers are never *creating* original speech, but only employing linguistic formulations that arose as possibilities in some prior age, and that the structure of the subject's existence is in part a reflection of that set of possibilities. This is one meaning of the de-centering of the self.

It entails that the Speaker-Hearer model be left behind for several reasons. Among other reasons there is Derrida's point (*Grammatology*, 1967) that "the European tradition connects the human voice with the *breath* rather than the *writing*, with the *spiritual* rather than with the *material*."[2] Concludes Broekman, "This is a precious anthropological insight, because someone who is hearing sounds listens to a voice. Listening is different from hearing. To listen is a spiritual occurrence and includes understanding and interpretation, whereas the hearing is mainly physiological fact" [Broekman (2019), p. 154]. (One is reminded of the robot that responds to commands by saying 'I hear and obey'; it would likely be a *very* different sort of robot that responded, 'I'm listening. . . .'). Thus the first-person Speaker as a fundamental reality has been set aside, and the Hearer has been identified as only a truncated conception of a person. Following a much more lengthy discussion than can be summarized here, Broekman concludes that

> Structuralism has underlined many ties between law and language. In its slogan concerning the decentralization of the subject, it has set out a complete antithesis for the centuries-old dominance of the Speaker-Hearer model [Broekman (2019), p. 169].

5 The Legal Subject's Linguisitic Position

Chapter Six is entitled "Alter's presence." It expands upon a further implication of the de-centralizing of the first-person subject, arguing that "*there exists no first person without another,* a second or a third position. Saying 'I' *is* saying 'He'/ 'She' [Broekman (2019), p. 172]. Among other aims, he pursues this theme as an explanation of the truth of Buber's doctrine of the "I-Thou" relation. At the same time, he points out that the doctrine was by no means exclusively Buber's discovery; Buber was in contact with the entire Amsterdam Significs circle, as well as Lady

[2] See Derrida (1967), pp. 29ff. (Broekman did not provide a page reference).

Welby, and the insight emerged from several sources. His discussion involves a re-examination of the Speaker-Hearer model, as well as a re-consideration of Austin's and Searle's speech act theories. Among other things, he concludes that speaking of "speech acts" restricts our understanding of language use to artificially designated "speakers" and "hearers," and instead recommends that we replace that expression with "speech *events*" in order to convey the much more fluid reality of ever-shifting arrangements of momentary speakers and listeners in which various individuals participate in the event on a basis of equal powers, and all are understood to be products in a certain sense of the pre-existing structure of possibilities for utterance made available by the language as a whole.

Chapter 7 ("What language, what law?") begins to apply some of the conclusions from previous chapters to the basic issue of the relation between legal discourse and the natural language in which it is couched. By now there are several grounds for doubting that the "I" uttered in legal discourse could be identified with the "I" uttered in natural language. The "I" in legal discourse refers equally to all possible "I"s, and is hence tantamount to the "legal subject." But the legal subject has at most a fluid relation to the personal pronouns of a natural language: it may be taken for the first, second or third persons depending on the circumstances. Hence, "*The fate of pronouns stemming from the mother tongue is dubious in law*" [Broekman (2019), p. 213].

Broekman develops this thought into the further conclusion that, "the concepts of legal discourse . . . are unable to describe the genesis of a Self or to take that Self in its uniqueness into account" [Broekman (2019), p. 216]. "*Law's authority does not embrace any singularity*" [Broekman (2019), p. 216]. Still more strongly,

> The "I," once articulated, is in law understood as the totality of every individual "I," which means all pronouns are incorporated in the "legal subject." Alter's presence is a necessary condition for the pronouns "I," "You," and all others to be in effect. Without that presence being incorporated, law cannot exist—and thus it can never be articulated, in any mother tongue. In other words, *pronouns have to be lost in law so that law can exist.* [Broekman (2019), p. 216].

Chapter 8 ("Word, seme, digit") presents something of a *coda* to the book as a whole. It raises the problem of whether the "word" is appropriately regarded as the basic unit of language, and concludes that it is not, despite the fact that numerous settled forms of discourse concerning language (including the Speaker-Hearer model and speech act theory) seem to push us in that direction. But Broekman insists, "*a word is not an act but an event*" [Broekman (2019), p. 248]. As an event it is not merely shaped by the rules of language, but also by relations of social power and status, and moreover usually has origins that are buried in a history of which we are not fully conscious.

> *But a word never has solely one specific meaning*—an observation that makes a word difficult to accept and even more difficult to maintain in the case of lawyers. It is their tendency to obtain justice and objectivity (or at least equilibrium) by means of unilateral meanings. But all our engagements with meaning and sense are complex and organic—no meaning of a word is ever fixed on one particular lingual utterance. As a consequence, *words are always participating in processes of change.* [Broekman (2019), p. 249].

And:

> Slowly becoming visible on the horizon is the idea that, belonging to the most vital components of language, *words are continuously and at all levels in motion*. [Broekman (2019), p. 254].

6 "Conversions" Between "Analog" and "Digital" Languages

Broekman expands this theme of words undergoing continuous transitions in meaning to include the subject of "conversions" (translations) between "analog" and "digital" languages, where natural languages are conceived as "analog" and computer languages as "digital." (To be sure, it is by no means clear to this writer why a natural language should be described as '*analog*'; it is merely *not* an artificial, *digital* "language").

As an aside, it should be noted that there are also "conversions" between analog and digital processes that do not necessarily involve "language" in any essential sense. For example, music that was once reproduced by an analog process (the movement of a needle in a groove generating a varying electrical current) is now mostly reproduced through a digital process *mimicking* the analog signal. Connoisseurs sometimes complain that the "conversion" is not exact, that a difference can be detected between the two types of reproduction. However, that detectable difference is not ultimately due to the fact of conversion, but rather to the fact that the "granularity" of the digital reproduction is too coarse. In principle, the granularity could have been so fine that no human ear could ever have detected a difference, but the cost in terms of computing power and the necessary storage capacity (the disk size) would have been prohibitive for a mass consumption technology. Thus, the complications don't necessarily stem from the mere fact of analog-to-digital *conversion* in itself, but from concerns specific to *language*, as Broekman repeatedly emphasizes.

He points out that the simple act of sending or receiving a text message on a cell phone involves multiple "conversions" of analog-to-digital followed by digital-to-analog. Computers are universally described as requiring "languages" for their programming, and Broekman takes this way of talking quite literally. However, he stresses that digital "languages" differ in some radical respects from natural languages. We seem driven to use digital languages ever more intimately in our daily activities, the activities of lawyers not excluded. He points to "datafication" as a phenomenon particularly significant for the legal profession. as many cases now involve extremely large data-bases (e.g., codifications of EU statutes, court decisions, etc.).

He claims that this phenomenon, also allied with developments in artificial intelligence, tends to undermine the very distinction between "natural" and "artificial" [Broekman (2019), p. 278]. Digital (i.e., "artificial") languages are now inextricably involved in our daily activities; we must "interact" with them continuously, and this cannot fail to have consequences for our very understanding of the concept of "language."

7 Conclusions

What remains to be considered is an actual *coda* to all of this in the form of the final chapter ("The flagship's wreckage"). The "flagship" allegedly facing wreckage is "speech" in our traditional conception of it. The principal ground for this declaration of immanent wreckage is the theme of "conversions" introduced in the previous chapter. The final chapter explores numerous apparently inescapable consequences of Broekman's analysis of analog-digital and digital-analog conversions. These consequences supposedly flow from the radical differences between any artificial digital language and any natural language. Most of them, however, seem to depend upon taking the idea of a digital "language" exceedingly literally, and not regarding the term as merely a convenient metaphor. Similarly, *words* in a natural language are said to be translated into "digital expressions," i.e., word-equivalents.

One can agree with many of Broekman's distinctions between natural and "digital" language:

> A major experience in speech is that language comes to the participant in speech events as a gift—*being a gift* is a bewildering antipode in this context: it destroys the might, pride, and uniqueness of the speaker's feelings. It strives for equilibrium between speaker and hearer, and within this state of equality also for the development of dimensions of *appreciated otherness*. . . . The discovered character of language as a gift annihilates the forces and dynamics of the Speaker-Hearer Model and unfolds a forceful grip on digital life in modern cultural and scientific experience. [Broekman (2019), p. 297]

On the other hand, digital "communication" is by definition inevitably based upon the Speaker-Hearer model: there is always some "sender" and some "receiver." [Broekman (2019), p. 306]. Further,

> The digital world does not know any 'subject matter' since it cannot support the differences, concealed variations, and other irregularities linked with the term. It therefore manages digital matters completely withdrawn from any such interpretive color and speaks solely of *data* in this context. The semantic differences between 'subject matter' and 'data' are essential to understand the gap between the two language types. [Broekman (2019), pp. 294–295].

He further points out that whereas *metaphor* is at home in all natural languages, it has no place in any digital language: "The expression/determination 'metaphorical' is not at home in a digital context; to qualify a lingual expression as 'metaphor' is an analog operation, which cannot become digital" [Broekman (2019), p. 286]. The digital world excludes *empathy*. "There is a clear lack of, and a technical impossibility to produce, feelings of empathy, sympathy, or what is called 'human warmth' in the digital world" [Broekman (2019), p. 300]. At his most dramatic, he doubts whether our conceptions of what it is to be human can survive our experience of living in a world dependent upon digital processes:

> But can the concept of 'Geist' still be maintained when its verbal expression has to pass two types of conversion, and is thus influenced by digital forces in a manner hitherto unknown and even today largely unknowable?" [Broekman (2019), p. 299].

Ultimately he claims, in what he describes as the "final thesis of the book," that,

> Once DA conversions become necessary to further life, these components [of human experience articulated in natural language] do *not* come back to analog life. The digital cannot reverse its own leading principles and techniques without dissolving into nothingness. . . . Here is the wrecking whirlpool ahead of the flagship speech: the languages of speech articulated after their AD conversions are lost for analog traditions and subtleties. In order to be a real word, one would say in analog language, it must be meant, intended, felt, heard, read, or linked to any form of human empathy. [Broekman (2019), p. 301].

8 A Doubt

Up to now, I have mainly confined myself with to attempting to follow the course of some of Broekman's many subtle and intriguing arguments, elucidating their deeper roots where possible, and have not been motivated to dispute his analyses. However, I find I cannot follow him in this last turn. The alarm over "AD and DA conversions" seems to me somewhat overdone. It appears to rest upon taking a notion of "digital thinking" quite literally, as though it is something computers are *actually doing* when carrying out operations in digital languages, somehow paralleling what *we* are doing when we communicate in natural languages, but in a manner forever opaque to us humans. (This seems vaguely akin to the notion of the Singularity, widely anticipated and/or feared in some circles. But that has to do with A.I. devices supposedly surpassing human levels of intelligence in some definitive way that would enable them to subordinate us humans in the long run.) It might be more realistic to say that at bottom the standard, familiar digital computers are being made to implement physical processes that we can view as nothing more than "adding" and "subtracting," however wonderfully complex and impressive the ultimate results of combining countless iterations of such processes may seem to be at some meta-meta-level.

However, we should remember that in the background there is a more innocent notion of "digital thinking," which is the sort of thinking that *humans* do as they *devise* digital "languages." It is true that the vast size and complexity of many digital computer programs by now is such that we find we cannot *predict* with certainty what will result from *running* them (that's why computers crash, and why we encounter "bugs," and why we have to run "beta" versions). Even where we have programmed computers to write digital programs for other computers, we can in principle still work out the logic of the individual steps when necessary. I.e., *human* intelligence is to be found at work on *both sides* of this analog/digital divide. From this perspective, I find the predictions of the immanent "wreckage of the flagship speech" unconvincing for the present age. They depend upon taking the notion of digital "*language*" in simply too literal a fashion. For the present it remains essentially a metaphor.

There is of course the further complication that, currently, all the most advanced devices for dealing "artificially" with language, as in machine translation of natural languages, speech recognition, and robot/human conversation, are not literally digital computers, but "deep" neural networks, i.e., those possessing multiple "intervening" layers between the input and output layers, inspired originally by the neural "wiring" of the human brain. (They are also the basis for the most advanced facial recognition devices as well as those for "visual" navigation in the real world). These devices are not *programmed* using digital languages, but rather *trained*, in processes that involve both digital and analog elements, so as to eventually match varying inputs with the appropriate ("successful") outputs. Moreover, the particular changing, complex electrical configurations within the successive *intervening* ("hidden") layers that emerge in practice (due to training) and which happen to lead to successful outputs, are simply unintelligible to us, and certainly not interpretable as a digital "language." Thus the discussion of "digital/analog conversion" may need to be significantly modified or expanded in some way so as to apply to the functioning of deep neural networks as well.

In conclusion, it would not be appropriate to expect a settled and definitive theory of law and language from Broekman's work; that was not its aim. And, given his nascent account of natural language as perpetually in transition, that would have been a rather surprising outcome in any event. Rather, he is attempting to open up a protracted discussion of the issue by bringing to the fore a significant number of unnoticed presuppositions shaping our standard thinking, attempting to introduce new contexts in which to consider the entire matter, and pointing to facets of current social experience that may well call for new thinking altogether about language as well as law. In all these respects it seems to me he has achieved his aims to a convincing degree.

If I may end on a personal note, it has been my privilege to have had many stimulating conversations with Professor Broekman over a number of years when he was teaching in the United States, to have participated in his seminar on legal semiotics at the Penn State/Dickinson School of Law, to have read numerous publications that grew out of that seminar, and, not least, to count him as a good friend.

References

Broekman J (2019) Rethinking law and language: the flagship speech. Edward Elgar Publishing, Northhampton

Derrida J (1967) De La Grammatologie. Les Éditions de Minuit, Paris

Il'in I (2014) On the Essence of Legal Consciousness (trans: Butler W, Grier P, Tomsinov V) (eds) Wildy, Simmonds & Hill Publishing, London

Jan Broekman and the Multicultural Self

Francis J. Mootz III

Abstract The EU once championed the cause of building diverse societies through a strategy that was named multiculturalism. When faced with the multicultural reality of migration patterns, however, the member states unceremoniously abandoned multiculturalism and declared it to be a threat to the liberal foundations of their political order. Decades earlier, Jan Broekman had warned that the nation states could not promote multiculturalism, because the transformation had to occur at the level of the individual. In short, the times demanded the emergence of the multicultural self. In this chapter I rehearse Broekman's insights, contrast them with the accounts provided by Charles Taylor and Jürgen Habermas, and conclude that Broekman's approach is best contextualized today by Michael Ignatieff's description of the "ordinary virtues" in a world rent with division.

It is an honor to contribute to this *Festschrift* celebrating the intellectual legacy of my friend and former colleague, Jan Broekman, on the very happy occasion of his ninetieth birthday. Jan's influential career will be the source of inspiration for scholars on many topics well into the future. His reinvigoration of the Roberta Kevelson seminar on law and semiotics was a profound event not just for the student participants, but also for faculty members such as myself who participated. As revealed in the seminar, the breadth and depth of Jan's work precludes a summary or facile reconciliation. In this essay I engage with Jan's very suggestive claim that we cannot hope to sustain our multicultural society until each of us becomes a "multicultural self."[1] The great depth in his observation is a helpful pole star as we

I wish to thank Frank Fleerackers and Anne Wagner for organizing this *Festschrift* for Jan Broekman.

[1] See Broekman (2001, 2003a, b).

F. J. Mootz III (✉)
University of the Pacific, McGeorge School of Law, Sacramento, CA, USA
e-mail: jmootz@pacific.edu

F. Fleerackers (ed.), *The Rearguard of Subjectivity*, Law and Visual Jurisprudence 9,
https://doi.org/10.1007/978-3-031-26855-7_8

continue to navigate the irreversible multicultural reality of today's world, apparently without the benefit of a vibrant theory of multiculturalism to serve as our sextant.

Because he wrote at the turn of the century, Broekman's take on the potential for multiculturalism to transform Europe will ring a bit hollow to the modern ear. Indeed, his arguments may appear to be naive from today's perspective. Scholars now pen eulogies of multiculturalism in light of its abandonment by Western European countries, offering at most a wistful and humble suggestion that the concept might hold some limited relevance going forward. It was less than a decade after Broekman voiced his enthusiastic support for the solidarity implied by multiculturalism that key European politicians casually rejected the experiment of multiculturalism. As Rita Chin summarizes in her recent history of multiculturalism,

> By 2010, the idea that multiculturalism simply did not work in Europe was so self-evident–so obvious–that national heads of state felt comfortable declaring its failure without qualifications or caveats. Yet the shear ease with which Merkel, Cameron, and Sarkozy issued their declarations also raised an important question: how, exactly did this view become a kind of political common sense? It was one thing, after all, to be skeptical about Muslim immigrants' ability to integrate or to raise doubts about Islam's oppression of women. It was quite another to assert that the previously open question European multiculturalism was now closed–a casualty of its tolerance of beliefs and practices incompatible with "Western" values.[2]

My goal is to revive Broekman's insights to address our post-multiculturalism world.

This essay proceeds in three parts. First, I revisit Broekman's articles from two decades ago and trace his conception of multiculturalism and its challenges, informing his account with Chin's excellent historical overview from a later perspective. I next argue that Broekman accurately diagnosed the forces that would ultimately result in prominent EU nations rejecting multiculturalism as a strategy, and contend that he persuasively explained that the way forward hinged on a genuine multiculturalism rooted in the solidarity of all persons. Finally, in the third section of the essay, I contextualize Broekman's intervention by considering Michael Ignatieff's contemporary work on natural rights in order to provide a democratic framework for achieving solidarity under the banner of multiculturalism.

1 Why Western European Multiculturalism Failed

Broekman emphasizes that the European Union is founded on the model of a market, in which citizens are afforded an equal opportunity to participate in the nation's market and the Union's common market.[3] But what of the promise of a global

[2]Chin (2017), p. 238.

[3]Broekman (2003b), pp. 1–2.

market, in which law operates without nation states and genuinely encompasses all people under the principle of solidarity? Broekman argues that any such approach requires the development of social forms of life that can replace the role currently played by the nation-state. Europe became multicultural after the trauma of World War II and in response to reverse migration patterns spurred by decolonization.[4] In response to the new multicultural reality, "multiculturalism" was proffered as a suitably ambiguous term that designated a variety of affirmative responses to cultural differences that could relieve the resulting social, economic and political stresses. However, the term never achieved a coherent and concrete theoretical justification. In contrast to the United States, which expressly embraces its legacy as a nation of immigrants,[5] European countries experienced difficulties responding to the relatively sudden multicultural reality that eventually was regarded as a fundamental threat to their national integrity.

Broekman identified several reasons that the attempt to pursue a multiculturalist agenda would prove to be difficult. First, the strong identification of the relevant market with nation states rather than a global market premised on solidarity of all persons hampered any true multiculturalism. Because the EU is built on the citizenship of member states, "*the concept of multiculturalism* remains dominated by *the concept of a Nation-State* and safeguarded by the EU . . .".[6] Second, countries made clear distinctions between undesirable economic immigrants who were expected to fill labor shortages and then return home, on one hand, and refugees who were welcomed as deserving political immigrants, on the other hand.[7] Finally, nations pursuing policies of multiculturalism failed to engender solidarity, as opposed to mere toleration, among all persons. As Charles Taylor famously emphasized, if multiculturalism is to accomplish anything it is necessary to "recognize" each other and not just tolerate the other's precarious presence in one's country.[8]

Broekman's diagnosis of these significant challenges finds support in Rita Chin's recent comparative history of multiculturalism in several European countries.

---

[4]Ibid., pp. 12–13.

[5]The United States has a long history of racist immigration practices and violent responses to the suggestion that it acknowledge the multicultural nature of its society, but multiculturalism did play out differently in light of its foundation being built predominantly by immigration (with important exceptions for the indigenous peoples who were nearly eradicated and those brought to the country as enslaved persons). Broekman takes a somewhat rosier view of the United States and its openness to multiculturalism; see Broekman (2003a), p. 18; Broekman (2003b), p. 14.

[6]Broekman (2003b), p. 9; Broekman (2001), p. 35.

[7]See Broekman (2003b), p. 13. This distinction, in practice, meant that "some migrants were allowed to participate in binding interpretations of the common good (and thus creating multiculturalism) whereas other were strongly and publicly denied such place and position." Broekman (2003a), p. 17. This distinction is, at heart, wholly malleable. As Broekman explains, "Governments can deliberately create poverty and famine, either to submit regions to their regime or to force a population to migrate. Is the result of such situations a *political persecution* that produces *political refugees* or the cause for *economic refugees*? To what category do civil wars or ethnic conflicts belong? Broekman (2001), p. 41.

[8]Broekman (2003b), p. 15.

Despite very different contexts and very different approaches, the history of multiculturalism played out somewhat uniformly. Chin first acknowledges the significance and importance of the debates about "multiculturalism," which were spurred by the disruption of the global economy in light of the 1970's oil crisis and the refusal of guest workers to return home. A vocabulary and principle that could engender a response was necessary, and multiculturalism seemed to fit that bill.

> Whatever its perceived deficiencies, however, the concept's arrival marked a critical new development in Europe, giving it an ideological touchstone with which to explicitly engage questions of national diversity. Indeed, it was only in the process of debating multiculturalism that Europeans began to formulate the first affirmative arguments for social diversity as a core value and policy issue.[9]

Governments had sought to address the economic concerns raised by immigration behind the scenes and without extensive politicization. However, right-wing politicians linked persistent economic distress to the perceived problem of immigrants refusing to participate in the host country's culture.[10] It became untenable to be tolerant of different cultural responses to the principles of liberal toleration. The Rushdie affair served as a powerful symbol of the impossibility of multiculturalism,[11] and concerns about the subordination of women by Islam were also a significant factor in painting a picture of unassimilable Muslims eroding liberal values.[12] The dismissive statements by Merkel, Cameron, and Sarkozy "effectively drew a line in the sand. Liberalism, each leader suggested, had to be defended at all costs. The very survival of European society was at stake."[13]

Chin concludes that the liberal value of equality that had originally provided an opening to respecting multiple cultures, in the end, became the very source of intolerance. "By writing off multiculturalism, Europeans have reduced a complicated discussion about how to deal with ethnic and cultural diversity to a simplistic demand that Muslim immigrants adopt liberal values as the crucial precondition to inclusion in European society."[14] In direct contravention to liberal principles that focus on individual rights, the liberal backlash constructed Muslims as a monolithic group that posed a fundamental threat to liberal democratic culture.[15]

The hopes for global solidarity were cast aside as nation-states were valorized more than ever before.[16] While this may have been psychologically comforting to traditionalists living in Europe, it resulted in a regression to the "mono-ethnicity" of liberalism.[17] Ulf Hedetoft articulates the situation in stark terms:

---

[9] Chin (2017), pp. 17–18.

[10] Ibid., p. 137.

[11] Ibid., pp. 178–191.

[12] Ibid., pp. 192–236.

[13] Ibid., p. 286.

[14] Ibid., pp. 288–289.

[15] Chin (2017), pp. 289–295.

[16] See Modood and Meer (2013).

[17] Hedetoft (2013), p. 328.

> At the end of the day the much-vaunted talk about the crisis of multicultural solutions and the backlash against diversity has little to do with failed models, abortive practices or problems deriving from cultural diversity in its own right. Multiculturalism in that perspective is little more than a straw man standing in for much more serious reasons underlying the European debacle. It symbolizes and legitimizes the political desire to champion value-based national cohesion within nation states increasingly exposed to global risks of fragmentation and cleavage, to recreate classic national-ethnic homogeneity, European style, in circumstances radically inimical to that ambition. ... In that sense, 'multiculturalism' is a fall guy for the ongoing decline of statist control, and the cultural backlash against it – a quixotic struggle against windmills.[18]
>
> 'Multiculturalism' in this context, therefore, should be regarded both as a symptom of the malaise and as an explicit sign that we face a fundamental problem waiting for new, thoroughgoing and future-oriented remedies that will help resolve the conceptual paradox and possibly even take us beyond multiculturalism. Such a highly complex toolbox still has to be constructed and deployed intelligently.[19]

Multiculturalism failed as a guiding philosophy, leaving us to search for another concept that could promote the flourishing of social life in the multicultural world.[20]

2 Who Is the Multicultural Self?

2.1 *Broekman's Description of the Multicultural Self*

In his essay, Broekman presciently described the waning fortunes of state-sponsored multiculturalism, but he also pointed the way beyond this impasse by emphasizing the necessity of personal transformation in response to the fact of multicultural societies. It pays to begin by quoting him at length, before unpacking his insights carefully.

> *Multiculturalism begins in our selves.* It does not appear as the result of stimuli provided by politicians. Identity formation is an essential prerequisite for performing tolerance, for performing a creative management of perceived differences...
>
> ....
>
> How do members of a society make tolerance concrete and perform their transition to a multicultural society? It is clear in the light of the above, that this does not only touch the promotion of social issues or of rights in the public space, but in the first place a transition in oneself, a transition of one's self and as a self! Recognition is a re-birth, notably the rebirth of

[18]Ibid., pp. 330–331.

[19]Ibid., p. 332.

[20]Some scholars argue that multiculturalism has failed as a slogan, but it continues in various programs and practices; see Banting and Kymlicka (2013); Bevelander and Taras (2013), p. 6. "Multiculturalism lurks in the nooks and crannies of all European states. At a time of a more general crisis and malaise, its relevance – like that of the euro – is being challenged. Is it just multiculturalism – or Europe itself – that may be entering its twilight years?" Bevelander and Taras (2013), p. 22.

> knowledge about what others contribute to my life, how they ground my life, its language, its norms and values, its goals and ideals. What Taylor called the *Politics of Recognition* is therefore a policy of *bringing forth* in myself a knowledge that emerges from others. This pertains to an altered self, *another* self that fits the categories of citizenship in European society better than traditional liberal individualism ever proposes. That other self is "the multicultural self."[21]

> Multiculturalism has a deep meaning. With its links to the virtues of the plural, to tolerance, to exodus and exile, it implies, despite all negative connotations, tolerance and solidarity as a powerful and overarching form of life in the Occidental civil society. The multicultural self is an achieved self. The slogan: "*The European Union will be nothing if not multicultural!*" shows the radical character of that achievement. The forceful change, which is inherent in multiculturalism, should be noticed. Its emphasis is not on the "politics" of recognition or any other outer-directed measures but rather on "solidarity." The role of a perceived otherness changes the receptor as the central agent of that perception. "Multiculturalism" is in that perspective not solely a legal and political expression. Its ultimate goal is rather an inward-directed expressiveness, which determines the life of all citizens. . . The EU has spent time, energy and capital to focus education to enhance the capacities of a "self" that exercises solidarity as the basis for multiculturalism. The global importance of that approach should not be underestimated.[22]

Multiculturalism will be effective only as a project of human development, rather than an economic program or political slogan.

How can individuals successfully become multicultural selves? Broekman suggests that this requires a transformation of the discourse of liberal politics and tolerance, and an invitation to genuine democratic activities. It requires that we recognize ourselves as formed through social experience that is defined through the encounter with difference.

> What is at the end the issue in multiculturalism: me, in my autonomy and inalienable rights– or me as constituted and receiving constitutive incentives from others, that is: me as a truly social being? The question focuses an inwardly directed politics of recognition, which is in my inner dialogue that prepares for accepting the plurality of others. That pertains to an altered self, another self that fits the categories of citizenship in European society better than traditional liberal individualism ever proposed. I name that other self "the multicultural self."[23]

> Identity goes with recognition, and sometimes emerges from the heroic attempt to break out of life long cherished prejudices and beliefs about others. To see the other, to see the other as an equivalent self, to see the other as a source of my own identity, to accept this figure as a value in my inner self, to enjoy the wealth of the 'non-me,' are forms of being an accomplished multiculturalist self.[24]

The question is whether the multicultural self remains a plausible goal in our modern, neo-liberal world that prizes abstract rights-bearing persons who are, at root, indistinguishable from each other.

---

[21] Broekman (2003b), p. 16.

[22] Ibid., p. 19.

[23] Broekman (2003a), pp. 20–21.

[24] Ibid., p. 21.

2.2 The Multicultural Self as a Hermeneutical Achievement

I begin by adding hermeneutical detail to Broekman's brief portrait of the "multicultural self." Hans-Georg Gadamer's philosophical hermeneutics presents a new conception of the self as being formed through social discourse. Understanding occurs only in the encounter with an "other," whether the other is a text or engaging another person in dialogue. Gadamer captures the ego-decentering thrust of this philosophy with a detailed phenomenological investigation of conversation as a metaphor for all understanding. Beginning with the observation that "the more genuine a conversation is, the less its conduct lies within the will of either partner," he argues that understanding something is "like and event that happens to us."[25] When we seek to understand,

> the interpreter's own horizon is decisive, yet not as a personal standpoint that he maintains or enforces, but more as an opinion and a possibility that one brings into play at puts at risk, and that helps one truly to make one's own what the [other] says. . . . [T]his is what takes place in conversation, in which something is expressed that is not only mine or my [dialogue partner's], but common.[26]

This "fusion of horizons" that occurs in every act of interpretation

> leaves behind it any starting point in the subjectivity of the subject, and especially in the meaning-directed intentions of the speaker. What we find happening in speaking is not a mere reification of intended meaning, but an endeavor that continually modifies itself, or better: a continually recurring temptation to engage oneself in something or to become involved with someone. But that means to expose oneself and to risk oneself. Genuinely speaking one's mind has little to do with a mere explication and assertion of our prejudices . . . it exposes oneself to one's own doubt as well as to the rejoinder of the other.[27]

The result is that the "I" is always already the representation of a "we," such that even silent thinking is an expression of a dialogical self.

Chris Smith has made this hermeneutical point forcefully, emphasizing that "we never think in wordless ideas, but only in the words we have first heard from others and then hear again in our thinking."[28] He explains:

> In other words, language, audible speech, is not invented by private individuals to signify thoughts they already have but is the gift of the community that allows the individual to think in the first place. Not *cogito ergo sum* ("I think, therefore I am") is the truth of the matter, rather *loquimur ergo cogito* ("We speak, therefore I think").[29]

If the thinking self is always a product of dialogical engagement with other persons, texts and the world, ethical imperatives certainly follow.[30] We must broaden

---

[25] Gadamer (1989b), p. 383.

[26] Ibid., p. 388.

[27] Gadamer (1989a), p. 26.

[28] Smith (2000), p. 741.

[29] Ibid., p. 736.

[30] See George (2020); Smith (1991), pp. 179–266.

ourselves and gain understanding by suffering our horizon of pre-understanding to the risk of dialogue. The primary ways of doing so are to engage with texts from a different historical period, or to engage with persons from other, seemingly distinct, cultures.[31]

As described by Fred Dallmayr, in a series of essays[32] Gadamer expressly embraced the need for hermeneutical engagements between participants in the different cultural traditions of Europe to navigate the multicultural reality challenging the traditional order.[33] Because the "porous relations between self and other" reside at the heart of his hermeneutical philosophy, Gadamer opposes a "hegemonic Westernization" in favor of "the alternative project of an interactive dialogue–perhaps an agonistic dialogue–among competing cultures"[34]

> For Gadamer, it is chiefly the multiplicity (or multiculturalism) of Europe which harbors the continent's legacy and promise for the world. ... In the face of ongoing efforts aimed at European unification, this multiplicity for Gadamer cannot and should not be expunged [because] the deeper significance of Europe resides in her multicultural and multilingual character, in the historical "cohabitation with otherness in a narrow space."[35]

In Gadamer's own words, he finds resonance with Broekman's notion of the multicultural self.

> The highest and most elevated aim that we can strive for is to partake in the other, to share the other's alterity. Thus, it may not be too bold to draw as the final political consequence of these deliberations the lesson that the future survival of humankind may depend on our readiness not only to utilize our resources of power and (technical) efficiency, but to pause in front of the other's otherness–the otherness of nature as well as that of the historically grown cultures of people and states; in this way we may learn to experience otherness and human others as the "other of ourselves" in order to partake in one another.[36]

---

[31] Gadamer emphasizes the hermeneutic significance of temporal distance (Gadamer 1989b, pp. 291–300), summarizing his point as: "*Understanding is to be thought of less as a subjective act than as participating in an event of tradition*, a process of transmission in which past and present are constantly mediated;" Ibid., p. 290. The encounter with tradition brings one's prejudices into view by challenging one's horizon of understanding. Importantly, Gadamer softened the text to admit that other forms of distance can also promote understanding, and his subsequent writings make clear that intercultural experiences are particularly important sources of understanding. Ibid., p. 298, n. 228. Broekman carries this insight forward in his contribution to this volume by recognizing that the "self" is both a result of an "I-thou" encounter, and also a product of the semiotic structures of language, which is the ultimate social encounter.

[32] Dallmayr translates from works written in German. Rendered to English, the titles are: "Who Am I and Who Are You?," "The Multiplicity of Europe: Legacy and Prospect," and the book, "The Inheritance [or, Legacy] of Europe."

[33] See Dallmayr (1993).

[34] Ibid., pp. 507–508.

[35] Ibid., p. 520.

[36] Dallmayr (1993), p. 521.

It is wholly insufficient for members of society to regard each other with neutral indifference and bare tolerance. It is necessary for all persons to appreciate each other's otherness from the vantage of their own limited horizon.[37]

We must note, however, that Gadamer readily admits that the ethical implications of hermeneutical philosophy are exceedingly demanding, claiming that

> hermeneutical philosophy understands itself not as an absolute position but as a way of experience. It insists that there is no higher principle than holding oneself open in conversation. But this means: Always recognize in advance the possible correctness, even the superiority of the conversation partner's position. Is this too little? Indeed, this seems to me to be the kind of integrity one can demand only of a professor of philosophy. And one should demand as much.[38]

Should we regard radical hermeneutic openness, the foundation of the multicultural self, as just a quixotic dream that only a very few enlightened persons might achieve?

3 The Multicultural Self as the Result of Democratic Politics

The multicultural self, who fully embraces the risk of hermeneutical openness to others, requires a space in which to interact freely. Surely there must be strategies that governments and civil society can employ through the social, political and economic infrastructure that provide the material conditions for hermeneutical exchanges that foster the development of multicultural selves. The abstract rights of liberalism have proven insufficient, as they were leveraged against Muslims and other groups that were characterized as profound dangers to the neutral political and legal frameworks of modern constitutional democracies. How then can we appropriately promote multicultural selves?

3.1 Between Taylor and Habermas: Ignatieff's Minimalist Approach to Human Rights

Charles Taylor's politics of recognition resolved this question by adopting a Gadamerian account of the dialogical character of understanding and selfhood to promote a more humble form of liberalism that didn't insist on the uniformity of supposed neutral rights.[39] He contrasts the personal level of dialogical engagement and the public politics of equal recognition, emphasizing that the latter still has an outer limit or breaking point.[40] As he concludes, liberalism "can't and shouldn't

[37]Ibid., p. 524.

[38]Gadamer (1985), p. 189.

[39]Taylor (1994), pp. 32–33, 67, 73.

[40]Ibid., p. 61.

claim complete cultural neutrality. Liberalism is a fighting creed. The hospitable variant I espouse, as well as the most rigid forms, has to draw the line."[41] His solution is a weaker form of liberalism that permits the recognition of groups, but all groups are still subject to nonnegotiable limitations grounded in a supposed universal approach to natural rights.

Jürgen Habermas critiqued Taylor's resolution, arguing that only a radical democratic dialogue can bring liberal principles to bear in individual contexts that are not artificially segmented into "group" rights. Rather than obeisance to rights as philosophical concepts, there must be a democratic actualization of those rights that eliminates the need to introduce collective rights to offset the limitations of liberalism.[42] And yet, Habermas appears to limit the principles of social organization to an utterly austere set of procedures for the political and legal systems, given the inability of democratic engagements unable to provide a substantive consensus about the lifeworld.[43]

It is sheer hubris for me to attempt to mediate these issues within the short confines of this essay, but I want to adumbrate an approach that might answer Broekman's call for a rejuvenation of multiculturalism through the project of a radical hermeneutical engagement between persons. I outline the means by which we can pursue the development of multicultural selves without falling prey to the hyper neutralism of Habermas's account, nor surrendering to the residual effort in Taylor's account to link multiculturalism and "group rights" of some kind.

To carry forward Broekman's insights, I begin by accepting a thin, nearly gossamer, version of individual natural rights grounded in our hermeneutic natures that provides the vocabulary for fostering the conditions for multicultural selves. Michael Ignatieff accurately captures this reality by focusing on the "ordinary virtues" of social interaction as opposed to conceptually determined formal individual rights.[44] Under this account, natural rights emerge from political contest. "Human rights might become less imperial, if it became more political, that is, if it were understood as a language, not for the proclamation and enactment of eternal

---

[41] Ibid., p. 62.

[42] Habermas explains:

> If a well-functioning public sphere with open communication structures that permit and promote discussions oriented to self-understanding can develop in such multicultural societies against the background of a liberal culture and on the basis of voluntary associations, then the democratic process of actualizing equal individual rights will also extend to guaranteeing different ethnic groups and their cultural forms of life equal rights to coexistence. This does not require special justification or an alternative principle. For from a normative point of view, the integrity of the individual legal person cannot be guaranteed without protecting the intersubjectively shared experiences and life contexts in which the person has been socialized and has formed his or her identity. Habermas (1994), p. 128.

[43] Habermas (1994), pp. 130–135.

[44] See Ignatieff (2017).

verities, but as a discourse for the adjudication of conflict.[45] Ignatieff explains what he means by politics:

> To be a rights-bearer is not to build some sacred inviolability but to commit oneself to live in a community where rights conflicts are adjudicated through persuasion, rather than violence. With the idea of rights goes a commitment to respect the reasoned commitments of others and to submit disputes to adjudication. The fundamental moral commitment entailed by rights is not to respect, and certainly not to worship. It is to deliberation. The minimum condition for deliberating with another human being is not necessarily respect, merely negative toleration, a willingness to remain in the same room, listening to claims one doesn't like to hear, for the purpose of finding compromises that will keep conflicting claims from ending in irreparable harm to either side. That is what a shared commitment to human rights entails.[46]

Human rights don't trump claims by the other; rather they are a language that creates the basis for democratic deliberation with the other.

By positing a stronger version of liberal rights and continuing to recognize state sovereignty, the West leads other cultures to believe that rights are just a shield for cultural domination and moral imperialism.[47] Human rights become idolatry when sundered from their historical development as a protection of individuals from the power of groups (family, religion, and state).[48] And, yet, ultimately there is a point beyond which member of the community cannot go; intolerable acts such as unprovoked murder must be addressed with force, for example, rather than be subjected to a dialogic inquiry about the acceptability of this behavior.[49] Ignatieff suggests that all we might hope to achieve through human rights discourse at this point in history is to join together in opposition to unmerited suffering and gross physical cruelty. This is not a strategic retrenchment, but rather an acknowledgment of the precarious state of politics in these disjointed and fractured days.[50] We can only hope to sustain the ordinary virtues of social interaction that holds the promise for a politics of rights.

In modern bustling, multicultural cities different people must coexist in practical ways, enacting ordinary virtues in daily life rather than looking to procedural principles that assume fundamental sameness. These virtues—"trust, honesty, politeness, forbearance, respect"—permit us to survive despite deep differences in our cultural lifeworlds. Ignatieff focuses not on what people were supposed to have in common, but rather on how they negotiate how they can live together.[51]

---

[45] Ignatieff (2001b), p. 20.

[46] Ignatieff (2001a), p. 84.

[47] Ignatieff (2001b), pp. 47–48.

[48] Ignatieff (2001a), p. 83.

[49] Ignatieff (2017), p. 220; Ignatieff (2001b), p. 22.

[50] Ignatieff (2001c), p. 173.

[51] See Ignatieff (2017), pp. 24–25. Compare with Lingis (1994), in which Adolfo Lingis argues that, beneath the unified and univocal rationalism of liberal theory, the real matter of importance is to heed the call of conscience and to acknowledge everyone else in their distinctive and irremediable otherness.

> What is common to human beings, we found, is virtue, defined as acquired practical skills in moral conduct and discernment, not shared values as such. Wherever we went, whatever language barrier we were working across, we were able to recognize generosity when we saw it. It did not require translation. We felt trust, even when we couldn't explain why it had been accorded to us.[52]

Even when people live, work and pray in separate sectors of a city, there must be an operating code of ordinary virtues to enable them to come together productively.

What, then, is the role of government if human rights are the practical virtues of co-existence? First, the "default settings of an operating system are not propositional, general, or theoretical. . . . When we live side by side with people from other races or religions, our question is not, What do I owe persons who are different from me as a general proposition? but simply, Do I trust this particular person?"[53] Ethnically diverse cities such as Los Angeles cannot be governed in command-and-control style. "Instead, they need horizonal governance, with power dispersed through networks of community and business leaders committed to the maintenance of its shared operating system"[54] Ignatieff suggests that looking to the ordinary moral virtues is a "strategy for making do, for getting on with life, for bracketing larger questions that do not admit of answers"[55] given that a "global ethic, applicable to all mankind, is essentially unimaginable and irrelevant."[56]

It may appear Pollyannaish to assume that such cross-cultural hermeneutical encounters can occur, but the "fusion of horizons" is not a matter of subjective will as much as an unavoidable and continuing result of the encounter with another. The ordinary virtues have developed as ways to permit human understanding through an encounter with other, and the best "test of public institutions is whether they make it possible for us to behave decently toward each other."[57] Multiculturalism, then, is not a state project of tending to foreign groups within one's secure culture. Multiculturalism must be a project of enabling and fostering individual persons to emerge from the ordinary exchanges of daily life as multicultural selves. As Broekman emphasized,

> An appropriate *management of differences* is one of the most important . . . issues. That management is not an innate property of humans, it has to be learned. . . . The leading idea is here that multiculturalism and altruism must be learned, especially in our highly individualistic society. The Union did hitherto nothing to specifically develop the frameworks and programs for such learning processes.[58]

This critical learning was, in the end, unfulfilled.[59]

---

[52] Ignatieff (2017), p. 27.
[53] Ibid., p. 56.
[54] Ibid., p. 67.
[55] Ibid., p. 71.
[56] Ibid., p. 202.
[57] Ignatieff (2017), p. 223.
[58] Broekman (2001), p. 9.
[59] Ibid., p. 45.

3.2 *Politically Enabling the Multicultural Self*

Is it facile to promote the development of multicultural selves when the world is rent with division and hostility? Is it feasible for multicultural selves to develop under modern conditions, in which prejudices and distrust appear to run rampant? Doesn't multiculturalism require a governmental intervention to make space for competing groups? I would hope that the answer to these questions is now apparent: multicultural selves living by the ordinary virtues are already commonplace, and it is the duty of the old world to get out of the way of these developments. In fact, it is remarkable that people are able to interact with some measure of curiosity and cooperation, given state-promoted terror unleashed against outsider groups.

Governments have expressed *de jure* hostility to groups in many instances, with the Jim Crow apartheid of American south being just one example among many. This threat has been supplemented by quasi-governmental terrorist groups such as the Ku Klux Klan for decades upon decades. Less bloody, but more effective, civil society has separated different groups of persons based on where they live, work and play. Even seemingly mundane issues such as the social planning of the location of highways and railroads has violently reinforced the isolation of cultural groups. Residential segregation and ghettoization are often the products of private actors acting in concert to protect what they deem as social values by merely tolerating (another) place for the "other." The unrelenting attack on a porous and intersectional reality in which multicultural selves could grow and develop leads to the perception that outsider group identities are rigid and unwilling to engage in legitimate understanding on the terms of Western liberalism. All of this counterproductive divisiveness is manifested most dramatically through the state-sponsored educational system, which views the other as a threat rather than a source of critical self-understanding. Education reinforces tribal values, rather than embracing openness to other traditions as the primary source of knowledge.[60]

And so, Broekman's plea that we embrace the necessity of multicultural selves is not a naive quest for an unattainable ideal. The world he envisions does not require elaborate support and direction from a sovereign. Instead, it requires that the sovereign step back and allow the people the opportunity for democratic control of their localized lifeworlds in which the ordinary virtues are all that we may hope to achieve. Multiculturalism has failed as the dying expression of the nation-state system to protect its legacy. Multiple efforts to undermine democratic engagement have created a difficult situation. It is now time to reject state-inspired multiculturalism efforts and to reinforce the democratic sphere of dialogue in which the multicultural self can flourish. Of course, the state or its replacement must provide a last bulwark if cultural balkanization leads to the breakdown of ordinary virtues and the eruption of social violence. There is no safety net that ensures success when one seeks democratic engagement.

---

[60]Martha Nussbaum argues for reform of the educational system to cultivate humanity in the manner in which I describe the development of multicultural selves. See Nussbaum (1997).

4 Conclusion

The Western European experiments with multiculturalism did not truly challenge the nation states and their associated mix of tribal sentiments and liberal individualism. Ultimately, multiculturalism degenerated into a characterization of the "Muslim problem," reducing Islam to an undifferentiated "other" that can only be feared and thereby avoided. Ironically, rights-based liberalism and its promise of universal equality in fact served to undermine the solidarity of different persons by characterizing Islam as a block that rejected, and posed a grave danger to, these universal and non-negotiable rights. The West had spoken, and no multicultural program would be permitted to undermine the foundational heritage of European liberalism. But this is not the way things had to unfold. Jan Broekman laid out the significant challenge facing us in his essays from two decades ago: we must achieve the democratic solidarity of multiculturalist selves if our social life is to progress. Broekman's wise guidance on this question, perhaps the most important challenge that we face as a species, continues to reverberate today. If only we can collectively take heed and act accordingly.

References

Banting K, Kymlicka W (2013) Is there really a retreat from multiculturalism policies? New evidence from the multiculturalism policy index. Comp Eur Polit 11(5):577–598

Bevelander P, Taras R (2013) The twilight of multiculturalism? Findings from across Europe. In: Taras R (ed) Challenging multiculturalism. Edinburgh University Press, Edinburgh, pp 3–24

Broekman J (2001) A foreigner in the EU. Persona y Derecho 44:35–51. Available at https://hdl.handle.net/10171/1464

Broekman J (2003a) Multiculturalism. Persona y Derecho 48:15–27. Available at https://www.corteidh.or.cr/tablas/r27028.pdf

Broekman J (2003b) Solidarity and multiculturalism. In: Ulen T (ed) Social science research network – law and economics papers. Available at https://papers.ssrn.com/sol3/papers.cfm?abstract_id=405600

Chin R (2017) The crisis of multiculturalism in Europe: a history. Princeton University Press, Princeton

Dallmayr F (1993) Self and other: Gadamer and the hermeneutics of difference. Yale J Law Humanit 5(2):507–529

Gadamer H-G (1985) On the origins of philosophical hermeneutics. In: Philosophical apprenticeships (trans: Sullivan RR). MIT Press, Boston, pp 177–194

Gadamer H-G (1989a) Text and interpretation. In: Michelfelder DP, Palmer R (eds) Dialogue and deconstruction: the Gadamer-Derrida encounter (trans: Schmidt DJ, Palmer R). State University of New York Press, Albany, pp 21–51

Gadamer H-G (1989b) Truth and method (trans: Weinsheimer J, Marshall DG), 2nd rev. ed. Crossroad, New York

George T (2020) The responsibility to understand: hermeneutical contours of ethical life. Edinburgh University Press, Edinburgh

Habermas J (1994) Struggles for recognition in the democratic constitutional state. In: Gutmann A (ed) Multiculturalism: examining the politics of recognition (trans: Nicholsen SW). Princeton University Press, Princeton, pp 107–148

Hedetoft U (2013) Multiculturalism: symptom, cause or solution? In: Taras R (ed) Challenging multiculturalism. Edinburgh University Press, Edinburgh, pp 319–333
Ignatieff M (2001a) Human rights as idolatry. In: Gutmann A (ed) Human rights as politics and idolatry. Princeton University Press, Princeton, pp 53–98
Ignatieff M (2001b) Human rights as politics. In: Gutmann A (ed) Human rights as politics and idolatry. Princeton University Press, Princeton, pp 3–52
Ignatieff M (2001c) Response. In: Gutmann A (ed) Human rights as politics and idolatry. Princeton University Press, Princeton, pp 161–173
Ignatieff M (2017) The ordinary virtues: moral order in a divided world. Harvard University Press, Cambridge
Lingis A (1994) The community of those who have nothing in common. Indiana University Press, Bloomington
Modood T, Meer N (2013) Contemporary citizenship and diversity in Europe: the place of multiculturalism. In: Taras R (ed) Challenging multiculturalism. Edinburgh University Press, Edinburgh, pp 25–51
Nussbaum M (1997) Cultivating humanity: a classical defense of reform in liberal education. Rev. Ed. Harvard University Press, Cambridge
Smith P (1991) Hermeneutics and human finitude: toward a theory of ethical understanding. Fordham University Press, New York
Smith P (2000) The uses of Aristotle in Gadamer's recovery of consultative reasoning: Sunesis, Sungnômê, Epieikeia, and Sumbouleuesthai. Chic-Kent Law Rev 76:731–750
Taylor C (1994) The politics of recognition. In: Gutman A (ed) Multiculturalism: examining the politics of recognition. Princeton University Press, Princeton, pp 25–73

Francis J. Mootz III earned his Juris Doctor from Duke University School of Law, his Master's in Philosophy from Duke Graduate School, and his Bachelor's Degree from the University of Notre Dame. He has written extensively on the hermeneutical and rhetorical dimensions of legal practice and the implications for critical legal theory. He has taught and presented papers in Africa, Europe and South America. Over his career he has taught at Western New England University School of Law, Penn State University Dickinson School of Law, William and Mary Law School, and University of Nevada Las Vegas, William S. Boyd School of Law. Currently, he is Professor of Law at McGeorge School of Law, University of the Pacific, where he formerly served as Dean. In addition to many articles and book contributions, he is author of *Rhetorical Knowledge in Legal Practice and Critical Legal Theory (2006)*, which has been translated to Portuguese.

Lady Justice's Crooked Teeth: Sustainable Judicial Empathy Through (Inter-)Personal Rela(xa)tion(s)

Bart Nelissen

Abstract (Verdicts of) Belgian courts do not usually garner the respect of their British or US-counterparts, and even within Europe, Belgium's judicial administration does not exactly stand-out in a positive way. It would therefore be fair to state that what comes out of Lady Justice's mouth is often being characterized as "baked air with a problematic whiff". The crooked-teeth-with-(meta-)braces metaphorical defiguration of Lady Justice proposed in this essay captures both what precedes and what results from subpar, halitosis-inducing breathing habits, a notoriously "understudied" topic in Western medicine (Cf. P. Gwin, "How ancient remedies are changing modern medicine", *National Geographic* January 2019, https://www.nationalgeographic.com/magazine/article/ancient-chines-remedies-changing-modern-medicine. See also: Macnaughton (Body Soc 26(2):30–54, 2020).) *a fortiori* in Western judicial human resources management.

Some widely-shared concerns as to Belgium's rather unenviable constellation and *dito* "management" of its legal system's admittedly most precious resources (i.e. the (wo)men administering justice) are coupled with some commonsensical thoughts on equally cardinal aspects of the judicial mind-set and what we usually associate with it, in order to help deal with *malaised* judicial officials (and others!). *In abstracto* or semiotically, this also seems to be the case regarding the justice system as a whole, especially considering how chronic collective stress affects empathy and soci(et)al/ (inter-)personal rela(xa)tions.

Lecturer Erasmus School of Law (Rotterdam, The Netherlands), attorney-at-law, former research fellow (2012–2021), KU Leuven Centre for Public Law. Unsurprisingly, this essay draws upon our *Van onafhankelijk magistraat tot rechter-bureaucraat: factor van rechtstatelijke (des)integratie?,* Brussels, Larcier, 2018, 445 p. Criticism being a gift, any feedback is warmly welcomed via nelissen@law.eur.nl.

B. Nelissen (✉)
Erasmus School of Law, Rotterdam, The Netherlands
e-mail: nelissen@law.eur.nl

F. Fleerackers (ed.), *The Rearguard of Subjectivity*, Law and Visual Jurisprudence 9,
https://doi.org/10.1007/978-3-031-26855-7_9

Pain in itself is not unbearable; failure to understand it is (Fulton Sheen)

There is no guaranty of justice except the personality of the judge (Eugen Ehrlich)

1 Introduction and Scope

The Brussels Palace of Justice[1] is probably one of Belgium's most renowned landmarks, albeit competing with *Manneken Pis*,[2] the statue of a continuously urinating toddler who is more often than not dressed to the nines. The Palace's sheer size was unseen at the time of its inauguration, yet '*noblesse obligeait*' given Tiny Little Belgium's considerable GDP in absolute numbers due to its early and very dense industrialization, not to mention the colonial revenue of its monarch Leopold II. To no one's surprise, the building's well overdue restoration in the eighties of last century necessitated scaffolding of similar magnitude, and recently the scaffolding itself required restoration,[3] once more vindicating Belgium's propensity to surrealism. Lady Justice in Belgium indeed not only wears braces, but even meta-braces if we take her seat's meta-scaffolding as a tell-tale sign of Belgium's soci(et)al withering.

Indeed, (verdicts of) Belgian courts do not usually garner the respect of, let's say, their British or US-counterparts,[4] and even within Europe, Belgium's judicial administration does not exactly stand-out in a positive way.[5] It would therefore be fair to state that what comes out of Lady Justice's mouth is often being characterized as "baked air with a problematic whiff" or as downright *halitosis*, especially given the dire state of several court houses and prisons, the latter in part due to their notorious over-crowding,[6] the former as a result of fungal infestations.[7] Considering furthermore that law somehow remains "crystallized politics" and bearing in mind

[1] A brief exposé on the *World Monuments Fund* can be found here: https://www.wmf.org/project/brussels-palace-justice.

[2] For the City's official website, please visit: https://www.brussels.be/manneken-pis. For Trip Advisor reviews, please visit: https://www.tripadvisor.com/ShowUserReviews-g188644-d196129-r729052838-Manneken_Pis-Brussels.html.

[3] "Scaffolding on Brussels Palace of Justice gets renovated", *The Brussels Times* 16 March 2021, https://www.brusselstimes.com/brussels/160259/scaffolds-on-brussels-palace-of-justice-get-renovated-federal-government-public-buildings-administration-place-poelaert-minimes-laines-wynants-mathieu-michel.

[4] For the latest relevant findings of the *World Justice Report*, see: https://worldjusticeproject.org/our-work/wjp-rule-law-index/wjp-open-government-index/global-scores-rankings.

[5] The European Commission's so-called 2021 *EU Justice Scoreboard* can be consulted here: https://eur-lex.europa.eu/legal-content/EN/TXT/PDF/?uri=CELEX:52021DC0389&from=EN.

[6] "Belgium has most overcrowded prisons in EU", *EU Observer* 8 April 2020, https://euobserver.com/coronavirus/148011.

[7] https://www.demorgen.be/nieuws/brussels-justitiepaleis-geteisterd-door-schimmelplaag~b5b6802b/.

how *Windy City* Chicago got its nick-name,[8] certain popular contempt should, *mutatis mutandis*, come as no surprise.

Professor Broekman's vast and diverse scholarship first caught my attention some ten years ago as I was trying to explore and make sense of the human and hence judicial condition while drinking coffee as a full-time federal civil (dis)servant pursuing a doctorate in my free(d) time. In order not to lose my wits—as unfortunately happens all too often among doctoral candidates in the humanities [9]—I used to go swimming during my lunch breaks followed by subsequent attacks, in genuine ginger hyena-style, of (the healthier sections of) a federal government agency's buffet near the former factory-turned-swimmer's paradise at the outskirts of Louvain-la-*Veuve*—the Flemish "widow" of the (until 1968) unified University of Louvain where Professor Broekman taught at two of its most renowned schools. In the margin of one of these swims, I met an older gentleman who seemed to come there at least as often as myself and whom I learned to be a retired Dean of the Institute of Philosophy. At some point I told the esteemed gentleman that I had not only been reading up on Professor Broekman, whom I surmised to be the Dean's contemporary, but also that I had noticed how he (i.e. Broekman) had never become "inactive", yet still remained a prolific scholar and law professor across the Pond, i.a. at Penn State. The Dean, who was himself in remarkable shape for someone in his late seventies, was surprised to learn that Broekman was still publishing and teaching, decades after having officially withdrawn at Belgium's mandatory professoral retirement age of sixty-five. Broekman, in short, already incarnated, *a contrario*, the Dutch expression *"rust roest"* (rest makes rusty).

Under the shower, I sang the praises of Broekman's unsurpassed *Recht en anthropologie* (1979!), as one is wont to do in the middle of a draining PhD trajectory when stumbling upon a mind-blowing book. However, when asking out loud how it was possible that this book had never been brought under my attention, despite me having been in Law School and at the Institute of Philosophy for over eight years at the time, the Dean told me that this could be explained by Broekman's analysis having been found "unorthodox and (too) difficult".

The patient and/or masochistic reader of this contribution will hopefully bear with our—ADHD-afflicted, ENFP-ridden ("wild association business"/"truth before tact") and *'productive stupidity'*-tainted (cf. Schwartz[10])—*prima facie* "à côté de

[8] 'Chicago's exposed location between the Great Plains and the Great Lakes - and the wind swirling amidst the city's early skyscrapers - lend credence to the literal application of the nickname, but the power lies in the metaphorical use of "windy" for "talkative" or "boastful". Chicago politicians early became famous for long-windedness, and the Midwestern metropolis's location as a host city for political conventions helped cement the association of Chicago with loquacious politicians, thus underlying the nickname with double meaning.' (Simon 2008, p. 1).

[9] Schmidt and Hansson (2018), p. 1508171. For a more recent take: Hazell et al. (2021), p. 305.

[10] '[I]f we don't feel stupid it means we're not really trying. [...] Productive stupidity means being ignorant by choice. Focusing on important questions puts us in the awkward position of being ignorant. One of the beautiful things of science is that it allows us to bumble along, getting it wrong time after time, and feel perfectly fine as long as we learn each time. [...] The more comfortable we become with being stupid, the deeper we will wade into the unknown and the more likely we are to make big discoveries' (Schwartz 2008, p. 1771).

la plaque" abuse of the crooked-teeth-with-(meta-)braces metaphorical defiguration of Lady Justice. On the contrary, we will suggest how it may help to capture both what precedes and what results from subpar, halitosis-inducing breathing habits, a notoriously "under-studied" topic in Western medicine[11] *a fortiori* in Western judicial human resources management.

Reflection surrounding these meta-braces as the hitherto most popular corrective orthodontic technique—cf. the tongue as scaffolding of the teeth[12]—, indeed merits transposition to Belgium's judicial enterprise in obvious demise under a far from evident socio-political opinion climate. Some recent exploration and self-experimentation led to the discovery and verification of several very helpful hints to improve sleep and breathing, reduce overall stress, and increase productivity. Persistent mouth breathing and associated chronic hyperventilation turned out to be at the basis of several performance-worsening ailments.

In this essay we will ventilate some widely-shared concerns as to Belgium's rather unenviable constellation and *dito* "management" of its legal system's admittedly most precious resources (i.e. the (wo)men administering justice), coupled with some commonsensical thoughts on equally cardinal aspects of the judicial mind-set and what we usually associate with it (Sect. 2).

Against this backdrop, we furthermore venture to (concisely) propose a (necessarily incomplete) *first aid approach* to the reigning *malaise*, inspired by the dominant ABCDE-protocol,[13] focusing on what compr(om)ises (judicial) empathy, and on *the benefits of nose-breathing as opposed to mouth-breathing*. The latter induces stress and exhaustion, which in turn further reinforces mouth breathing. Several insights by Dr. Buteyko and his successor Patrick McKeown not only seem transposable but even prove beneficial *in concreto* when it comes to dealing with *malaised* judicial officials (and others!). *In abstracto* or semiotically, this also seems to be the case regarding the justice system as a whole, especially considering how chronic collective stress affects empathy and soci(et)al/ (inter-)personal rela(xa)tions (Sect. 3).

[11] Cf. P. Gwin, "How ancient remedies are changing modern medicine", *National Geographic* January 2019, https://www.nationalgeographic.com/magazine/article/ancient-chines-remedies-changing-modern-medicine. See also: Macnaughton (2020), pp. 30–54.

[12] The image comes from Patrick McKeown, as interviewed on the popular British *Dr Rangan Chatterjee Podcast*: "How Breathing Through Your Nose Will Change Your Life with Patrick McKeown", https://www.youtube.com/watch?v=FdXQ6K0zIj4.

[13] Thim et al. (2012), pp. 117–121.

2 Belgium's Un-enviable Politico-judicial Constellation: Legal Positivism as Cartesianism *in legalibus*

The Belgian politico-judicial constellation could aptly be characterized as a *risk-averse* (Hofstede[14]) and *consociational* (Popelier and Lemmens[15]), somehow "failing" democracy, with a *morally compromised judicial system* (Engels[16]), where juridization of social relations,[17] judicialization of politics,[18] and attempts to bureaucratize the judiciary[19]—sure enough at odds with human nature (von Mises[20])—are both rampant and smothering. Also, freedom of conscience is far from being

---

[14]Cf. www.geert-hofstede.com/hofstede_belgium.shtml where one reads i.a.: 'High Uncertainty Avoidance indicates the society's low level of tolerance for uncertainty. In an effort to minimize or reduce this level of uncertainty, strict rules, laws, policies, and regulations are adopted and implemented. The ultimate goal of this population is to control everything in order to eliminate or avoid the unexpected. As a result of this high Uncertainty Avoidance characteristic, the society does not readily accept change and is very risk averse'.

[15]I.e. 'Government by elite cartels to safeguard stabilities in divided democracies through power-sharing, veto rights and segmental autonomy' (Popelier 2013, p. 501, with references). Lemmens (2015), p. 112: 'As a consociational democracy, the institutional design and politics of Belgium are based on permanent negotiations and agreements between different linguistic, philosophical and ideological groups in society'.

[16]Engels (2015), pp. 11–15.

[17]*Res ipsa loquitur.*

[18]Cf. *mut. mut.* the sharp wording of the American theologian Randall Smith: 'There will be no true justice – and no real political discourse -until the Rawlsian illusion of neutrality is rejected and the Rawlsian tyranny of strangling political discourse is overthrown, The freedom to say only what the elites schooled in political liberalism deem acceptable is no freedom at all. For its own good, the public should be a lot more attentive to the political philosophy underlying a potential judge's future decisions rather than checking whether he or she got one or two key questions "right". The judge who affirms on Rawlsian principles that your "right" to own a gun is "not subject to political bargaining or the calculus of social interests" may turn right around and affirm on the same basis that government-mandated contraception coverage or same-sex marriage cannot be subject to the prudential judgments of democratically elected legislative bodies. The result is legislation from the judiciary in the name of "rights" and the beginning of the end of deliberative, representative government of the sort intended by the framers of the Constitution' (R. Smith, "Neutered by Neutrality: The Abiding Influence of John Rawls, Part Two", *The Public Discourse* 17 juni 2016, www.thepublicdiscourse.com/2016/06/17068/, 3).

[19]Cf. Mises some 75 years ago, stating that a bureaucrat is '[a]n officer bound by various instructions. The criterion of good management is not the approval of the customers resulting in an excess of revenue over costs but the strict obedience to a set of bureaucratic rules. The supreme rule of management is subservience to such rules', all the while indicating how '[t]he subordinate depends on the superior's judgment of his personality, not of his work. As long as the office clerk can rely on his chances of getting a job with private business, this dependence cannot become so oppressive as to mark the clerk's whole character. But it is different under the present trend toward general bureaucratization' (von Mises 1983, p. 68). See also our Nelissen (2014), pp. 914–929.

[20]'German Marxians coined the dictum: If socialism is against human nature, then human nature must be changed. They did not realize that if man's nature is changed, he ceases to be a man. In an all-round bureaucratic system neither the bureaucrats nor their subjects would any longer be real human beings' (*Ibid.*, 112).

respected as much as possible, [21] and the list of "hateful things" denizens have to finance with their taxes is too long to enumerate,[22] amidst quite unsettling societal occurrences of depression (especially among youngsters), substance abuse, and suicide.[23]

Ultimately, being "pragmatic" (described by evil tongues as a *salonfähig* concept for show(cas)ing lack of principle) has been the standard for proper policy-making in Belgium from the outset. The related and increasingly dominant 'liberal-pragmatic' concept of tolerance is nonetheless far from innocuous since it induces a 'sentimentalist anthropology', as Broekman's retired-yet-still-active-colleague Professor Herman De Dijn forewarned almost three decades ago:

> Man is seen here not primarily as a being geared towards goodness and truth, but as a being trying first and foremost to avoid pain, but also to acquire pleasure as much as possible; it is in line with this sensitivity, that man develops all sorts of subjective preferences which he wants to implement freely. Restrictions on this freedom can only be accepted because of possible harm to another's sensitivity. Society, more particularly the State, is seen here as a sort of mega-machine which pragmatically organizes the coordination of all these sensitivities with the least possible interference[24]

Such dominant anthropology is not without risk of excesses down the road, as De Dijn argued:

> [P]eople will be asked more and more to be tolerant of others and not to impose 'unreasonable' demands on others. This inflation in turn may lead to eruptions of intolerance under the stress of the requirements of social adaptation. Finally, if tolerance is reduced to 'letting everybody think and do as he likes', it is not astonishing that tolerance as a positive virtue, i.e. as the ability to bear what is really unacceptable, would be lost[25]

More generally, (Cartesian) Enlightenment thinking, of which 'Napoleonic' legal systems are the crystallized upshot, clearly seems to have resulted in the opposite of its laudable aims, i.e. liberation and emancipation, as Polish philosopher Kołakowski astutely noted:

> The Enlightenment [...] has turned against itself. In retrospect we can clearly trace its suicidal steps, starting with Hume in the eighteenth century. Hume's rules of empiricism eventually became the basis for epistemological nihilism, which recognizes no reason to cling on to the conception of truth in the traditional sense [of adequatio]. If practical considerations are the only authority we have for judgments about the world that go beyond individual perceptions, then the concept of truth is useless; utilitarian criteria are perfectly adequate, both in science and everyday life. But the Enlightenment saw itself as the bold and

[21] Cf. more generally: Nelissen (2015), pp. 137–158.

[22] B. Nelissen, "Belastingen: waarom betalen we voor zaken die ons degouteren", *Trends* 12 december 2017, https://trends.knack.be/economie/beleid/belastingen-waarom-betalen-we-voor-zaken-die-ons-degouteren/article-opinion-934769.html?cookie_check=1645433796.

[23] Cf. most recently: Mental Assessment Group, *Mental Health of Belgian Population: (25/01/2022)*, https://fdn01.fed.be/documents/1a770733c18a42d6d7db89e37920540f/20220207_GEMS_MAG%20%281%29.pdf.

[24] De Dijn (1994), p. 28.

[25] *Ibid.*, 28.

> relentless pursuit of truth – the whole truth, as Hume required. Truth was supposed to defeat and supplant religious superstition, Christian myths, tradition and history as sources of certainty. And we can see how this struggle for truth in secular culture reached a cultural impasse, leaving us to confront, unarmed, a new situation where truth is absent, degraded, in pragmatist thinking, to the status of an old superstition. But the philosophy that killed-off truth proclaims unlimited tolerance for the 'language games' (i.e., opinions, beliefs and doctrines) that people find useful. The outcome is expressed in the words of Karl Kraus: 'Alles ist wahr und auch das Gegenteil'. 'Everything is true and also its opposite'[26]

This 'feasibility paradox' was furthermore pointed out by a plethora of authors, from Fulton Sheen,[27] to William Fulbright[28] and requires no further corroboration, although the 'Paradox of Modern Man' as illustrated by Alisdair McIntyre is too poignant to be left unmentioned:

> Each of us, individually and as a member of particular social groups, seeks to embody his own plans and projects in the natural and social world. A condition of achieving this is to render as much of our natural and social environment as possible predictable and the importance of both natural and social science in our lives derives at least in part – although only in part – from their contribution to this project. At the same time each of us, individually and as a member of particular social groups, aspires to preserve his independence, his freedom, his creativity, and that inner reflection which plays so great a part in freedom and creativity, from invasion by others. [...] It is necessary, if life is to be meaningful, for us to be able to engage in long-term projects, and this requires predictability; it is necessary, if life is to be meaningful, for us to be in possession of ourselves and not merely to be the creations of other people's projects, intentions and desires, and this requires unpredictability. *We are thus involved in a world in which we are simultaneously trying to render the rest of society predictable and ourselves unpredictable*, to devise generalizations which will

[26]Kołakowski (2012), pp. 317–318.

[27]'It is one of the curious anomalies of present-day civilization that when man achieves greatest control over nature, he has the least control over himself. The great boast of our age is our domination of the universe: we have harnessed the waterfalls, made the wind a slave to carry us on wings of steel, and squeezed from the earth the secrets of its age. Yet, despite the mastery of nature, there perhaps never was a time when man was less a master of himself. He is equipped like a veritable giant to control the forces of nature, but is as weak as a pigmy to control the forces of his passions and inclinations' (Sheen 1936, p. 49).

[28]'We know so very much more about things than we do about people, so very much more about the workings of jet planes and nuclear missiles than about our own inner needs. We are exploring the mysteries of outer space while we remain puzzled and ignorant about the mysteries of our own minds. Far more than supersonic airplanes or rockets to the moon, we need objective perceptions of our own fears and hopes and a broader perspective about our own society, our relations with others and our place in the world. [...] Until about two centuries ago there was no great disparity between progress in technology and progress in human relations, between man's understanding of things and his understanding of himself; both were progressing very slowly indeed. Then, with the Industrial Revolution, man achieved a gigantic breakthrough in his technology, a breakthrough which was followed by rapid and accelerating progress to which there is no end is yet in sight. There has been no comparable breakthrough in human relations; in the last two centuries our understanding of ourselves has progressed somewhat, perhaps a bit more rapidly than before, but not nearly as fast as our understanding of the physical world. The result of this disparity has been the development of an enormous gap between our facility with tools and our facility with ideas, between our control of the physical world and control of ourselves' (Fulbright 1966, p. 170).

> capture the behavior of others and to cast our own behavior into forms which will elude the generalizations which others frame[29]

The highly fashionable idea of judge-made law being, at least conceptually, clearly at odds with the transparency-centered, so-called hyper-enlightened 'Napoleonic DNA',[30] promoting this idea, especially in continental systems, amounts to swearing in a house of worship. At any rate, Broekman's analysis helped to better understand the genealogy of this taboo and how to deconstruct it. His insights were most welcome as I was getting increasingly frustrated by a topic that should be straightforward but nonetheless remained elusive. I painstakingly wondered how to make sure that the right kind of people (successfully apply to) become judges and how to subsequently keep them happy and productive or, in other words: how to contribute to their and, indirectly, our own flourishing.

Heaps of management literature, applied psychology, but inevitably also metaphysics (What is human *nature*, let alone what is *being*?) almost naturally supplemented my reading list. In doing so, I devoured Broekman's aforementioned *Law and anthropology* and (more than one of) his (many) *clés de lecture*—legal positivism being equated to Cartesianism *in legalibus*—came across as truly eye-opening and visionary. [31] I realized that reductionist views, however appealing they may be, about (wo)men called upon to judge their fellow (wo)men ultimately won't yield the sought-after, robust answers. Similarly, the aforementioned De Dijn stated that care-giving, when undergirded by erroneous anthropology, can never be truly effective.[32] Or, to quote *The Underground Thomist*, 'Any moral theory that fails to take account of excuses, rationalizations, and self-deceptions will badly misunderstand the human condition'.[33]

As long as we rely on people, rather than AI, [34] to judge others, we would, in short, be remiss if we stopped investing in an ever more accurate assessment of the human condition in which we all partake, and Professor Broekman's impressive *parcours* testifies to a more-than-ever-crucial relentless search for truth and *dito* exploration.

Following Alain de Botton's dictum—"education serves to save us time and to spare us from errors"[35]—Broekman appears as the *educator par excellence*: his

---

[29] MacIntyre (2012), p. 120.

[30] Damaška (1986), p. 36.

[31] Not at all to my surprise, Law and Economics trailblazer Guido Calabresi, whom I had the pleasure of meeting during his interview with my then fellow visiting researcher at Columbia Law School, Marco Bellia, stated that, were he to start over, he would focus on *law and anthropology*: Bellia (2013), pp. 26–42, and more specifically pp. 34–35.

[32] De Dijn (2011), p. 215. *Mutatis mutandis* one could claim the same about economics, which Hazlitt aptly described as an art '[which] consists in looking not merely at the immediate but at the longer effects of any act or policy; it consists in tracing the consequences of that policy not merely for one group but for all groups' (Hazlitt 2011, p. 5).

[33] Budziszewski (2011), p. 199.

[34] Oimann (2021), pp. 375–402.

[35] de Botton (2012).

polytopic activities allow for (clashes of) different viewpoints engendering theoretical novelties (theory here understood as "professionalized common sense"), in turn rendering possible much-needed relief *in concreto*. Absent such avenues to (help) imagine what brings us together *via* what transcends us, ideological claustrophobia and solipsism are looming on the horizon. Or as Fulton Sheen would have it:

> Formerly, man lived in a three-dimensional universe where, from an earth he inhabited with his neighbors, he looked forth to heaven above and to hell below. Forgetting God, man's vision has lately been reduced to a single dimension; namely, that of his own mind. Where can the soul go, now that a road block has been thrown up against every external outlet? Like a city which has had all its outer ramparts seized, man must retreat inside himself. As a body of water that is blocked turns back upon itself, collecting scum, refuse, and silt, so the modern soul (which has none of the goals or channels of the Christian) backs upon itself and in that choked condition collects all the sub-rational, instinctive, dark, unconscious sediment which would never have accumulated had there been the normal exits of normal times. Man now finds that he is locked up within himself, his own prisoner. Jailed by self, he now attempts to compensate for the loss of the three-dimensional universe of faith by analyzing his mind[36]

The stakes in such "battles of ideas" can hardly be overstated, as the Canadian evolutionary psychologist Gad Saad recently affirmed.[37] This polemic author states that 'the pursuit of knowledge does not always neatly fit clean dichotomies' and he coined the term *dichotomania* to designate '[t]he penchant of many researchers to map phenomena into binary realities'.[38] He specifically blames academia for the intellectual climate's quick deterioration through sentimentalization:

> The problem arises when domains that should be reserved for the intellect are hijacked by feelings. This is precisely what plagues our universities: what were once centers of intellectual development have become retreats for the emotionally fragile. The driving motto of the university is no longer the pursuit of truth but the coddling of hurt feelings[39]

Saad's *envoi* merits to be quoted as well:

> Any system that is built on a false understanding of human nature is doomed to fail. Building a society where the primary objective is to protect one's fragile self-esteem from the dangers of competition will only lead to a society of weakness, entitlement, and apathy. Life is necessarily competitive; society is necessarily hierarchical. It does no one any favors to pursue a utopian vision of society where no one's feelings are hurt[40]

---

[36] Sheen (1958), consulted online.

[37] 'Unless we win the battle of ideas, the enemies of reason, together with the mind viruses they promulgate, will lead our free societies to lunatic self-destruction' (Saad 2021, p. 22).

[38] *Ibid.*, 24.

[39] *Ibid.*, 27.

[40] *Ibid.*, 190.

Whomsoever is not prepared to adapt her/his views to reality, but rather does the opposite, [41] as Newspeak-retailing ideologues are known to do (cf. Frankfurt[42] and Scruton[43]), perhaps does not belong in academia and should be kept even further away from the bench, especially if the person is lacking *empathy*,[44] admittedly a crucial, yet risky "judicial virtue".[45] Indeed, being empathic appears not only to be the flipside of the being-prone-to-burn-out-coin (cf. *infra*, Sect. 3), it may also get

[41] Fleerackers (2012), p. 248 (our translation): 'Law's effectiveness rather rests on the extent to which this instrument adaptively relates to its object, reality, than on its internal logic'. Cf. Kletzer (2013), p. 98: 'Philosophy has nothing to tell the law which the law would not know from itself. If there is to be law then it is by necessity. Put differently: viewed from the point of view of the law, the law exists necessarily and the validity of the law leaves open no meaningful questions to be answered by legal philosophy. Viewed from the point of view of philosophy, however, there can be no positive law and no legal validity. Relative positivism is but the law viewed from the point of view of philosophy. The irresolvable paradox it faces is that, for it, there can be no valid law at all. So it is the positive law itself that has fulfilled and completed a task which philosophy has set itself and which it necessarily failed at completing, since a law that is in need of a constitution through philosophy cannot be positive law. Relative positivism is a philosophical doctrine which thinks it is a doctrine about the law, but which actually is a doctrine about its own, i.e., philosophy's, supreme competence, a doctrine, however, which conflicts with its own positivistic commitments. As a theory of the supreme competence of philosophy and reason, relative positivism is actually closer to a natural law theory than it might think. Whereas relative positivism takes reason and its mouthpiece philosophy to be the final arbiter of all formal questions relating to the law, natural law theory takes reason and its mouthpiece philosophy to be the final arbiter of all questions relating to the law. In relation to natural law, relative positivism has given up some competences over the positive law. Absolute positivism surrenders all competences over the positive law. Absolute positivism is thus aware that it is a philosophical doctrine about philosophy, about the limits of philosophy. As such a philosophical doctrine about the limits and incompetence of philosophy, absolute positivism to a certain extent has to be both a reflexive and also an anti-philosophical doctrine'.

[42] [S]ocieties cannot afford to tolerate anyone or anything that fosters a slovenly indifference to the distinction between true and false. Much less can they indulge the shabby, narcissistic pretense that being true to the facts is less important than being "true to oneself" (Frankfurt 2012, p. 33). Cf. the Italian priest and pedagogue Giussani (1922–2005) characterizing a society as less or more 'ideological' to the extent it 'tends to put a freeze on every true search. Such a society uses power as an instrument to contain such research within certain limits of realization and expression. A dictatorship is never concerned that research regarding man be free research because it is the most dangerous limit to power; it is a potentially uncontrollable source of opposition' (Giussani 2011, p. 51).

[43] 'Newspeak occurs when the primary purpose of language – which is to describe reality – is replaced by the rival purpose of asserting power over it. The fundamental speech-act is only superficially represented by the assertoric grammar. Newspeak sentences sound like assertions, but their underlying logic is that of the spell. They conjure the triumph of words over things, the futility of rational argument, and also the danger of resistance.' (Scruton 2019, p. 9).

[44] The empathy literature displays 'virtual consensus that the empathizer (1) understands, (2) feels, and (3) shares the other person's feelings (4) with self-other differentiation' (Eklund and Meranius 2021, p. 302).

[45] See more generally: Colby (2011), pp. 1944–2015; Lee (2014), pp. 145–206; Weinberg and Nielsen (2012), pp. 313–352.

someone labeled as "an activist judge" in light of the parallel drawn by SCOTUS Justice Roberts' between judges and umpires.[46]

More still, empathy and other "soft values", however often associated with the dealings of effeminate or syssified bèta-males or so-called *soy-boys*, nevertheless seem to require, just as the virtue of tolerance does, (self-)confidence, proper judgment, awareness of one's surroundings including the (hardening) opinion climate, and the willingness to communicate one's epistemic vulnerability as well as risk-taking (i.e. the risk to be disappointed should one's trust and resulting mildness be betrayed). Empathy admittedly does not stand on itself and its study/practice should always be embedded in other virtues such as integrity,[47] not to mention a well-developed moral imagination,[48] e.g. through the judicious consumption of novels ("Law and Literature"). We take the liberty to quote the unsurpassed West on this last point:

> [t]o create better communities we probably should learn [. . .] to become better readers of the classical cultural and legal texts that (partly) constitute our communal life. Improving the quality of our reading will improve the quality of our 'textual community'. But we also ought to improve the quality of our 'interactive community', and to do that, we need to become not just better readers, but better people. We need to concern ourselves not just with the worth of the 'principles' expressed or unexpressed in a legal text, but also with the subjective quality of the lives which that legal decision – our legal decision – will affect. [. . .] We need to listen, then, not just to the great stories and classic texts that constitute our cultural and legal tradition. We also need to listen to the lawyers, legal academics, lay people, poets, novelists, [. . .]. By learning to listen to the outsider, we expand and improve our interactive community. Ultimately, we expand and improve ourselves[49]

Finally, underscoring the importance of empathy is clearly at odds with what Fissell labeled the "anti-empathic turn" as a form of "neo-orthodoxy". The author concluded his 2016 assessment as follows:

> The source of public law (the legislature or the people, and not the judiciary) makes it either too haphazard and incoherent, or too vague, to admit of formal conceptual order. Thus, public law cannot be determinate, and no right or wrong legal answers will flow from a neutral or scientific rationalism. With all of this lost, this type of "adjudication" (if it can be called that at all) is but another form of politics – no necessary right and wrong, jus winners

[46] Cf. Jill Suttie, "Do We Need More Empathetic Judges?", *Mind&Body* June 16th 2016, Do We Need More Empathic Judges? (berkeley.edu).

[47] Cf. recently: Stępień (2021), p. 102: '[J]udicial empathy becomes much less controversial when it is complemented by judicial integrity. [. . .] [F]or the emergence and proper functioning of judicial empathy ('proper', which means that it co-collaborates in the implementation of procedural principles) as a kind of judicial virtue or attitude, a number of conditions needed to be fulfilled, including the development of judicial integrity. In other words, from a developmental perspective, which emphasises the process of becoming the mature judge, the emergence and functioning of judicial empathy require bolstering the integrity of judges. Thus, the abilities, skills, and virtues that enable the judge to 'go outside' their perspective to 'resonate with others' or 'enter the situation of others' require the simultaneous building of many other types of 'judicial crafts' and the forming of a specific set of them that together make up 'the whole' of the judge.'

[48] Hasnas (2011), pp. 26–48.

[49] West (1988–1989), p. 156.

> and losers. Thus, while the anti-empathic thinkers strenuously insist on a separation of law and politics, legal science – as understood on its own terms – cannot preserve the law and politics divide when applied to the area of most interest to them: public law. The anti-empathic consensus demands logical-formal reasoning (like classical legal orthodoxy), but unlike its progenitor the new theory allows for this reasoning to act upon a "law" that has no conceptual order (something orthodoxy would have thought was a necessary first principle)[50]

This chapter is far from being first, nor will it be last, at evoking some 'metaphysical crisis' within jurisprudence. At this point, we deliberately conceive of 'metaphysics' as broadly as possible since it caters to a stubborn need of ours.[51] Jean Grondin, to mention but him, rightly emphasizes that '[o]ne need not adopt a particular doctrine (like one joins a political party or a religion) to practice metaphysics. One simply needs to realize what one is doing when one attempts to understand our world and the meaning of one's experiences'.[52]

We furthermore assume that one cannot (continue to) retail/display what has not been received beforehand, that tolerance presupposes self-confidence, rationality and a sustainable, reliable and verifiable self-image (in short: anthropological realism and epistemic humility/vulnerability).[53] In other words, 'a judge must understand that what is reasonable can be other than what he or she instinctively believes to be so. Empathy can serve as a "corrective" to a judicial point of view that may be uninformed or unaware of the mistakes judges are inclined to make because of their own position of privilege and stereotypes'.[54] Ehrlich was, in short, visionary when he stated well over a century ago that '[t]*here is no guaranty of justice except the*

---

[50] Fissell (2016).

[51] Cf. Mootz III (2011), p. 15: 'Stephen Smith has articulated law's quandary in an unsettling and straightforward manner, describing: "how our understanding of law has deteriorated due to our wanton neglect (or, rather, our systematic suppression) of its ontological dimensions" [. . .]. Smith argues that law's quandary follows from the fact that legal practice outstrips the ontological presuppositions of both everyday experience and natural science with its reference to "The Law," but the only other available option – the ontological inventory of religious concepts, as epitomized in Aquinas's natural law theory – is irredeemably divorced from law in our (post)modern age [. . .]. More precisely, our quandary is that the discourse of law depends on some form of transcendent reality, but we expressly disavow such an ontological grounding despite the undeniable character of our practices [. . .].'

[52] Grondin (2012), p. xviii. Toward the end of his book, the author captures the two "hallmarks" of metaphysics: '[I]t strives to understand the whole of reality and its reasons. By the nature of its query, metaphysics is oriented toward universality and reason' (Ibid., 248). Also illuminating is what he calls the 'metaphysical assumption': '[T]he more universal the perspective is, the more it aids us to understand our world and our experience' (*Ibid.*).

[53] Cf. '[R]ationality is "the capacity to become aware of reality according to the totality of its factors". This is why a person always ought to perceive himself, in all sincerity and humility, as continually searching. The more lively and humble the search, the more insightful the results, since everything positive and useful which a person has found will be used in this endeavor' (Giussani 2001, p. 105). For a positive approach to epistemic vulnerability manifested by 'the willingness to be honest and open to learning by accepting one's own fallibility', see Meyer et al. (2017), pp. 221–235.

[54] Negowetti (2014), p. 750.

personality of the judge'.[55] What counts for personality seems equally *ad rem* for someone's character.[56]

Accordingly, we all cannot but benefit from well-rested, tolerant, open-minded judges willing to engage in (unavoidable) risk-taking and possessing and maintaining genuine authority.[57] Further still, trust is a so-called 'reactive attitude'[58] (Onora O'Neill) and judges should ideally venture to be(come) 'moral exemplars'[59] (Linda Zagzebski). Finally '[w]hat's important in this business is to manage the environment – you don't need to manage the people. If you have to manage the people, they shouldn't be here' (Russ Reynolds).[60]

3 Judicial Empathy Fatigue, Chronic Stress and Social Rela(xa)tion(s)

Let us now (re)turn to our amateur-level, perhaps even foolish,[61] semiotic endeavor using (a specific feature of) Lady Justice—her crooked teeth—by way of "eisegesis", to help mitigate at micro-level (i.e. the individual judge's situation) the undeniable malaise characterizing (probably not only) the Belgian legal system as a

[55]Ehrlich (1917), pp. 65–66.

[56]Budziszewski (1997), p. 45: 'Aristotle says more than that laws should be based on true moral ideas. He argues that they should be used to shape character – to make men virtuous. For good character is not inborn but an acquired characteristic. We are born with the ability to acquire virtue, he thinks, but we are not born with virtue itself. There is something in us that finds virtue attractive and wants to have it, but that is not the same as having it'.

[57]'We experience authority when we meet someone who possesses a full awareness of reality, who imposes on us a recognition and arouses surprise, novelty and respect'. (Giussani 2001, p. 64).

[58]Cf. O'Neill (2018), pp. 293–300.

[59]The Oklahoma-based philosophy professor Linda Zagzebski defines a *moral exemplar* as 'a person who is most admirable. We identify the admirable by the emotion of admiration. I assume that our emotion of admiration is generally trustworthy, but I do not assume that we always trust it. When we do, we take the object of admiration to be admirable. A person who is admirable in some respect is imitable in that respect. This is rough because there are many reasons why we do not or cannot imitate the admirable. But the feeling of admiration is a kind of attraction that carries with it the impetus to imitate. The ways in which the exemplar are admirable, and hence imitable, can be used to give us both a way of understanding significant moral concepts and a way of using those concepts as a way of making ourselves and our lives conform to the admirable' (Zagzebski 2010, p. 54).

[60]Reynolds (2012), p. 73.

[61]Cf. Peterson (2021), p. 18: 'The beginner, the fool, is continually required to be patient and tolerant – with himself and, equally, with others.His displays of ignorance, inexperience, and lack of skill may still sometimes be rightfully atttributed to irresponsibility and condemned, justly, by others. But the insufficiency of the fool is often better regarded as an inevitable consequence of each individual's essential vulnerability, rather than as a true moral failing'.

consequence of an admittedly distrusted,[62] risk-averse, ever-more bureaucratized[63] and hence stressed-out judiciary as a whole.

Risk-aversion, lack of empathy, and, more generally, intolerance are undoubtedly induced and aggravated by a plethora of factors, and we do not purport to exhaustively grasp the many intricacies involved. However, (chronic) *occupational stress*, itself a "loaded" concept, appears to stand out[64]:

> In general, occupational stress has many causes, including perceptions of injustice in procedures (e.g. decision-making in promotions), interpersonal matters related to employment (e.g. feeling respected) or lack of variety in job tasks. Judges experience occupational stress, typically scoring at least moderately high on a variety of measures of depression, stress and burnout. Their stress scores are often even higher than those of scores of people who work in other high-stress occupations like prison wardens and physicians. Common stressors include high caseloads; time limitations; social isolation; lack of privacy; the pressure of making legal decisions, including political pressure; publicity associated with trials; poorly prepared or disrespectful counsel; exercising judicial discretion; safety concerns; lack of resources; job security, especially for judges who face reelection or retention votes; long, boring trials and trials with frequent interruptions; and tension among colleagues and staff. Many of these stressors are related to occupational burnout. [. . .] This experience of others' trauma, often called secondary traumatic stress or vicarious trauma, adds to judges' stress[65]

Isaiah Zimmerman, who has been working on the topic since the eighties of last century,[66] furthermore illustrated how judges may even be more susceptible to stress-related ills than professional categories, such as front-line workers who are ususally associated with it:

> When we say frontline workers, people often think of emergency medical professionals, law enforcement, child welfare caseworkers, therapists, and residential staff for mental health facilities or prisons. Rarely do people think of the often quiet and even-tempered people who wear robes and sit behind a bench for a living: judges. Our public perceptions of the judge are as a person of ultimate neutrality who dispenses justice. But in reality judges also experience not only stress, but also vicarious trauma. Vicarious trauma refers to distress associated with working directly with traumatized people[67]

It is furthermore well-documented how stress, and more specifically the human "fight or flight state of mind" pertaining to our sympathetic nervous system, affects the quality of our sleep as it relates to upper-chest, fast and shallow *mouth breathing* which in turn contributes to chronic hyperventilation, sleep apnea, high(er) blood-pressure, halitosis, crooked teeth (especially within young children), tooth decay, obesity, increased cortisol levels, and both physical and academic underperformance, not to mention brain fog, agitation, restlessness, and both erratic

[62] Cf. recent calls for judicial self-government in the Belgian context: Leloup (2022), pp. 3–24.

[63] Cf. our Nelissen (2014), pp. 914–929.

[64] See also: Penney and Spector (2005), pp. 777–796.

[65] Millera et al. (2018), pp. 603–604, omitting manyfold references.

[66] Zimmerman (1981), pp. 5–8.

[67] Excerpt from a recent article with the author's input: Rahul Kumar, "Judging 'under stress': What it does to judges", *The Daily Guardian*, 11 September 2020, https://thedailyguardian.com/judging-under-stress-what-it-does-to-judges/.

Table 1 Common symptoms of Hyperventilation Syndrome (Timmons and Ley (1994) cited by Mckeown)

Respiratory	Shortness of breath, irritable cough, tightness or oppression of chest, inability to take a deep breath, excessive sighing
Muscular	Cramps, muscle and neck and shoulder pains, stiffness
Psychic	Tension, anxiety, 'unreal feelings', panic, phobias, agoraphobia
Gastrointestinal	Difficulty in swallowing, globus (having a lump in one's throat, dry mouth and throat, acid regurgitation, heartburn, flatulence, belching, air swallowing, abdominal discomfort, bloating
General	Weakness, exhaustion, impaired concentration, impaired memory and performance, disturbed sleep (including nightmares), emotional sweating

behavior (e.g. ADHD) and risk-aversion),[68] all of which we do not (want to) wish upon the (wo)men rendering justice on a daily basis.

Even, and perhaps even more likely, the kindest, most empathetic, diligent and professional judges with the ideal personality can fall prey to these 'personality-altering' ills, associated with the concept of *Compassion Fatigue* or *Empathy Fatigue*. The phenomenon is described as 'a work-related stressor that results from exposure to others who have experienced trauma; it is often called secondary traumatic stress disorder or vicarious trauma [. . .]'.[69]

Judicial self-reporting furthermore allows to draw a list of tell-tale signs of stressed-out judges. See for example the plethora of complaints reported in a study of the AMERICAN JUDGES ASSOCIATION back in 2009.

The medical literature indicating how the likeliness of mouth breathing increases with age should therefore not be overlooked. Somewhat surprisingly, the negative effects of mouth breathing were already documented by the late Russian physician, Dr. Konstantin Buteyko (1923–2003). His successor Patrick McKeown, himself a recovering mouth breather, continues to retail these insights both throughout books and podcasts as well as media appearances, together with unbelievably easy methods to provide much-needed relief,[70] i.e. with breath-holds, mouth-taping, and the gradual exposure to so-called "air-hunger", all resulting in higher Breath Oxygen Level Test-scores (BOLT[71]), but more importantly, in more restful sleep and (considerable) alleviation of the above-stated symptoms. Incidentally, these

[68]McKeown (2015). See more recently, McKeown (2021). For more resources, see www.oxygenadvantage.com and https://buteykoclinic.com/books/. Cf. also *The Joe Rogan Experience*, Episode 1506 (with James Nestor), where it was laid out, in a concise, fifteen-minute segment, why being a "mouth-breather" is bad for you: https://youtu.be/zWQxNoqKE6E.

[69]Millera et al. (2018), p. 604, with references.

[70]For a stimulating, recently aired podcast: "Patrick McKeown meets Dan Brule", *Oxygen Advantage*, 21 April 2020, https://www.youtube.com/watch?v=6RJWvRfZohc (@41:45). For a more comprehensive overview, see also Mackeown (2021), 534 p.

[71]Cf. Dr. Rangan Chatterjee, "How To Measure Your Bolt Score With Patrick McKeown", *Oxygen Advantage*, 26 February 2020, https://www.youtube.com/watch?v=f1pOYDukrXo; In order to improve it, see: Patrick McKeown, "How To Improve Your Bolt-Score", *Oxygen Advantage* 5 January 2022, https://www.youtube.com/watch?v=slIrMpKJtas.

Table 2 Mouth breathing versus nose breathing (*pace* McKeown)

Mouth breathing	Nose breathing
Heavy/Fast/Shallow breathing	Light/slow/deep
Upper-chest	Abdominal/diaphragmatic
Fight-or-Flight	Rest-and-Digest
Sympathetic nervous system (SNS)	Parasympathetic nervous system (PNS)

Table 3 Practical versus repetitive thinking (*pace* McKeown)

Practical thoughts	Repetitive thoughts
Not draining	Draining
Positive	Negative
"Focussed on the task at hand"	"Stuck in your head"
Problem-solving	Problematic

symptoms are closely related to so-called *hyperventilation syndrome* and a brief overview of common symptoms should suffice to make this point (Table 1).

Persistent excessive breathing or hyperventilation, even in its mildest form, should thus not be taken lightly: human breathing is indeed supposed to *be light, effortless, soft, through the nose, diaphragmatic, rhythmic and gentle, and paused on the exhale*, as McKeown summarizes in almost every media appearance. Slow/Low (nose-)breathing stimulates the *vagal nerve*,[72] causes secretion of (the neurotransmitter) acetylcholine and slows down the heart rate, interpreted by the brain that the body is safe. Mouth breathing tragically displays the exact opposite dynamics (Table 2).

Persistent mouth breathing, especially at a young age, therefore has detrimental effects on a person's cognitive and physical (i.a. cranial) development. [73]

Mouth breathing also appears to be related to so-called repetitive (negative) thinking (RNT[74]) as opposed to so-called practical thinking (Table 3).

Mouth breathing, in sum, seems to make for less well-rested judges who are more irritable, erratic, risk averse, and, even more worrisome, less empathetic, cognitively impaired and generally under-performing judicial officials who cannot but (further) defigure an already out-of-shape Lady Justice.

(Re)considering (the findings of) some important work on judicial stress(ors)[75] while duly noti(ci)ng the reported symptoms as listed in Fig. 1, it thus seems at least

[72]'The vagal nerve, as a proponent of the parasympathetic nervous system (PNS), is the prime candidate in explaining the effects of contemplative practices on health, mental health and cognition', Dutch neuroscientists Gerritsen and Band explained in a recent, widely-read article: Gerritsen and Band (2018).

[73]M. Higgins, "Mouth Breathing In Children & Adults – The Importance Of Correct Resting Tongue Position", https://www.martinhigginsphysiotherapy.co.uk/how-to-stop-mouth-breathing-in-children/ (consulted February 22nd 2022).

[74]Gil-Luciano et al. (2019), pp. 53–59.

[75]Bornstein et al. (2018).

Statement	M, Mdn, SD
Having upsetting or images about the trial	1.56; 1.00; .79
Feeling distant or cut off from people around you	2.29; 2.00; 1.09
Feeling emotionally numb	1.64; 1.00; .90
Feeling irritable or having fits or anger	2.15; 2.00; .95
Having trouble concentrating	1.87; 2.00; .87
Being overly alert	1.68; 1.00; .97
Being jumpy or easily startled	1.57; 1.00; .93
Note: (1 = not at all; 5 = extremely)	

Fig. 1 Judges' experience with stress symptoms (Flores et al. 2009, p. 81)

worthwhile to contemplate changing one's breathing and sleeping habits in order to *mind our minds.*

To this end, Patrick McKeown explains how, especially in the West, we have (not) been trained to (stop) think(ing), i.e. to create gaps in between thoughts. Rather, the author recalls, we have been feeding into a racing mind. The mind, however, remains the bodily organ through which quality of life is perceived. It is no coincidence that many top executives—including the late Steve Jobs (1955–2011)—incorporated mindfulness in their lives, McKeown notes. All this is not about turning an individual into a plant or *to cater to the tree-hugging, open-sandals-brigade,* the recovering mouth breather quipped more than once.

4 Conclusion

Research often boils down to *me*-search (i.e. introspection[76]), inevitably co-consists of *we*-search, and Professor Broekman clearly acquired mastery over both. Let us incessantly strive to emulate the curiosity and open-mindedness displayed by this prolific and epistemically humble scholar, and may his scholarship be cherished as a shining example and highly sourceable toolbox to probe the Rule of Law and to advance both our judges' well-being as well as our own flourishing.

Rather than stating that "decadence is the necessary condition of a renaissance" and merely bracing for impact, a first helpful step in the right direction might be a switch to nose-breathing by all those who could benefit from Broekman's unwavering commitment to both the exploration and amelioration of the human

[76]To this end, cultivating a taste for (moments of) silence appears to remain very conducive and perhaps even paramount: Sarah (2017).

condition, not in the least our judicial officials and those who have to (in)form them. Well-rested, (self-)confident, tolerant jurists may well turn out to be (and remain) the resilient "agents of peaceful change" (cf. Irish Nobel laureate Seamus Heaney) our fractured, late-modern society so desperately needs.

References

Bellia M (2013) The future of law and economics: interview with Guido Calabresi. Philosophical News, pp 26–42

Bornstein BH, Edwards CP, Reichert J, Miller MK (2018) Judges and stress: an examination of outcomes predicted by the model of judicial stress. Judicature, Iss. 3, https://judicature.duke.edu/articles/an-examination-of-outcomes-predicted-by-the-model-of-judicial-stress/

Budziszewski J (1997) Written on the heart. The case for natural law. InterVarsity Press Academic, Downers Grove, p 45

Budziszewski J (2011) The line through the heart. natural law as fact, theory, and sign of contradiction. ISI Books, Wilmington (Delaware) [2009], p 199

Colby TB (2011) In defence of judicial empathy. Minnesota Law Rev 94:1944–2015

Damaška M (1986) The faces of justice and state authority. A comparative approach to the legal process. Yale University Press, New Haven, p 36

de Botton A (2012) Religion for Atheists: a non-believer's guide to the uses of religion. Pantheon, New York

De Dijn H (1994) Tolerance, loyalty to values and respect for the law. Ethical Perspect:27

De Dijn H (2011) Vermaatschappelijking van de zorg. In welke maatschappij? Streven, p 208

Ehrlich E (1917) Judicial freedom of decision: its principles and its objects. Sci Leg Method:47

Eklund JH, Meranius MS (2021) Toward a consensus on the nature of empathy: a review of reviews. Patient Educ Couns 104(2):300. https://doi.org/10.1016/j.pec.2020.08.022

Engels P (2015) Mensonges d'État. Entre fraude, corruption et terrorisme: La justice belge en faillite. Renaissance du Livre, Waterloo, pp 11–15

Fissell BM (2016) Modern critiques of judicial empathy: a revised intellectual history. Mich State Law Rev 817. https://scholarlycommons.law.hofstra.edu/faculty_scholarship/1182

Fleerackers F (2012) Over levensbeschouwing, rechtsdenken en juridische vorming. In: Fleerackers F, Van Ransbeeck R (eds) Recht en levensbeschouwing. Reeks 'AdVocare' Interdisciplinair Cahier 20.1, Gent, p 245

Flores DM et al (2009) Judges' perspectives on stress on stress and safety in the courtroom: an exploratory study. Court Rev: J Am Judges Assoc 45:76. https://digitalcommons.unl.edu/cgi/viewcontent.cgi?article=1295&context=ajacourtreview

Frankfurt HG (2012) On truth. Alfred A. Knopf, New York, p 33

Fulbright JW (1966) The arrogance of power. Pelican, New York, p 170

Gerritsen R, Band G (2018) Breath of life: the respiratory vagal stimulation model of contemplative activity. Front Hum Neurosci 12. https://www.frontiersin.org/article/10.3389/fnhum.2018.00397

Gil-Luciano B et al (2019) How are triggers for repetitive negative thinking organized? A relational frame analysis. Psicothema 31(1):53–59. https://doi.org/10.7334/psicothema2018.133

Giussani L (2001) The risk of education. The Crossroad Publishing Company [1995], New York, p 105

Giussani L (2011) The religious sense. McGill-Queen's University Press [1997], Montreal, p 51

Grondin J (2012) Introduction to metaphysics. From Parmenides to Levinas (trans: Soderstrom L). Columbia University Press [2004], New York, p xviii

Hasnas J (2011) Is moral imagination the cure for misapplied judicial empathy? Bandes, Bastiat, and the quest for justice. Washburn Law J 51:26–48

Hazell CM, Niven JE, Chapman L et al (2021) Nationwide assessment of the mental health of UK doctoral researchers. Humanit Soc Sci Commun 8:305. https://doi.org/10.1057/s41599-021-00983-8
Hazlitt H (2011) Economics in one lesson. Ludwig von Mises Institute [1946], Auburn, p 5
Kletzer C (2013) Absolute positivism. Neth J Leg Philos, Afl. 2, p 98
Kołakowski L (2012) Our Merry Apocalypse. In: Idem, Is God Happy? Selected essays. Penguin [1997], London, p 313
Lee R (2014) Judging judges: empathy as the Litmus test for impartiality. Univ Cinc Law Rev 82(1):145–206
Leloup M (2022) Judicial self-government in de Belgische rechtsorde: over rechterlijke onafhankelijkheid, rechterlijke verantwoordelijkheid en de scheiding der machten. TBP (1):3–24
Lemmens K (2015) (S)electing judges for Strasbourg. A (dis)appointing process? In: Bobek M (ed) Selecting Europe's Judges. A critical review of the appointment procedures to the European Courts. OUP, Oxford, p 95
MacIntyre A (2012) After virtue. Bloomsbury [1981], London, p 120
Mackeown P (2021) The breathing cure. Exercises to develop new breathing habits for a healthier, happier and longer life. OxyAt Books, Dublin, 534 p
Macnaughton J (2020) Making breath visible: reflections on relations between bodies, breath and world in the critical medical humanities. Body Soc 26(2):30–54. https://doi.org/10.1177/1357034X20902526
McKeown P (2015) The oxygen advantage: the simple, scientifically proven breathing technique that will revolutionise your health and fitness. Hachette, London
McKeown P (2021) Atomic focus: harness the true power of your brain, develop resilience against stress, and get focused with simple breathing exercises to change your mental and physical state. OxyAt Publishing, Dublin
Meyer F, Le Fevre DM, Robinson VMJ (2017) How leaders communicate their vulnerability: implications for trust building. Int J Educ Manag 31(2):221–235. https://doi.org/10.1108/IJEM-11-2015-0150
Millera MK, Reichert J, Bornstein BH, Shulmand G (2018) Judicial stress: the roles of gender and social support. Psychiatry Psychol Law 25(4):602
Mootz FJ III (2011) 'Die Sache': the foundationless ground of legal meaning. In: Broekman JM, Mootz FJ III (eds) The semiotics of law in legal education. Springer, New York, p 5
Negowetti NE (2014) Judicial decisionmaking, empathy, and the limits of perception. Akron Law Rev 47(3):693. http://ideaexchange.uakron.edu/akronlawreview/vol47/iss3/3
Nelissen B (2014) Het Grondwettelijk Hof en de rechterlijke pensioenwrevel. 'Verambtenariseert' onze rechtspraak? NJW, Afl. 313, 914–929
Nelissen B (2015) Judicial policy vs. freedom of (judicial) conscience: friends or foes? In: De Bruyne J, de Potter de ten Broeck M, Van Hiel I (eds) Policy within and through law. Reports of the third ACCA conference. Antwerp, Maklu, pp 137–158
O'Neill O (2018) Linking trust to trustworthiness. Int J Philos Stud 26(2):293–300
Oimann A-K (2021) Krijtlijnen voor een artificiële rechter. Tijdschrift voor Filosofie (3):375–402. https://doi.org/10.2143/TVF.83.3.3289987
Penney LM, Spector PE (2005) Job stress, incivility, and counterproductive work behavior (CWB): the moderating role of negative affectivity. J Organ Behav 26(7):777–796. https://www.jstor.org/stable/4093955
Peterson JB (2021) Beyond order. 12 more rules for life. Penguin, London, p 18
Popelier P (2013) The Belgian Constitutional Court: guardian of consensus or venue for deliberation? In: Alen A, Joosten V, Leysen R, Verrijdt W (eds) Liberae Cogitationes. Liber amicorum Marc Bossuyt. Intersentia, Antwerpen, p 499
Reynolds R (2012) Heads. Business lessons from an executive search pioneer. McGraw Hill, Columbus, p 73

Saad G (2021) The parasitic mind. How infectious ideas are killing common sense. Regnery, Washington DB, p 22
Sarah R (2017) La force du silence. Contre la dictature du bruit. Fayard, Paris
Schmidt M, Hansson E (2018) Doctoral students' well-being: a literature review. Int J Qual Stud Health Well-being 13(1):1508171. https://doi.org/10.1080/17482631.2018.1508171
Schwartz M (2008) The importance of stupidity in scientific research. J Cell Res:1771
Scruton R (2019) Fools, frauds and firebrands. Thinkers of the new left. Bloomsbury [2015], London, p 9
Sheen F (1936) The moral universe. Bruce Publishing Co, Milwaukee, p 49
Sheen F (1958) Go to heaven. McGraw-Hill, New York
Simon S (2008) Windy city: a novel of politics. Random House, New York, p 1
Stępień M (2021) On the relationship between judicial empathy and the integrity of judges. Krytyka Prawa 13(3):98. https://doi.org/10.7206/kp.2080-1084.474
Thim T, Krarup NHV, Grove EL, Rohde CV, Løfgren B (2012) Initial assessment and treatment with the Airway, Breathing, Circulation, Disability, Exposure (ABCDE) approach. Int J Gen Med 5:117–121. https://doi.org/10.2147/IJGM.S28478
Timmons BH, Ley R (1994) Behavioral and psychological approaches to breathing disorders. Springer, Boston. https://doi.org/10.1007/978-1-4757-9383-3
von Mises L (1983) Bureaucracy. Libertarian Press, Grove City [original edition: New Haven, Yale University Press, 1944]
Weinberg JD, Nielsen LB (2012) Examining empathy: discrimination, experience, and judicial decisionmaking. South Calif Law Rev 85:313–352
West R (1988–1989) Communities, texts and law: reflections on the law and literature movement. Yale J Law Humanit:129
Zagzebski L (2010) Exemplarist virtue theory. Metaphilosophy, vol 41, Afl. 1–2, p 41
Zimmerman IM (1981) Stress: what it does to judges and how it can be lessened. Judges' J 20(4):5–8

Narrativity and Memory. Towards an Ethics of Testimony

María Lucrecia Rovaletti

Abstract When survivors of Nazi concentration camps said that what kept them going in life was the need to tell others about the horror, they were expressing a need for an 'ethics of testimony'; the salvation of victims by keeping their memory alive.

Ricoeur argues that 'time becomes human time when it is articulated in narrative form', demonstrating that narrative plots constitute a 'privileged means with which to reconfigure our confused, shapeless and often muted temporal experience.' In spite of this, an experience is not always enough to be the subject of a narrative, as its traumatic nature often prevents the subject from assimilating their personal history. There is a powerful temptation to deny that it ever took place or it is experienced as something that happened to someone else. On these 'dark nights of the soul', when one suffers periods of extreme abnegation, 'the question of *who I am* does not lead to nullity but the difficult nature of the issue' (Ricoeur, 1990, p. 197, SMA).

In order to prevent it from becoming an unbearable sequence of events, we tell a story and try to find its meaning, not to condone or forget but to win "the privilege of judgement" (Arendt, 1990, p. 91). If forgetting leads to the rupture of tradition, the truth is not a discovery that destroys the secret but the revelation that does it justice and allows it to be passed on to future generations.

Narratives thus move on from being the life of one individual to become part of the ethical and cultural heritage of a people.

> The relevance of the issues of memory, including what one might call a duty to memory, are based on a brutal event, an extreme situation for society and its institutions: the terrorism and criminalization of the state occurring on a scale never before seen in the country. And the importance of memory has acquired a public space proportional to the enormity of crimes

---

M. L. Rovaletti (✉)
Buenos Aires University (UBA), Buenos Aires, Argentina

CONICET (National Council for Scientific and Technical Research), Buenos Aires, Argentina

2nd Chair of 'Psychology, Ethics and Human Rights' and 2nd Chair of 'Phenomenological Psychology', School of Psychology (UBA), Buenos Aires, Argentina

Department of Medical Humanities, School of Medicine (UBA), Buenos Aires, Argentina

F. Fleerackers (ed.), *The Rearguard of Subjectivity*, Law and Visual Jurisprudence 9,
https://doi.org/10.1007/978-3-031-26855-7_10

that undermined the basic values on which a sense of belonging and a shared history are based (Vezzetti 2007, p. 3).

1 Narrative Plots and Fragmentary Documents

From the second half of the twentieth century onwards, the concept of 'narrative' has acquired great importance in the fields of the social and human sciences. Philosophy, especially hermeneutic phenomenology, has focused on the temporal facet of narrative, seeking to establish links between the structure of subjectivity and the form of the story given that the latter occurs as a means of organizing events in time. Time becomes human when it is expressed in a narrative form and narrative is also significant in the ways in which it describes the temporal aspects of the human experience.

In fact, a story represents a form of 'temporal logic', a network of indications and implications that connect events in time in a certain way, from a certain perspective. All human experience consists of being surrounded by stories (Schapp 1983) and, as Ricoeur notes, these stories have a narrative structure. In fact, there is a link between the construction of a subjectivity and a narrated story. This is what is called a 'narrative identity'.

In *Temps et Récit* (*Time and Narrative*), Ricoeur shows how stories provide a unique basis for the 'chaining together or connection of a life'. Storytelling imbues linguistic scope to the temporal human dimension: the human experience becomes understandable *within* and *because of* the story. But a narrative is not simply an aid to understanding, it is an ontological measure; this is why identity *is* narrative, the product of a story dynamic that develops during the plot. The knowledge that a human being can have of themselves is never direct, it always occurs through the medium of language.

Narrativity, as a part of the human condition, possesses the dual nature of being both historical and fictional. The story that each person tells weaves together different plots related to their life and as this occurs they make choices, remove and distort certain aspects, which is to say they interpret events in order to obtain a version that presents them at an advantage in the given circumstances.

Although the subject *learns* to become the narrator of their life, they never fully become its author. Essentially, they arrive at the story because it has already been told by others. As Hannah Arendt says: 'No one has a life worthy of consideration if a story can't be told about it.' One discovers who 'they are' in others: hence the move from biography to autobiography.

When Ricoeur suggests that 'time becomes human time when it is articulated in narrative form' (Ricoeur, *TR I,* 1983, p. 17), he is saying that narrative plots constitute a 'privileged method by which we can reconfigure our confused, shapeless and at its extreme, mute temporal experience.' (*op. cit.*, 13). Essentially, one cannot reach *themselves* except through the medium of our stories or the way we assimilate them and the way they take shape, whether this is through modulation or becoming inextricably linked to them.

The understanding that each of us has of ourselves is a narrative because it cannot be interpreted outside of time. The story transforms human events that are not necessarily connected to one another into the structure of a plot that shall be the *configured imagination* that provides *meaning*. Thus dissimilar elements that might have been forced upon us, that are beyond our control or that were undesired interact with one another...

At first sight, it would appear that narrative intrigue created by a summary of heterogeneous and discordant occurrences has achieved a definitive victory over the *un-meaning* contained within certain negative determinations. Essentially, different planes exist within every plot, some of which have a dynamic effect on their development while others remain stable but also make a contribution to determining the *meaning* of a story. It is thus impossible to imagine absolutely transparent communication. As Schleiermacher demonstrates, misunderstandings form part of the work of understanding. In reality, we only describe the different ways in which stories can arise or recur, some of which have been anticipated for some time while others appear abruptly: understanding a story, taking part in it in one way or another, means being open to their multiple horizons.

However, events or facts do not always become the subject of a story because the *traumatic experience* sometimes prevents the subject from accepting their personal history leaving only silence in its place. Thus:

> The majority of people who have been tortured, once freed, describe different feelings related to the horror they suffered: shame, pity, anger, bewilderment, hatred, etc. but they cannot communicate their more private experiences of the event. (Kordon et al. 2002a, p. 93)

There is even a powerful temptation to deny that said reality ever took place, or it is regarded as something that occurred to someone else. Clinical psychotherapy is full of examples of this kind. The task of the self consists of transforming these *fragmentary documents* into a historical construction that provides the author and their audience with the sensation of *temporal continuity* (Aulagnier 1992, p. 290). 'Talking about one's suffering' can be a means *for oneself* of accepting that suffering and lending it meaning.' (Maury-Rouan and Vion 1994)

However, cohesion can't be definitively understood or achieved. Narrative identity arises out of a fragile identity (Ricoeur, *TR III* 1985, p. 358).

2 An Identity Constructed Between the Cracks

Narrative identity is also the field in which one occasionally experiences the extreme sense of one's lack of identity. On these 'dark nights' of the soul, these moments of extreme abnegation. 'the question *who am I* no longer leads to nullity but the difficulty of the question itself' (Ricoeur 1990, p. 197).

For instance, a patient is recorded telling her therapist that not being named or seen was one of the worst experiences of her life, it made her feel that she no longer existed for the other:

> She constantly said to herself: "My name is Silvia and I'm 24 years old" to continue to feel herself. A guard would occasionally give her a cigarette or take her by the hand. The experience of having one's hand held has been recovered as a memory. (Kordon et al. 2002b, p. 120)

Analyzing certain stories, one realizes that 'every experience is synonymous with a trauma too violent to articulate' and 'that is thus more disruptive to the "assimilation of heterogeneity" that leads to narrative intrigue.' (Greisch 2001, p. 196).

Sometimes, these 'inconsistencies' refer to the retroactive development of the traumatic effect of events from the 'past' that are *only* subsequently actualized under certain conditions: this is what Freud calls *Nachträglichkeit*,[1] or *retroactivity*. These inconsistencies produce something very valuable: the presence/absence of what is 'out of time', *Zeitlos*. Freud saw the devastating effects of incurable, open wounds as something 'extemporaneous', phenomena that destroy the self-regenerative capacity of the psyche. They are like 'saturated phenomena' (Marion 1992), traumas that are '*inconclusive events*' (Figueiredo 1998), which prevent reassembly of meaning and history due to the damage they do to the psyche. And so they become a kind of *non-event* or *un-fact* meaning that they are perhaps what is most radically 'timeless'.

This is not delayed action ("*deferred action*", "*après coup*", or *a posteriori*) but the '*work of memory*' by a 'wounded memory' (*blessé),* as Ricoeur says (2000). But does a true reconstruction really occur? Or is it the *shadow* that forever accompanies a person without ever being fully integrated? Is it not rather the presence of a Void? The presence of the un-narratable. Is it possible, then, to create a process that constructs and reconstructs the *meaning* of that experience? Is it possible that the 'timeless' in all its incarnations can be recognized and experienced as an integral and indivisible part of the flow of experiences? These *emotional frameworks* which belong essentially to the experience of remaining in life, which create a footprint of emptiness and denial, remain in the lives of survivors.

One doesn't have unlimited freedom to assemble new stories because often '*the meaning*' of one's personal identity resides in the *cracks*, the minor strategies one employs to resist pressure, supported by *solidity* and *trust* in their world and their ideals.

It is the identity of the *ipse,* which is expressed in the unpredictable and multi-vocal story able to *support a promise*, which translates into 'fidelity to one's self', providing evidence of the permanence of subjectivity.[2] In essence, regardless of their

---

[1] J. Lacan is right to call attention to the importance of this issue.

[2] Ricoeur suggests that the story of a unique individual is never the monotonous and monolithic story of an *idem.* He thus distinguishes 'identity' from 'selfness', the persistence of qualities, properties or characteristics that only indicate the ersistence of a unvarying core of personality: character. In humans, however, there also exists the identity of the *ipse* as the human capacity to maintain *a promise*. He calls this kind of identity *Selfhood* or *Selbstheit* in German.

Selfness expresses the permanence of the 'what (*quoi*)', and *selfhood* represents the permanence of the 'who' in spite of any variations that may have occurred. If this wasn't so, human subjectivity would disappear every time there was a radical change in a way of life. The dialectic between *selfness* and selfhood is what creates 'human identity'.

individual characteristics and circumstances (*idem*), each victim tried and generally succeeded in supporting themselves *within* and *out of their fidelity to themselves* (*ipse*); their life project, which is why:

> When "silence" is experienced as the best way to protect oneself from the destruction one fears from the outside world, said mechanism is used not only in relation to anything directly connected to the traumatic experience but it becomes a "natural" way of relating with the world. (Martín 2002, pp. 208–209)

As a means of liberation, the victim tries to continue with the strategies that helped them to survive the repressive context. This is why those who have been incarcerated for long periods of time have had to recreate in prison—in their own way—a non-damaging bond with the world.

However, the destructive experience they have suffered often makes rejoining society difficult: they live as though they were in a 'situation of formal, unreal liberty, haunted by the ghostly threat that the cycle of terror will return' (Martín 2002, p. 209). Hence the inclination towards detachment and solitude, as though that might protect their liberty even if they actually only end up restricting it.

In their therapy, they also demonstrate a need to protect themselves from a re-activation of their traumatic experiences even if this defensive strategy takes up so much of their time and libido that they are prevented from becoming a part of the dialectic of giving and receiving.

In spite of the varied nature of the experiences and their associated clinical histories, some recurring shared parameters can be established that, when compared with the general population, can be considered meaningful: the traumatic experience remains present creating difficulties with forming bonds and in some cases generating organic diseases with greater intensity and frequency. However, this issue only becomes apparent when an apparently neutral stimulus unconnected to the painful experience presents itself in the history.

On other occasions, even though these people do not display an express pathology, the effects of the terror remain in a disguised form, meaning they require therapeutic support. In fact:

> Torture may well constitute one of those extreme experiences in which the ghost of death is always present. In some cases, it occurs as a result of the torture. When this happens, the ghost then hovers over everyone in the same situation. (Kordon et al. 2002a, p. 92).

Feelings of embarrassment, shame or humiliation silence the context of torture because certain private experiences have been compromised, producing a rupture in the image the person previously had of themselves.

In these critical situations, there is always an inability to testify. As Agamben shows in *Remnants of Auschwitz* (Agamben 2000), the truth of what happened is very difficult to talk about and can even be disbelieved.

There are horrors and terrors that words cannot do justice and which no ears are capable of hearing. This is the 'inhuman' dimension of horror. It becomes human again when it is put into words, albeit with all the difficulties that entails. Therein lies the courage to reclaim what remains of humanity after an inhuman experience to which no one is immune.

The survivor never knows for certain why they survived and although they torment themselves looking for an answer, they'll never fully have it: living now means the personal work of dealing with the guilt of having survived while others, often a majority, died. It feels as though one were usurping an existence that doesn't fully belong to them, an existence that perhaps should belong to someone else.[3] This is why a patient says: 'I was surprised to hear a friend tell me that I've always described myself as a survivor because if not I'd have to think more about living than surviving.' (Kordon et al. 2002a, p. 96)

At the clinic we are often confronted with the unsayable, the incommunicable.[4] If one word can sum up this horror-induced failing it is unjustifiable, incomprehensible, un-analyzable because the analyst is confronted with mutilations of psychic capital and potential that are beyond their power to 'repair' and that *they are unable to reveal to the patient.* But we are not then reduced to filling in the gaps: to the contrary we must take in the difficult task of enabling subjects to re-invent the mediums, objects and projects that combat the continued effect of Thánatos, the force responsible for these definitive mutilations. Like the *work of grief* 'as regards reconciliation with the loss itself, the work is never fully completed' and so 'patience with oneself becomes seen as a virtue' (Ricoeur 2000, p. 107). Ricoeur admits that the unity of the plot of a story is constantly in conflict with all the contingent elements introduced by the delays created during the previous period of life. Human actions have a dispiriting contingency given the irreversibility and irrevocability of past actions the how and why of whose origins are a mystery to us, as is the unpredictability of future actions.

Conventional narratives into which meaning has been carefully woven aren't sufficient to represent human *temporality.* Essentially, the extemporaneous will inevitably emerge because it is *from* these emergences and *within* these emergences that *time is temporalized.* Every 'moment' shall always be *pointing to* and *attracted by* other moments in the creation of a *fractured story* and *over-determined* by a 'before' and an 'after'. This does not displace the constructive function of the story, it seeks to establish the conditions and means by which the *extemporaneous* can to some degree be included and in some cases configured and in others left free for an unpredictable but enriching activity.

In order for it not to become an unbearable sequence of events, we tell a story and seek meaning, not to condone or forget but to obtain the 'privilege of judging' as Hannah Arendt suggests.

> If the truth is not put into words, it is expressed in symptoms. These symptoms point to the unsayable and also keep it hidden within an indecipherable language. These symptoms speak through the human body, they are metaphors for the experience that continues to cause

[3]Guilt can also be experienced by those who never experienced torture or terrorism as K. Jaspers notes in *El problema de la culpa* (The Problem of Guilt), Barcelona, Paidós, 1999.

[4]It is also impossible to create a correspondence between the representation and the thing being represented; it is difficult to theorize an 'object' that is necessarily elusive and un-objectifiable such as the 'subconscious'. This is a possible correlation between 'interpretations', 'reconstructions' and 'factual history.'

> pain. Or they are social metaphors that must be placed in context in order to understand their meaning and consequences. (Lira Kornfeld 1996, p. 153).

If oblivion leads to the breakdown of tradition, the truth, in contrast, is not 'a discovery that destroys the secret, but the revelation that does it justice' (Arendt 1999, p. 163) and allows it to be communicated to future generations. The truth makes itself present within an ethical and political horizon, or to go further, it is a truth that '[...] can't be found but is instead made' (Martín Baró 1998, p. 297).

> However, atrocities are not easy to repress. The effort to deny in order to forget is always unsuccessful. Remembering and saying – and knowing – the truth is a necessary condition for the recovery of the social order and the recovery of victims. Speaking the truth – speaking about what has happened – or keeping it a secret are often contradictory trends that are generated by traumatic experiences. (Lira Kornfeld 1996, p. 153)

The damage to victims, meanwhile, is not primarily the harm to economic goods and possessions that might have been lost and it is greater than physical and emotional damage; it is damage to oneself, to one's *own life project* and everything that affects it. Its extremity is based on the fact that it damages a person's right to choose their own fate, the freedom of a subject to choose a means of self-realization. It is thus an irreparable or close to irreparable loss or serious hindrance to their personal opportunities (Fernández Sessarego 1996) that can only achieve symbolic recovery when it includes guarantees that it can never be repeated, a 'never again'.

In contrast to the disturbance caused by post-traumatic stress[5] which is related to a disruptive event or incident, the experiences suffered by victims of state terrorism last for much longer and involve multiple disruptive episodes.

For instance, the abduction of children during the dictatorship is not simply a 'traumatic episode', but a process that involves a large part of their lives. For relatives of the disappeared, or families looking for children that are adults today, the crime continues to be committed, which is why they are considered crimes to which no statute of limitations can apply. They have a similar effect on mental health because the traumatic event continues to occur.

Finally, it is fundamental for the recovery of these traumatic situations to be able to place the events in a context that encompasses more than individual experience. Here symbolic reparations enacted as policies of the state become important. As Vicario de la Solidaridad de Chile[12] say:

> ...truth, justice and reparation of the harm caused to victims and society are essential elements to achieving true reconciliation. The whole nation must commit to a future process of democratization and construction of a shared society with unrestricted respect for human and civil rights so that they become the cornerstones of institutions (*La Tercera* newspaper, Chile, 25-11-1989; cited in Lira Kornfeld 1996, p. 63).

---

[5]Post-traumatic stress syndrome also does not explain the multiple symptomatic manifestations of trauma or the profound and persistent alterations in personality it causes. Neither does it account for the *meaning* of the traumatic events to the victim. Crimes against humanity intensely and directly affect the dignity of a person and their life project over time.

3 The Duty of Memory as a Duty to Do Justice

When

> [. . .] prisoners in the Nazi concentration camps explain what kept them going they say it was the need to tell people about the horror; what they envisaged was the salvation of the victims by keeping their memory alive. They didn't just want to remember the dead, they wanted to save them. (Reyes Mate 2003, p. 115).

The memory that seeks to process the loss of so many abducted, tortured, murdered, and exiled bodies must revise and salvage the failed promises of a time dominated by the fury of combat and the irreversibility of death but it must also seek to revive ideas and passions.

> [. . . .] memory is not a spontaneous record of the past, it requires a framework for recovery and meaning in the present as well as expectations for the future (Vezzetti 2010, p. 3).

Although 'totalitarian domination' always seeks to create 'pockets of oblivion' inside which 'all events, both good and bad' disappear, they are destined to fail as 'there are too many people to make oblivion possible. There will always be someone left alive to tell the story' (Arendt 1990, p. 352). The truth will always filter through the cracks left by a supposedly omnipotent power. *Remember so as not to repeat*, said Adorno (1982).

> But what does it mean, then, to bring justice to the victims? What does it mean to bring justice to the injustices that lie within the realm of memory? How can we bring back those who are gone, not because they left but because they were made to leave: disappeared? (Reyes Mate 2009, p. 21).

Full justice for personal harm —death, kidnapping, torture, threats— is impossible to achieve, all that is left is a modest but fundamental form of justice, which is achieving complete awareness of 'the irreparable'. Confronted with political damage —the murdered or disappeared person is denied their right to citizenship— the only solution is to return that right. Repairing or doing justice in response to damage to a society— when society has been fractured and impoverished by violence—means identifying the victims and the perpetrators.

We are historically responsible for what we have done and what we cease doing. When Primo Levi (Levi 2003) asked himself *what we can do*, he answered that if witnesses were to disappear, then there would be no memory and thus no possibility of justice. Hence the need to continue remembering the witness, maintain awareness of an injustice that requires that justice be done and even transform ourselves into 'witnesses'.

And so memory—the struggle against oblivion—allows us to keep the rights that were once denied to the victims alive and relevant. 'The duty of memory is the duty to do justice, for the memory of people other than oneself' (Ricoeur, MHO 2000, p. 108) while oblivion implies the approval of injustice. As Todorov (2002) argues, genuine memory is always exemplary insofar as it takes responsibility not only for preserving the past but also committing to prevent a repeat of the horrors that occurred in the present. The concept of 'retrospective responsibility' means that one is responsible for the results of certain behaviours, especially those produced intentionally through action or omission; 'prospective responsibilities' means that one has an *a priori* responsibility when faced with potential events that one is obliged to be aware of prevent.

The suffering of a people cannot be forgotten because narrative keeps it alive and present. Narratives must thus be passed on from individual lives to become part of the ethical and cultural heritage of a people.

Memory, *anamnetic justice*, as Reyes Mate calls it (2003, pp. 100–125) is what brings our gaze back to the *repressed* as an ongoing process that reclaims forgotten histories and affirms from the beginning that *responsibility* is the first essential ethical step towards assimilating one's fate. As León Gieco sang (Gieco 2001):

> Todo está escondido en la memoria
> Refugio de la vida y de la historia
> La memoria estalla hasta vencer
> a los pueblos que la aplastan
> y no la dejan ser. . . .

> (Everything is hidden in memory
> Refuge of life and history
> Memory bursts forth until it overcomes
> the peoples who crush it
> and try to stop it)

References

Adorno TW (1982) Minima moralia. Reflexiones desde la vida dañada (Minima Moralia. Reflections on a damaged life). Taurus, Madrid

Agamben G (2000) Lo que queda de Auschwitz. El archivo y el testigo. Homo Sacer III (The Remnants of Auschwitz. Archive and testimony. Homo Sacer III). Pre-textos, Valencia

Arendt H (1990) Hombres en tiempo de oscuridad (Men in dark times). Editorial Gedisa, Barcelona

Arendt H (1995) De la Historia a la acción (Between past and future). Editorial Paidós, Barcelona

Arendt H (1999) Eichmann en Jerusalen (Eichmann in Jerusalem). Lumen, Barcelona

Aulagnier P (1992) El aprendiz de historiador y el maestro brujo (The Historian's Apprentice and the Master Wizard). Amorrortu, Buenos Aires

Fernández Sessarego C (1996) El daño al proyecto de vida en la jurisprudencia de la Corte Interamericana de Derechos Humanos (The damage to life project in the jurisprudence of the Inter-American Court of Human Rights). Derecho PUCP, N° 56, (Lima). Diciembre, pp 659–700

Figueiredo LC (1998) Temporalidad y narratividad en los procesos de subjetivación de la clínica psicoanalítica (Temporality and narrativity in processes of subjectification in clinical psychoanalytics). In: Rovaletti ML (ed) Temporalidad. El problema del tiempo en el pensamiento actual (Temporality. The problem of time in current thinking). Lugar Editorial, Bs. As., pp 271–282

Freud S Repression. In: The standard edition of complete psychological works of Sigmund Freud, vol 14. Hogarth Press, London, pp 141–158

Gieco L (2001) La memoria (Memory). Song. Available on 09/03/2023 at: https://youtu.be/nS6IWj3XJDQ

Greisch J (2001) Paul Ricoeur. L`itinerance du sens. Millon, Grenoble

Kordon D, Edelman L, Lagos D, Kersner D (2002a) Trauma social y psiquismo. Consecuencias clínicas de la violación de los derechos humanos (Social trauma and the psyche. Clinical consequences of the violation of human rights). In: Kersner D, Madariaga C (comp.), o.c., pp 85–100

Kordon D, Edelman L, Kersner D (2002b) Impacto psíquico y trasmisión inter y transgeneracional. In: Kersner, D & Madariaga C (comp.), Trauma social y psiquismo. Consecuencias clínicas de la violación de los derechos humanos (Social trauma and the psyche. Clinical consequences of the violation of human rights). In: Kersner D, Madariaga C (comp.), Paisajes del dolor, senderos de esperanza: salud mental y derechos humanos en el Cono Sur (Landscapes of Pain, paths to hope: mental health and human rights in the Southern Cone). Buenos Aires-Equipo de Trabajo e Investigación Psicosocial y Grupo Tortura Nunca Mais-Río de Janeiro. CINTRAS- SERSOC, pp 109–128

Levi P (2003) Si esto es un hombre (If this is a man). El Aleph, Barcelona

Lira Kornfeld E (ed) (1996) Reparación, Derechos Humanos y Salud Mental (Recovery, human rights and mental health). Ediciones ChileAmerica CESOC, Santiago de Chile

Martín A (2002) El fracaso del leteo o la imposibilidad del olvido (The failure of Lethe or the impossibility of forgetting). In: Kersner D, Madariaga C (comp.) o. c, pp 203–214

Martín Baró I (1998) Psicología de la Liberación (The psychology of liberation). Editorial Trotta, Madrid

Maury-Rouan C, Vion R (1994) Raconter sa souffrance: gestion interactive de la tension narrative. In: Jacques Bres (dir.) Le Récit oral, Montpellier, Université Paul-Valéry - Montpellier III, pp 215–226

Reyes Mate M (2003) En torno a una justicia anamnética (Regarding Anametic Justice). In: Mardones J, Reyes Mate M (eds) Laética ante las víctimas (The ethics of victims). Anthropos, Barcelona, pp 100–125

Reyes Mate M (2009) Justicia y memoria, la significación política de las víctimas (Justice and memory, the political significance for its victims). Nuestra Memoria (Bs. As.), Año XV, N° 32, pp 17–26

Ricoeur P (1983) Temps et Récit. L'intrigue et le récit historique. TR, I. Du Seuil, Paris

Ricoeur P (1985) Temps et Récit; Le temps raconté, vol III. Du Seuil, TR, III, Paris

Ricoeur P (1990) Soî-meme comme un autre. Du Seuil, Paris (SMA)

Ricoeur P (2000) La memoire, l'histoire, l'oubli. Seuil, Paris

Schapp W (1983) In Gewchichten verstrickt. Zum Sein von Mensch und Ding. V. Klostermannn, Frankfurt

Todorov T (2002) Memoria del mal, tentación del bien. Indagación sobre el siglo XX (The memory of evil, the temptation of good. An examination of the 20th century). Península, Barcelona

Vezzetti, H (2007) Conflictos de la memoria en la Argentina. Un estudio histórico de la memoria social. In: Anne Pérotin-Dumon (dir.) Historizar el pasado vivo en América Latina. Universidad Alberto Hurtado, Santiago de Chile, pp. 1-44. http://etica.uahurtado.cl/historizarelpasadovivo/es_contenido.php. Accessed 18 August 2013

Vezzetti H (2010) Sobre la violencia revolucionaria. Memorias y olvidos, de reciente aparición (Regarding revolutionary violence. Recently appeared memories and oblivion) (México, Ed. Siglo XXI); 2007 "Conflictos de la memoria en la Argentina. Un estudio histórico de la memoria social" (Conflicts of memory in Argentina). In Anne Pérotin-Dumon (dir.) Historizar el pasado vivo en América Latina (Writing the History of the Living Past in Latin America) (Santiago de Chile, Universidad Alberto Hurtado), o.c.: 1–44. Available on 18-08-2013 at: http://etica.uahurtado.cl/historizarelpasadovivo/es_contenido.php

Juridical Dignity and (Inter)subjectivity: Semiotic and Normative Levels

Ana Margarida Simões Gaudêncio

Abstract Conceived from the idea of human dignity, juridical dignity—as a condition and as a substrate for conferring the entitlement of rights and duties to a subject—faces nowadays decisive challenges both to its intentionality and to its content: once the human being ceases to be the constitutive basis of the conditions of possibility and meaning of the concept of Subject of Law, the intelligibility matrix of juridicity will be at stake, entailing a theoretical and practical shift in the characterization of juridical subjectivity and intersubjectivity—with the consequent obsolescence of the reciprocal recognition of personhood as a specific condition for juridicity, both as a discursive resource and, mostly, as a normative concept. In this regard, the meaning of Subject of Law will be reflected through a dialogue with the conceptions of Subject (Self-Person) presented by Jan Broekman and by Castanheira Neves.

1 Human Dignity and Juridical Dignity

Conceived from the idea of human dignity, juridical dignity represents a culturally traditional condition and substrate for conferring the entitlement of rights and duties to a subject. This is the starting point of the present reflection, mostly as the acknowledgment of the nowadays decisive challenges both to its intentionality and to its content: once the human being ceases to be the constitutive basis of the conditions of possibility and meaning of the concept of Subject of Law, that characterization of juridical subjectivity and intersubjectivity will be at stake, entailing a theoretical and practical shift in the intentionality and in the intelligibility matrix of juridicity.

The presently evident changes in the *atmosphere* of subjectivity crucially reflect on the sense of Subject of Law and on the expression *juridical subject*. Under such

A. M. S. Gaudêncio (✉)
Faculty of Law, University of Coimbra, Coimbra, Portugal

UCILeR – University of Coimbra, Institute for Legal Research, Coimbra, Portugal
e-mail: anagaude@fd.uc.pt; https://apps.uc.pt/mypage/faculty/anagaude

F. Fleerackers (ed.), *The Rearguard of Subjectivity*, Law and Visual Jurisprudence 9,
https://doi.org/10.1007/978-3-031-26855-7_11

circumstances, rethinking the significance of juridical dignity—both as a normative condition and as a semiotic tool for understanding its content and contours—aims at re-understanding the meaning of juridical subjectivity and intersubjectivity. Of course, considering human dignity as a *value* in the foundation of law requires distinguishing ahistorical-natural from historical-axiological constructions, on the one hand, and, consequently, on the other hand, moral and juridical conceptions of the origins of the content and meaning of human dignity in law, as well as its nature—as value or as rank.

1.1 Juridical Dignity and Juridical (Inter)subjectivity

Starting from a culturally constructed idea of human dignity—as value and as rank (Barak 2015; Waldron 2012, 2015)—, juridical dignity—as a condition and as the substrate for attributing ownership of rights and duties, on the one hand, and as a content protected by law, on the other hand—and juridical intersubjectivity—as the establishment and treatment of juridically relevant relationships—are currently facing decisive challenges both to their entitlement, their intentionality and their content. And this, especially with regard to diversely fragmented assimilations by the law within different *forms of life* (Wittgenstein 1953)—and their different environmental and cultural implications—and/or other forms of intelligence—in multiple, so-called post-human, conjugations. Such a consideration of the relations which are relevant to law, not only between people, but also between people in their different environments and with their different environments, aims at questioning the meanings of *subject* and of *object* of law(s), towards a plural consideration of the normatively based construction of the normativity of law.

The ubiquitous intervals(-gaps) between disaggregation and aggregation, and between non-identification and identification, threaten nowadays the delimitation of juridical intersubjectivity capable of stabilizing a notion of juridical responsibility on the basis of a recognizable centre of reference identified with a human being. There will be, in such scenarios, perhaps, phenomenona of *eccentricity*. On the one hand, as reaffirmations of identities, microscopically stated—though, plural in character...—by counter-hegemonic identifications of convictions compensating for the disaggregation of referents; and, on the other hand, as denials of differentiations, macroscopically—not always, however, hegemonic...—supported by the rejection of hegemonic identifications of aggregative convictions. The current ubiquitous gaps between disaggregation and aggregation and between non-identification and identification threaten the delimitation of juridical intersubjectivity as a stabilizing signifier to juridical responsibility based on a recognizable reference centre identified with a human being. Distinguishing humans and non-humans as juridical subjects implies decisive challenges to the intentionality and content of juridical dignity, subjectivity and intersubjectivity, specifically considered through an ethical-juridical sense of reciprocal recognition. And, therefore, assuming that this reciprocal recognition of a specific sense of human dignity is understood in the civilizational context of law—then, historically presupposing both the notions of community and of society as origins of the qualities of human subjects of law in relation.

1.2 Juridical Subjects, Subjectivity and Intersubjectivity Within the Validity *of Law*

Considering law, in the occidental civilizational circumscribed experience, as a complex normative network—presupposing foundational sedimented valuations, expressed through a special language, with very different *signifier* and *signified* signs, and specific requirements for the self-understanding of man in time and space, as to the conformation of praxis—, the necessary answer of rules to a technological and globalized society should not obviate the pertinence of the possibility of the an axiologically filtered and specifically historically-spatially determined juridical sense, conferring to law an independent place in the immense ocean of discourses.

In this regard, the meaning of the expression Subject of Law will be reflected through a dialogue between two specific conceptions of Subject—the conception of the Self as proposed by Jan Broekman (2011, 2019) and the notion of the Person as presented by Castanheira Neves (2002, 2013). Such a reflection will mostly consider the reciprocal recognition of personhood as a specific condition for juridicity and rethink the significance of juridical dignity beyond that reciprocal recognition.

Regarding the contemporary dematerialization of social relations and of their subjects, the atomizations of intersubjectivity are illustrated in multiple scenarios as paradoxical deconstructions of subjectivities. As if, in a critical-reflexive retrospectivity, individuality would overshadow personality. And this, within a political point of view, as the participation in the *polis*, on the one hand; but also, on the other hand, as a consequence of the recognition of a person from a specifically juridical point of view, and thus, as a *subject* of law. As if the entire cultural construction which generated reciprocal recognition as the source of intersubjectivity, in general, and juridical intersubjectivity, in particular, would have glimpsed in (a)critical spraying... Such a *recognition* of the human being as a Person—understood as an axiological acquis, with but still beyond the biological structure—, constitutes, then, for Castanheira Neves, the "ethical imperative of the law" (Neves 2002, p. 866).

All this can only make sense through a *reciprocal recognition* between persons, of the *person* as a subject of non-eliminable ethical dignity. From such a statement, two main implications will follow—as axiological and normative inferences, that is, as conditions of axiological and normatively essential possibility to the constitution of law: first, the principle of equality and, second, the principle of responsibility. And this within two main presuppositions: first, the human-*person* originally presented as *the* subject of rights and duties (Neves 2002, p. 867); and, second, the understanding of law as *validity* (Neves 2002, p. 868; Neves 2013). Posing a basic intersubjective alternative for building the validity and objectivity of law, not built on a heteronomy of determination of objectively assimilated validity but on an autonomous intersubjectively rooted valuation—which transforms it into a specific and indispensable dimension of human practice, in order to mobilize a self-transcendence of meaning—or even a practical-cultural transcendentality—as an essential referent, allowing it to react, with the normatively adequate movement, at the pragmatically agglutinating speed of practice (Neves 2003, pp. 146–147).

Therefore, law, within a cultural context in which it constitutes a comparative intersubjectivity and a corresponding tertiality, represents an axiological and culturally constructed experience of these types of subjectivity and intersubjectivity. Such an axiological, cultural and constitutive construction of juridical subjectivity and intersubjectivity, as well as their realization, constitute the foundations of a materially autonomous sense and meaning of law (Neves 2002, pp. 869–870; Neves 2008a, pp. 10–14; Neves 2008b; Linhares 2008, pp. 426–427; Linhares 2012; Marques 2009, p. 566; Gaudêncio 2020a, b).

2 For a Reconstruction of the Relationship Between Juridical Dignity and Human Dignity, Within Difference and Recognition

Such configurations of subjectivity, and, consequently, of intersubjectivity—and, within it, of the substantive meanings and of the consequent structural boundaries of juridicity—will then be taken as cornerstones of a reconstruction of the meaning for juridical dignity. Here, different compensatory phenomena will be observed... which will imply, at least, two centrifugal oscillating movements, or, perhaps, in centripetal engagements, or, potentially, on a collision course... on the one hand, of microscopically re-affirming differences as identities—not all, however, plural...—enunciated through counter-hegemonic identifications of compensatory convictions of disaggregation of referents; and, on the other hand, of denials of differences, macroscopically—notwithstanding, not always hegemonically...—sustained through the rejection of hegemonic identifications of aggregating convictions (Gaudêncio 2012)... And as such taken here as *object*, as a result of the current observation of the hypertrophy of subjectivity, in a growing axiological and social disaggregation, in the context of intersubjectivity—whether microscopically or macroscopically projected. In an accentuation of *differences* which elevates the possibilities of *forms of life*, perhaps even with the affirmation of *difference* as a practical standard in the experience of intersubjectivity. *Difference*, whose meanings are here multiplied in terms of options, of discourses and of deviations of convictions, always in relation to the *other*, who, as *another*, in his/her *otherness*, is different, and different insofar as found itself in relation. A *difference* actually also *in discourse*, which immediately manifests itself in *correlation*, as in *nested opposition*—in the words of Jack Balkin (1990)—, of reciprocally imbricated *signifier* and *signified*.[1] Fixing this, from the outset, as proposed by Jacques Derrida (1972, 1994), on difference-*différénce* as only intelligible exactly in relation, and therefore dependent on deference-*déférence*, in reciprocal connection, and while in relation, *différance*.[2] And *difference* to be understood, on the other hand, in the reading which Jacques Derrida offers of Martin Heidegger, as *Unterschied*, *Differenz*, but also *Austrag*, and even *diaphora*. And, thus, a *difference* which—in its *différance*—is also and simultaneously *relation*-relationship. A relationship that implies reporting, referring to something-other, and, simultaneously, taking (-carrying), taking the other, *tragen* and *austragen*, *taking-bringing* which also implies taking with and carrying out[3]... But *difference* also as an *obstacle* and an effective *absence* of dialogue, in a register of *impossibility of communication*. Thus,

[1] See Balkin (1990, 1994a, b), p. 1152. "When we deconstruct conceptual oppositions like public and private, we are not necessarily trying to show that they form a false dichotomy. We are trying to show that they form a *nested opposition*. A nested opposition is a conceptual opposition in which the two terms "contain" each other." (Balkin 2005, p. 729). See also Linhares (2004), pp. 97–98, n. 89, and Gaudêncio (2013), pp. 110–122, 142–147, 177–190, 262–270.

[2] "(...) la différence marquée dans la "différ()nce" entre le *e* et le *a* se dérobe au regard et à l'écoute, cela suggère peut-être heureusement qu'il faut ici se laisser renvoyer à un ordre qui n'appartient plus à la sensibilité. (...) L'ordre qui résiste à cette opposition, et lui résiste parce qu'il la porte, s'annonce dans un mouvement de différance, (avec un *a*) (...)." (Derrida 1972 ("La Différance"), pp. 1–29, p. 5).

[3] "(...) als Hören der Stimme des Freundes, den jedes Dasein bei sich trägt." (Heidegger 1927, § 34, p. 163, the motto to Derrida's *"L'oreille de Heidegger. Philopolémologie (Geschlecht IV)"*). See also Derrida (1994), pp. 341–419. And, specifically on *tragen*: "Mais que veut dire «porter» *(tragen)* dans ce cas? porter non pas au sens de porter en soi, comporter, mais porter près de soi *(bei sich)*, porter sans porter, porter l'autre? (...) Pour commencer à lire la portée de ce *«Tragen»* avec la gravité qu'il appelle, il ne faudrait rien négliger de l'attention pensante que Heidegger accorde à la sémantique allemande du *Tragen* (...), puisqu'il ne s'agit de rien *de* moins que la différence, de l'un des noms qu'il donne à la différence *(Unter-schied* ou *Differenz)*, à savoir *Austrag*." (Derrida 1994, p. 347). "Et plus loin, toujours dans *Die Sprache*, suivant encore le motif du *Geviert* qui rassemble (...) *das Dingen der Dinge*, Heidegger s'avance dans l'espace qui rapporte ou réfère *Tragen* à *Austragen* comme portée, gestation, mise au monde conduisant à terme ou à la naissance, et à *Austrag* comme différence ou *diaphorá*. La *diaphorá* signifie à la fois la différence *(Unterschied)* mais aussi le différend, le dis- par lequel on *se porte* de côté on s'écarte en *s'emportant* dans le discord. Dans *diaphorá*, comme dans rapport, référence, différence, il y a référence à la férence, à la portée, au *phérō* grec ou au *fero* latin, à *diaphérō* (je diffère, je sépare et je porte jusqu'au bout)." (Derrida 1994, p. 349). "Or l'autre nom de ce qui porte le monde au monde et à terme dans l'*Austrag*, c'est l'unité ou l'intimité rassemblée de la dif-férence *(Unter-Schied* que Heidegger écrit ici en deux mots) ou de la *diaphorá*." (Derrida 1994, p. 349). "La sémantique allemande du *Tragen, Austrag, nachträglich,* que nous suivons ici comme problématique de l'*Unter-Schied* ou de la différence et que je cherche à traduire dans la sémantique latine du *port,* du *rapport,* de la *relation,* de la *portée,* du *porter à terme,* du *comportement,* etc., en vue de problématiser et de mieux interroger la phrase de *Sein und Zeit* que nous ne perdons pas de vue *(das Hören der Stimme des Freundes, den jedes Dasein bei sich trägt)*, Heidegger tend à vouloir la protéger, justement, contre une certaine latinisation." (Derrida 1994, p. 351). "Il marque que tout ce qu'*«Unter-Schied»* n'est pas, tout ce dont on doit soigneusement distinguer de l'*«Unter-Schied»* se dit en latin: *«Der Unter-Schied ist weder Distinktion noch Relation»:* «L'*Unter-Schied* n'est ni distinction ni relation»." (Derrida 1994, p. 352).

perhaps, turning now to Jean-François Lyotard (1979, 1983), above all, in difference as *differend*—*irreconcilable* (language) conflict due to the impossibility of mobilizing a *rule* capable of transposing the *incommunicability-incommensurability* between *genres of discourse*, incommensurable in terms of specifically the respective *phrase regimens*.[4] An understanding of *difference* pertinent in terms of *discourse deviations*—even if *apparent*—, convoking the (im)possibility of fixing substantial meaning, and as a search for the respective fixation *among the discourses*. And difference, besides, also understood in the sense of expression of divergence of options or *forms of life*, of *deviation* from some *normality* or *normalities* (Galeotti 2002). [5] Sometimes arousing direct, sometimes indirect, *opposition*, sometimes even *indifference*, sometimes even *tolerance*, as omission of the opposition to what is *different*, from which one disagrees and against which one could potentially react. Which inexorably poses a fundamental question, after all, perhaps, utopian, on tolerance—that Michael Walzer, exemplarily, enunciates in the following way: "What exactly do we do when we tolerate difference?" (Walzer 1997, p. 13).

Recognition and tolerance constitute deeply distinct notions and contents. The recognition of the difference will imply, from the outset, on a pre-juridical point—even a trans-juridical point (moral, or ethical, for instance...)—, admitting the *other* as *different*, in order to reasonably decide on the position to be taken in face of such difference. Therefore, recognition may underly tolerance, thus constituting a true presupposition of tolerance, insofar as the former will be relevant in the fundamental substantiation of intersubjectivity—and, so, assumed as reciprocal recognition, under such conditions. Which will also imply, in this approach, a relationship which may conform to it as a *translation*, in the sense proposed by James Boyd White (1990).[6] And, consequently, understood as a set of practices capable of constituting a standard of justice, in the awareness of the impossibility of completely understanding the other—a practice that will mean translation as integration, in the sense that it also implies, per se, tolerance.

[4]"L'incommensurabilité, au sens de l'hétérogénéité des régimes de phrases et de l'impossibilité de les soumettre à une même loi (sauf à les neutraliser) (...). L'incommensurabilité affecte-t-elle la relation entre les régimes de phrases ou la relation entre les genres de discours? – A chaque régime de phrase correspond un mode de présentation d'un univers de phrase. Un genre de discours inspire un mode d'enchaînement des phrases les unes avec les autres, ces phrases pouvant être de régime différent." (Lyotard 1983, p. 187). See also Lyotard (1979) and Drolet (1994).

[5]"Since the 'different' is by definition what diverges from 'the normal' the 'different' shares the semantic ambiguity of 'normal', which vacillates between a descriptive and a normative use." (Galeotti 2002, p. 91).

[6]"(...) the activity I call 'translation' – making texts in response to others while recognizing the impossibility of full comprehension or reproduction – becomes a set of practices that can serve as an ethical and political model for the law and, beyond it, as a standard of justice." (White 1990, p. 258). "Translation is thus a species of what in the opening chapter I called 'integration': putting two things together in such a way as to make a third, a new thing with a meaning of its own." (White 1990, p. 263. See also pp. 3–4 (1. «*Intellectual Integration*», pp. 3–21).

Intrinsically ambiguous, not allowing for a compartmentalized characterization, despite the recognition in it of different facets, tolerance, as a category of intelligibility, roams—in search of its transcendental conditions, foundation, rationality, subjects, objects and objectives—among different domains of human practice: religion, ethics, philosophy... In a convergence of meanings that, despite with varied accentuations, contributes to the establishment of a clear and specific meaning of what this category is, in theoretical determination, and how it should operate, in its practical dimension—there would be no tolerance unless at the confluence of those multiple meanings (Gaudêncio 2019, pp. 108–142, 350–437).

If the juridical valuation of socially interfering behaviours (and the materially underlying *meaning* of them) ceases to reside in the axis of *relativization* and *comparability* of the corresponding subjects—thus, presupposing *difference*, and therefore, *diversity*, and, when so, allowing for, at least, *tolerance* (Broekman 2011, pp. 182–185 and 187–194; Wagner and Bhatia 2009, pp. 1–7; Gaudêncio 2016, 2019, pp. 35–40, 143–169, 437–442, 629–635)—, there will be not only a change in the positioning of the defining line of juridical intersubjectivity, but an effective change of *meaning* of juridicity itself... with a *displacement effect*—more, perhaps, than a *décentrement effect*, which would represent a linguistic expression of a positioning of the subject that would bear a specific cultural heritage, expressively and impressively, in which a presupposed *centre* would be *decentred.* And, thus, subjectively and objectively opening a radically new space to the substantialization and delimitation of what is a *subject of law* (Broekman 2011, 2019, specially ch. 5, 6). Actually, the reciprocal recognition of personhood as a specific condition for juridicity may become obsolete, both as a discursive resource and, and mostly, as a normative concept.

As a semiotic resource, and considering Broekman's proposal (Broekman 2019), once the *subject* is a growingly plural reference, meaning a plurally *signified* within a singular *signifier*, its cultural content and semiotic role respectively represent the construction of a set of *meanings* and of the *rationale* of intersubjectivity (Broekman 2019, pp. 135–171). As the construction of a set of *meanings*, signifying that there shall now be included the countless discourses on crucial identity elements—meaning the uniqueness of each one, in the specific characteristics naturally presented and culturally achieved, and the pertinence to a community or group. And, consequently, as the construction of the *rationale* of intersubjectivity, signifying that the element subject is the cellule and the condition of possibility of relationship, and, so, of intersubjectivity. Which represents the consciousness of the relational structure of the subject, and requires the understanding of its constitution and content in a pluralistic scenario as the one we contemporarily are immersed in. This is a first step for the comprehension of the multiple possible correspondence between the meanings and contents of the Self—and the relationship between I and Self—and those of the Person, as subjects, on the one hand, and, on the other hand, for the comprehension of the similarities and of the differences between these two *signs*—in *signifier* and *signified*—, and their practical consequences, both in culture in general, and, especially, in law (Broekman 2011; Broekman and Backer 2013, ch. 11, 12; Broekman and Backer 2015, pp. 141–145).[7]

As a normative concept, in fact, juridical *subjectivity*, and *intersubjectivity*, presupposing a dialectic between a pole of *suum*—of autonomy—and a pole of *commune*—of responsibility—, now following the proposal of Castanheira Neves (Neves 2012, p. 16; Neves 1995, pp. 415–416), require, among human juridical subjects, that reciprocal recognition. Such a dialectic, and, thus, the sense and the borders of the juridicity it weaves together, when admitting other kind of subjects of law, will have to be, at least, re-equated, both in the meaning and in the content of the reciprocal protection and requirement ascribed to the subjects of law—something (since) always debatable, and debated. . .—, or as to what can be assumed as juridical dignity, on the one hand, in correspondence-analogy with human dignity. Or, on the other hand, if/when in the absence of such a referent—insofar as the requirements of valuation presuppose different instantiations—, establishing totally different meanings and contents to the ownership of rights and duties and the repositioning of the respective material and formal limits. In such a shift, the core question will not be establishing the criteria to recognize juridical personality to non-human beings, namely to artificial intelligence constituents, but to human beings.

So, if we start from the configuration of juridical subjectivity as an expression of the Self, in its atmosphere and in its contextual meaning, on the one hand, and the notion of Person, within the reciprocal recognition it entails, we shall re-propose the meaning of the juridical subject as a substantial core and as a tool of understanding, in order to look for the practical and normative consequences of the establishment of new subjectivities in juridical practice—from other animal species to vegetables, on the one hand, and to artificial intelligence, on the other.

The *paradigm* remains, for now, in *being a person*, as, furthermore, it means, first, personhood, and, then, personality. . . Such a juridical personhood—and then, juridical personality—is specifically taken here in the *sense* proposed by that reciprocal recognition, presupposing a civilizational *sense* of human dignity (Dupré 2015; Barak 2015; Waldron 2012, 2015). Which means an axiologically-culturally created element, constitutive of juridical subjectivity and

[7] "Emphasis on the engenderment as a condition for human identity has its general and in particular philosophical implications. They focus, as said in the introductory remarks, the drive of Occidental culture to give priority to dissection, fragmentation, analysis or atomizing instead of a view on the process, the unfolding or the entirety of reality around us. This is of greatest importance for any philosophy of law, who only seems to be possible as analysis or dissection as a basis for articulation of laws and legal discourses. But we are now confronted with the fact that relationships between I and Self are extremely essential for the wiring of the discourse of Law in its entirety, as it may be for all types of discourses, eventually in all languages and cultures. Today, we are careful not to claim global conclusions, but exactly with the I-Self relation as a central datum, we could venture that from here *all* human discourses unfold—as indeed Plato suggested from his cultural viewpoint. This would give even more credit to Welby's reflections on I and Self, as if they were foreshadowing Lacan's intuitions." (Broekman and Backer 2015, p. 144).

intersubjectivity—and of their settlement (Neves 2002, 2009). Whilst the condition to be a subject of law presupposes *being a person*, and, therefore, a human being—or a collective composition of human beings—, that will constitute the fundamentally measuring characteristic of the quality of holder of juridical subjective rights and duties. This is a crucially prior question, which will correspond, consequently—provided the dogmatically constructed requirements—, to the construction of the meaning of juridical personality, and, within it, of the ability to enjoy and to act within juridical subjective rights, and, concomitantly, to the accomplishment of juridical duties—, implying the identification of a rational centre of imputation, traditionally assumed in an element of the human species. When/if the subject of law is not necessarily a person—or a collective of persons—, it is not just an alternative sense of juridicity that will be at stake. There will then be a remarkably different sense of intersubjectivity itself—not just juridical, in particular, but also social, in general... An intersubjectivity sense in which personality would no longer entirely lead, but which would be developed in a gradation of rational imputation centres—thus allowing for selection among beings, whether humans and non-humans, as more and as less capable of intellection and of construction of autonomous reasoning and decision (Gaudêncio 2020a, b).

The normatively constitutive continuum within the *suum/commune* dialectic, and, concomitantly, its semiotic effects, requiring bilaterality, comparability and tertiality as contextually constitutive characteristics of juridicity, project the essential discussion on the (de)limitation of responsibility to the fundamental stage of normative principles, and, consequently, to the critical-reflective stage of the limits of the law (Neves 2009). Correspondingly, those propositions express the dialectic and dialogic construction and reconstruction intersubjectively contextualized by the fundamentals of delimitation of the intersubjectivity interval concerning juridicity. Which means setting the fundamental conditions of possibility for determining such constitutive dimensions, on the one hand, of the subjects of law, and on the other, of the practically and normatively adequate meaning(s) and content(s) for assimilating a correspondently specific sense of equality and of responsibility—substantially and formally inherent to the law, as the frontiers of reciprocal demandability, and, therefore, practically-normatively and reflexively-dialectically constituting juridical intersubjectivity, presupposing juridical dignity.

References

Balkin J (1990) Nested oppositions. Yale Law J 99:1669–1705

Balkin J (1994a) Being just with deconstruction. Soc Leg Stud:393–404

Balkin J (1994b) Transcendental deconstruction, transcendent justice. Mich Law Rev 92(5): 1131–1186

Balkin J (2005) Deconstruction's legal career. Cardozo Law Rev 27(2):719–740

Barak A (2015) Human dignity. The constitutional value and the constitutional right. Cambridge University Press, Cambridge

Broekman J (2011) Signs, diversity, and tolerance: a review article. J Comp Law 6:169–208

Broekman J (2019) Rethinking law and language. The Flagship 'Speech'. Elgar
Broekman J, Backer L (2013) Lawyers making meaning: the semiotics of law in legal education II. Springer
Broekman J, Backer L (2015) Editorial 5: I and Self (Welby, Lacan). In: Broekman J, Backer L (eds) Signs in law – a source book: the semiotics of law in legal education II. Springer, pp 141–145
Derrida J (1972) Marges de la Philosophie. Minuit, Paris
Derrida J (1994) Politiques de l'amitié. Galilée, Paris
Drolet M (1994) The wild and the sublime: Lyotard's post-modern politics. Polit Stud XLII(2): 259–273
Dupré C (2015) The age of dignity. Human rights and constitutionalism in Europe. Hart, Oxford and Portland
Galeotti AE (2002) Toleration as recognition. Cambridge University Press, Cambridge
Gaudêncio AM (2012) From centrifugal teleology to centripetal axiology(?): (In)adequacy of the movement of law to the velocity of Praxis. Boletim da Faculdade de Direito da Universidade de Coimbra LXXXVIII(I):91–103
Gaudêncio AM (2013) Entre o centro e a periferia. Lumen Juris, Rio de Janeiro
Gaudêncio AM (2016) Fraternity and tolerance as juridical boundaries. Boletim da Faculdade de Direito da Universidade de Coimbra XCII(II):849–865
Gaudêncio AM (2019) O intervalo da tolerância nas fronteiras da juridicidade: fundamentos e condições de possibilidade da projecção jurídica de uma (re)construção normativamente substancial da exigência de tolerância. Instituto Jurídico da Faculdade de Direito da Universidade de Coimbra, Coimbra
Gaudêncio AM (2020a) "Jurisdictional realization of law" as Judicium: a methodological alternative, beyond deductive application and finalistic decision. Int J Semiot Law 33(1):133–146
Gaudêncio AM (2020b) Responsabilidade como princípio e limite(s) da(s) intersubjectividade (s) jurídica(s): reflexões em torno da proposta de Castanheira Neves. Revista de Direito da Responsabilidade 2:771–790
Heidegger M (1927) Sein und Zeit (Max Niemeyer, Tübingen 1979)
Linhares JMA (2004) O logos da juridicidade sob o fogo cruzado do ethos e do pathos – da convergência com a literatura (Law as literature, literature as law) à analogia com uma poiêsis-technê de realização (Law as musical and dramatic performance). Boletim da Faculdade de Direito da Universidade de Coimbra LXXX:59–135
Linhares JMA (2008) A "abertura ao futuro" como dimensão do problema do direito": um "correlato" da pretensão de autonomia? In: Nunes AA et al (coord) O Direito e o Futuro. O Futuro do Direito. Coimbra, Almedina, pp 391–429
Linhares JMA (2012) Law's cultural project and the claim to universality or the equivocalities of a familiar debate. Int J Semiot Law 25(4):489–503
Lyotard JF (1979) La condition postmoderne: rapport sur le savoir. Minuit, Paris
Lyotard JF (1983) Le Différend. Minuit, Paris
Marques MR (2009) A dignidade humana como prius axiomático. In: Andrade MC et al (org) Estudos em Homenagem ao Prof. Doutor Jorge de Figueiredo Dias IV. Coimbra Editora, Coimbra, pp 541–566
Neves AC (1995) O princípio da legalidade criminal. O seu problema jurídico e o seu critério dogmático. In: Digesta – Escritos acerca do Direito, do pensamento jurídico, da sua metodologia e outros I. Coimbra Editora, Coimbra, pp 349–473
Neves AC (2002) Coordenadas de uma reflexão sobre o problema universal do Direito – ou as condições da emergência do Direito como Direito. In: Ramos RMM et al (org) Estudos em homenagem à Professora Doutora Isabel de Magalhães Collaço II. Coimbra, Almedina, pp 837–871
Neves AC (2003) A crise actual da Filosofia do Direito no contexto da crise global da Filosofia. Tópicos para a possibilidade de uma reflexiva reabilitação. STVDIA IVRIDICA 72. Coimbra Editora, Coimbra

Neves AC (2008a) O direito interrogado pelo tempo presente na perspectiva do futuro. In: Nunes AA et al (coord) O Direito e o Futuro. O Futuro do Direito. Coimbra, Almedina, pp 9–82
Neves AC (2008b) O problema da universalidade do direito – ou o direito hoje, na diferença e no encontro humano-dialogante das culturas. In: Digesta – Escritos acerca do Direito, do pensamento jurídico, da sua metodologia e outros III. Coimbra Editora, Coimbra, pp 101–128
Neves AC (2009) Pensar o direito num tempo de perplexidade. In: Dias AS et al (org) Liber Amicorum de José de Sousa e Brito, em comemoração do 70.° Aniversário. Coimbra, Almedina, pp 3–28
Neves AC (2012) Uma reconstituição do sentido do direito – na sua autonomia, nos seus limites, nas suas alternativas. Revista da Faculdade de Direito da Universidade Lusófona do Porto 1(1)
Neves AC (2013) O direito como validade: a validade como categoria jurisprudencialista. Revista da Faculdade de Direito da Universidade Federal do Ceará 34(2):39–76
Wagner A, Bhatia VK (2009) The international dual nature of law: tolerance and diversity. In: Wagner A, Bhatia VK (eds) Diversity and tolerance in socio-legal contexts: explorations in the semiotics of law. Farnham, Burlington
Waldron J (2012) Dignity, rank, and rights. Oxford University Press, Oxford, New York
Waldron J (2015) Is dignity the foundation of human rights? In: Cruft R et al (eds) Philosophical foundations of human rights. Oxford University Press, Oxford, pp 117–137
Walzer M (1997) On toleration. Yale University Press, New Haven/London
White JB (1990) Justice as translation. The University of Chicago Press, Chicago/London
Wittgenstein L (1953) Philosophische Untersuchungen/Philosophical investigations (trans: Anscombe GEM). Blackwell, Oxford

The Performance of (the Declaration of) Independence

Political Theatricality in 1776 and Beyond

Klaas Tindemans

Abstract This essay analyzes the American Declaration of Independence (1776) as a performative speech act, in a double sense, linguistically and performatively. This foundational act of the first transatlantic republic performs the independence of the thirteen colonies, by making the leap from constituted power—referring to 'we, the people', the source of sovereignty—to constituent power. This is a radical perlocutionary speech-act, as Hannah Arendt and others observe. But the 'founding fathers' could only perform this revolution by making use of 'natural acting', by their awareness of the theatricality of their actions. The Declaration of Independence could be politically successful through the acknowledgment of the performative and openly theatrical character of its expression. This successful performance created the nation, or even 'we, the people' as a political community. Even if the theatrical illusion is upheld that the people made the independent nation, the founding fathers knew—skilled actors/politicians as they were—that it was the other way round: the declaration made the people.

Years ago, I asked theatre students to read the Declaration of Independence, as a dramaturgical exercise. I asked to read it as a performance text, not as a document with considerable historical and political value. They cut up the text, they restructured it, as if it was a chorus of an ancient Greek tragedy. They highlighted certain phrases, took them out of context and confronted them with contemporary material. As a result, decontextualized sentences such as "for the sole purpose of fatiguing them into compliance with his measures" and "to harass our people, and eat out their substance"[1] are framing a long description of the so-called 'enhanced interrogation techniques'—the euphemism of the Bush-administration for torture

[1] National Archives (2022).

K. Tindemans (✉)
RITCS | Royal Institute for Theatre, Cinema & Sound (Erasmus Brussels University of Applied Sciences and Arts), Brussels, Belgium
e-mail: klaas.tindemans@ehb.be

F. Fleerackers (ed.), *The Rearguard of Subjectivity*, Law and Visual Jurisprudence 9,
https://doi.org/10.1007/978-3-031-26855-7_12

on ‘unlawful combatants’, i.e. their enemies in the war on terror.[2] The contrast between the bureaucratic harassments these words of Thomas Jefferson decry in dramatic terms and the harsh reality of waterboarding, prolonged sleep deprivation, sensory deprivation and sensory bombardment—to name but a few techniques—resulted in an exercise of ‘counter-rhetoric’. One might suggest that a performative transformation produces clearer insights than an academic close reading or a deconstructive analysis of the Declaration of the Independence of 1776. This is a point indeed, but not the one I will try to make here. The pedagogical exercise was meant to confront a political text—probably the most influential foundational text of North-Atlantic political history—with a series of rhetorical gestures, sometimes radically critical, sometimes mildly ironical. It was not a gratuitous performance, since the Declaration of Independence itself is essentially a rhetorical and a performative effort, starting with Thomas Jefferson’s draft. As a performative event, it could be approached from two different angles: as a constituting act, and as a theatrical act.

The Declaration of Independence is a ‘performative speech act’ or, more precisely, a ‘perlocutionary speech act’, as JL Austin calls it: a speech act with necessary real consequences in the real world.[3] Both the nature of the Declaration, as a rebellious act, and its tremendous impact, its ‘real consequences in the real world’ have turned this event into a cornerstone of political and, more specifically, constitutional theory. The Declaration of Independence raised, almost explicitly, the central question of the relationship between constituent power, constituted power and authority, an issue that remains relevant in our post-political times.[4] It is also the key subject in Hannah Arendt’s ground-breaking study of the political nature of revolution as an historical phenomenon—United States of America 1776, France 1789.[5]

The Declaration of Independence can also be approached as a performative event in a more theatrical sense. Many aspects of the ‘fabrication’ of the Declaration should be understood in the context of eighteenth century cultural practices—practices which were, seen from a cultural-historical point of view, in a process of structural transformation: rhetorical skills, acting practices, the role of the audience, the relationship between text and delivery. Performative practices, such as rituals and mimicries, are often deployed, most often not deliberately, to bridge the gaps in profound societal change. The emancipation of the thirteen colonies constitutes such a change, and the performance of the Declaration of Independence, as a linguistic speech act and as a performative action, corresponds to that function. But its performative character and impact reaches beyond the simple speech act. Anyhow, this act/action reduces the complexity of the process of bourgeois emancipation and

[2]These techniques were based upon the so-called SERE (Survival, Evasion, Resistance, Escape) program of the US Department of Defense, a program of counter-interrogation for the military (Human Rights Watch 2011, p. 23). See also Ralph (2013), pp. 114–135.

[3]Austin (1975), pp. 117–118; Searle (1969), p. 25.

[4]Lindahl (2007), pp. 485–505.

[5]Arendt (1990), pp. 141–178.

political independence, it 'surrogates', in the terms of Joseph Roach, [6] the contradictory and often suppressed tendencies that lead to the iconic event of declaring independence.

1 Performing a Constitution

Hannah Arendt situates the revolutions of the late eighteenth century in the context of an important paradigmatic shift that started with early Modernity.[7] The early Modern theory of the 'King's Two Bodies', developed during the Renaissance and radically implemented during the English Civil War,[8] implied already a source of sovereignty apart from divine legitimacy, by dividing kingship between a contingent physical embodiment—the actual king—and an eternal dynasty, royal domain and *auctoritas*. Early Modern absolutism kept the link with theology, in its philosophical analogies and in the demi-god status of the monarch, but the French revolution replaced this royal sovereignty with the sovereignty of the nation. Although Robespierre, following Jean-Jacques Rousseau,[9] makes it clear that this nation of *citoyens* cannot exist with the cult of a 'supreme being', the analogy with classical political theology can be seen as purely formal or symbolic. The early ideologue of the French Revolution, abbé Sieyès, saw the Nation as the source of sovereignty as the sole constituent, and thus as the direct successor to royal, absolutist sovereignty.[10] For Arendt, the continuity of the French state, in its necessity to point out a place of absolute sovereignty—even in a symbolic way—marks a meaningful difference with the American Revolution. The 'founding fathers' didn't fight an absolute, the British regime was already a 'limited government'. The colonial regime was already based on a series of balances between discretionary power and rule of law. As Caroline Winterer explains, the ideas of 'enlightened' government, including the reference to Montesquieu's famous separation of powers, circulated widely on both sides of the Atlantic.[11] The framers of the American constitution designed a construction that fully reflected this spirit.[12] This starting position doesn't explain the difference in

[6] Joseph Roach defines 'surrogation' as follows: "A performance offers a substitute for something that pre-exists in it. It stands in for an elusive entity that it is not but that it must vainly aspire both to embody and to replace." Roach (1996), pp. 2–4.

[7] Arendt (1990), pp. 154–165.

[8] The distinction between the 'body politic' and the 'body physic' of the (English) king, allowed the Parliament to revolt against a king who, allegedly, had cut himself of from a Parliament that considered itself as an inseparable part of the 'body politic' (Kantorowicz 1957/2016, p. 20).

[9] Rousseau (1762/2014), pp. 156–163.

[10] Sieyès (1989/1988), pp. 11–146.

[11] Winterer also notes that Montesquieu's (smaller) chapter on slavery was the most debated part of his book, in British America, as it exposed basic ambiguities of enlightened thought (Winterer 2016, p. 153).

[12] Arendt (1990), p. 157.

solidity of the revolutionary outcome, but it creates a different context, i.e. a context in which the distinction between *constituent* and *constituted* power is a crucial element in the rhetoric, the dramaturgy and the theatrics of the Declaration of Independence as an event. The leap from 'constituting' to 'constituted'—the escape from Sieyès' vicious circle, as Arendt puts it[13]—is probably the most perlocutionary speech act thinkable, at least in the political domain.

For Bonnie Honig, the crucial contribution of Hannah Arendt to political theory is her claim for an distinct realm for political action, a literal and metaphorical space for 'public liberty'.[14] A space defined both against the idea of sovereignty—with its theological heritage—and, quite arguably, against the idea of 'biopolitics', the Foucault paradigm.[15] The iconic action to provide such a space is the American Declaration of Independence which, in Arendt's eyes, clears the ground for the subsequent Constitution, with its accent on the institutional, federalist framework. It is structurally important, Arendt underlines, that the Bill of Rights is the first amendment to the Constitution: the institutional building comes first, the subjective rights of the citizens are the second issue.[16] The French Revolution followed the inverse logic, with the dramatic consequences we all know. So, it is perfectly understandable that Arendt's—and Honig's—attention focuses on the foundational action, the performance of declaring independence. Precisely the strong performative character of the American Declaration of Independence, in its very phrasing, makes it an argument to start political action, to create a framework for public liberty. But at the same time, the sentence "we hold these truths to be self-evident" is highly ambiguous, as a performative speech act. The reference to "self-evident truths" is a *constative* speech act,[17] actually a reference to the aforementioned "laws of nature" and nature's God, and per se not political. It is the verbal form "we hold" that transforms "these truths" into a performative, and thus in a political statement.[18] Since the Declaration requires an audience, present and future, as it is the very constituent act of the polity itself, it cannot exist but as a performative if it claims *potestas*, as Spinoza calls the power of subsistence of a given political order.[19] The question is however, says Honig, if the suppression of the constative aspect, its reference to truths outside the act of constitution itself, solves the theoretical problem of the foundation, as Arendt seems to expect (or to wish)—the preamble should be

---

[13] Arendt (1990), pp. 183–184.

[14] Honig (1993), pp. 79–83.

[15] Michel Foucault uses the term (or its corollary, 'bio power', *bio-pouvoir*) to explain a shift from a regime of political control on abstract subjects towards politic control and discipline on physical bodies: he sees this evolution as a fundamental characteristic of capitalism and (neo)liberalism (Foucault 2004, pp. 3–6).

[16] Arendt (1990), pp. 133–134.

[17] 'Constative' speech acts are, in Austin's terms, utterances that report a fact—true, untrue or nonsensical—which are not intended to have material consequences in the real world, in contrast with 'performative' speech acts (Austin 1975, pp. 2–3).

[18] Honig (1993), pp. 99–100.

[19] Terpstra (2011), p. 32.

sufficient.[20] The pure performative character of the Declaration should, in Arendt's eyes, provide security against the tendency, of any revolution, to imitate the structure of legitimacy of the previous regime—as Sieyès did by replacing the kingship with the nation as source of sovereignty. The Americans however created a different kind of authority, i.e. a self-referential rule of law within an appropriate institutional framework. Jacques Derrida, in his comprehensive analysis of the act of signing of the Declaration of Independence,[21] sheds a light on the problem. He makes clear that it makes no sense to try to get out of Sieyès' vicious circle. A constituted power should exist without reference to its founder, but the foundation itself cannot exist without a signature. The health of the institution depends, one could argue, on its capacity to mourn for and to commemorate the lost signer(s).[22] But who is/ are this/ those signer(s)? Thomas Jefferson was the 'draftsman', but he didn't sign as an editor, only as a representative. He acted as a secretary of the content provided by the representatives. Are these representatives the ultimate signers? No, they do not sign for themselves, they represent—self-evidently—the people of the United States. The true signer is thus the 'good people', i.e. the people who intentionally declare themselves independent from Britain, by their very signature-by- proxy.[23] Consequently, it remains unclear whether their act of signing—and by extension, their authorship—*states* independence or *produces* independence. Did they free themselves and does the text—and the rhetorical gesture—confirm this fact? Or is the declaration itself an act of liberation? In terms of a speech act: is the utterance of the 'good people' and their proxies/representatives a constative or a performative speech act? In fact, says Derrida, this confusion is complicated by another one. The new signatures dissimulate another tacit performative, i.e. the dissolution of an existing colonial contract—which could be symbolized by the Mayflower Compact of 1620, considered by Arendt as an anticipation of the concept of power for the independent Union.[24] But this double signature cannot hide definitively the fact that the signers constitute themselves, as an independent community, by the act of signing: before the Declaration, as a text, the signers didn't exist, as a polity.[25] This performative act is thus the very kernel of the 'constituent' operation, in the framework of a revolution. Even when it relies, in last instance, upon God who guarantees the rectitude of the popular intentions. It is this reference to God which conjoins the constatation and the prescription, the 'is' and the 'ought' of this foundational speech act.[26] But if this Declaration, and, subsequently, the Constitution of the United States of America, want to bar any return to political theology, this text, as a political action, should be qualified as 'undecidable', insofar as an original

[20]Honig (1993), pp. 101–102.
[21]Derrida (1986), pp. 7–15.
[22]Derrida (1986), p. 8.
[23]Derrida (1986), p. 9.
[24]Arendt (1990), p. 107.
[25]Derrida (1986), p. 10.
[26]Derrida (1986), p. 11.

law is required in the first place. Perfect legitimacy, *pace* Arendt's desire, does not exist. It is the undecidability itself that marks the revolutionary momentum and thus, as Arendt advocates, political action conceived as public liberty.[27] It was no coincidence that the issue of the *Grundnorm*—Hans Kelsen's term[28] (Kelsen 2008, pp. 77–84)—has continued to haunt American courts until Martin v. Hunter's Lessee (1816), where the Supreme Court re-enacted the 'constituent' momentum by assuming the American people as the sole source of the law.[29]

2 Theatricalizing a Declaration

However, an analysis of the Declaration of Independence, 1776, as a constituent speech act and as a textual event cannot be limited to its legal-philosophical vulnerability. It should also be considered as an integral part of the eighteenth century rhetorical and theatrical tradition, as Jay Fliegelman does.[30] Fliegelman opens his essay with a textual curiosity, a printing proof of the official Declaration based upon Jefferson's own reading copy. The printer misread Jefferson's marks as emphases instead of pauses. The fact that Jefferson marked his pauses makes sense, since he considered himself, in contrast to the talented orator and fellow 'founding father' Patrick Henry, as a poor rhetorician: a precise preparation could indeed compensate, partly at least, his lack of a rhetorical delivery.[31] In Jefferson's time, orators were convinced that writing should be transformed into drama, that the text should be divided into units of self-evidence: "we hold these truths to be self-evident"— actually very literally. But Jefferson's important oratorial exercise—he had to convince the representatives in the Continental Congress to constitute a nation, even a state—should also be understood in the larger context of theatricality in the eighteenth century. Richard Sennett, among others, has explained how eighteenth century theatre, on stage and in the audience room, functioned as the laboratory for new 'bourgeois' conventions of public propriety in an urbanizing society.[32] This function was made possible by material conditions—separation of stage and parterre, fixed seats, policing, etc.[33]—and by important esthetical and dramaturgical shifts. In this transformation Denis Diderot's *Paradoxe sur le*

[27] Honig (1993), p. 107.

[28] The *Grundnorm* ('basic norm') is the hypothetical cornerstone of a given legal and normative order, it bridges the gap between the normative 'desire' of a given regime (especially a revolutionary regime) and the actual and factual range of the power of this regime (Kelsen 1934/2008, pp. 77–79).

[29] Lindahl (2007), pp. 492–496.

[30] Fliegelman (1993).

[31] Fliegelman (1993), pp. 4–7.

[32] Sennett (1977), pp. 89–122.

[33] Ravel (1999).

Comédien[34] serves as a crucial document, even when it was only published in 1830. Diderot's dialogue discusses a popular brochure, *Garrick ou les acteurs anglais*,[35] about the qualities of the good actor. David Garrick was the most famous actor of his time, in Great Britain and on the continent. His name and fame are only a pretext for Diderot's characters to talk about the histrionic skills needed to communicate sensitivity on stage. For the authors on rhetoric the American political orators read in preparation of their political-rhetorical efforts, Garrick also serves as an icon. He stood for the rejection of 'grand style', in favor of naturalistic acting—perfectly fit for the emerging genre of 'bourgeois tragedy'.[36] He embodied, quite literally, an important shift in representation of both feelings and ideas, on the public stage in its largest sense. The feelings of the actor shouldn't be communicated anymore, but the experience of those feelings, the affects, should be enacted. Represented sentiments weren't something mysterious anymore, but visible physical consequences of definable behavior.

Naturalist acting, in the eighteenth century and up to and including Stanislavski's so-called system, was clearly based upon a materialist psychology.[37] The paradoxical result, in the sense of Diderot's dialogue, was the blurring of the line between expressing an emotion and counterfeiting it. Put another way: theatricality was the essence of natural behavior. Anti-theatrical authors, Jean-Jacques Rousseau as their most vocal mouthpiece, denounced this posture, but some American commentators, like 'founding fathers' John Adams and Benjamin Franklin saw the political profit of these ideas—something more than just theory, but a practice tested by Garrick and others.[38] The paradigm of representation, as conceived by a socially ambitious and secularized bourgeoisie, not only influenced the theatre—in itself a social institution—but also the idea of politics and public liberty. Empiricist philosophy suggested that the natural world was transparent, that it should not be mediated by Platonic ideas in order to be understood, that it was not designed but only set in motion by God.[39] Language, as a pragmatic tool, reflects this insight, meaning that the truthfulness of a proposition should not depend anymore on its consistency with another proposition, but on its consistency with experience and facts. This implied that the classical formulas of rhetorical construction, borrowed from Aristotle and Quintilian, had lost their meaning.[40] Diderot's paradox, translated in terms of political rhetoric, meant that the alleged transparency of societal facts, meticulously

[34]Diderot (1830/1991).

[35]Published as an anonymous book, 'translated' (or more precisely: plagiarized) by a certain Antoine-Fabio Sticotti from Aaron Hill's *The Actor*. Sticotti intervenes with his (Hill's) book in the ongoing discussion about the sensitivity of the actor. For Diderot this book is the ideal pretext to develop his thesis of radical and consequent non-sensitivity as a requirement for the good actor (Chouillet 1970, pp. 209–226; Sticotti 1770/2007).

[36]Fliegelman (1993), p. 81.

[37]Roach (1993), pp. 116–217.

[38]Fliegelman (1993), pp. 81–82.

[39]Winterer (2016), p. 42.

[40]Fliegelman (1993), pp. 48–52.

observed and skillfully translated into sentiments, could prompt convincing arguments and create sincere empathy for a political cause. When John Adams describes American republicanism in terms of theatricality—"America was designed by Providence for the Theatre, on which Man was to make his true figure"—he subscribes implicitly the paradox of theatrical naturalism, based upon observation and reconstruction of both facts and affects.[41] Adams goes even further by insisting that representative institutions should be seen as the political operation of sympathy, since they are "in miniature, the exact portrait of the people".[42] Naturalistic ('true') eloquence, says a rhetorician in 1774, translates the sublimity of kingship into a power consistent with republicanism.[43] This translation, which probably would be subscribed wholeheartedly by Hannah Arendt, assumes the vulnerability of the foundational act, it factors in the risk of replacing the free will of the sovereign by the free will of the citizens. In contrast with the *Déclaration des droits de l'homme et du citoyen*, which informed the French citizens about their natural rights, the Declaration of Independence expresses these rights, these 'self-evident truths' by real men, real speakers. Jefferson proposed, as the title of the document, "a declaration of the representatives (...) in Congress assembled", to make this point. Political negotiation led to the more abstract, more 'sovereign' formula of "the unanimous declaration of the thirteen united States of America", thus eliminating the idea of representation, truthful but per se imperfect.[44]

A conclusion invites for more research questions. Let us assume that certain influential political documents, such as the Declaration of Independence, are necessarily performative speech acts, performative events. This means that they must confront the central question of political foundation, they must take the posture of a 'constituent body' in order to be politically relevant in the first place. A theory of natural rights, rights existing outside the realm of the rule of law itself, is not acceptable anymore and can be denounced as a softly secularized version of political theology. But how can a political community, in the very moment of its coming into existence, escape from this theoretical deadlock? Honig, with Derrida, insists on the importance of performativity, on the undecidability of the foundational gesture. Fliegelman, without addressing specifically this philosophical issue, insists on the cultural context of this gesture, in all its concreteness—Jefferson's pauses. Does this cultural analysis show us an escape route from Sieyès' vicious circle? Possibly, but many questions, epistemological and others, should be dealt with previously.

[41] Quoted by Fliegelman (1993), p. 91.

[42] Quoted by Fliegelman (1993), p. 43.

[43] Quoted from the manual of James Burgh (*The Art of Speaking*) by Fliegelman (1993), p. 31.

[44] Fliegelman (1993), p. 65.

References

Arendt H (1990) On revolution. Penguin Press, London

Austin JL (1975) How to do things with words, 2nd edn. Oxford University Press, Oxford/New York

Sticotti AF (1770/2007) Garrick ou les acteurs anglois. Ouvrage contenant des observations sur l'Art Dramatique, sur l'Art de la Repré sentation et Ie Jeu des Acteurs. https://gallica.bnf.fr/ark:/12148/bpt6k738548.image. Accessed 5 Sep 2022

Chouillet J (1970) Une source anglaise du "Paradoxe sur le comédien". Dix-huitième Siècle 2:209–226

Derrida J (1986) Declarations of independence. New Polit Sci 7(1):7–15

Diderot D (1830/1991) In: Laubreaux R (ed) Paradoxe sur le comédien. Précédé de Entretiens sur Le fils naturel. Flammarion, Paris

Fliegelman J (1993) Declaring independence. Jefferson, natural language & the culture of performance. Stanford University Press, Stanford

Foucault M (2004) Sécurité, territoire, population. Cours au Collège de France. 1977-1978. Seuil/Gallimard, Paris

Honig B (1993) Political theory and the displacement of politics. Cornell University Press, Ithaca/London

Human Rights Watch (2011) Getting away with torture. The Bush Administration and Mistreatment of Detainees. https://www.hrw.org/report/2011/07/12/getting-away-torture/bush-administration-and-mistreatment-detainees. Accessed 15 Aug 2022

Kantorowicz EH (1957/2016) The King's two bodies. A study in mediaeval political theology. Princeton classics edition. Princeton University Press, Princeton/London

Kelsen H (2008) In: Jestaedt M (ed) Reine Rechtslehre. Studienausgabe der 1. Auflage 1934. Mohr Siebeck, Tübingen

Lindahl H (2007) The paradox of constituent power. The ambiguous self-constitution of the European Union. Ratio Juris 20(4):485–505

National Archives (2022) Declaration of independence: a transcription. https://www.archives.gov/founding-docs/declaration-transcript. Accessed 2 Sep 2022

Ralph J (2013) America's war on terror. The state of the 9/11 exception from Bush to Obama. Oxford University Press, Oxford

Ravel JS (1999) The contested parterre. Public theater and French political culture 1680-1791. Cornell University Press, Ithaca/London

Roach JR (1993) The player's passion. Studies in the science of acting. University of Michigan Press, Ann Arbor

Roach JR (1996) Cities of the dead. Circum-Atlantic performance. Columbia University Press, New York

Rousseau JJ (1762/2014) In: Bernardi B (ed) Du contrat social. Flammarion, Paris

Searle JR (1969) Speech acts. An essay in the philosophy of language. Cambridge University Press, Cambridge/New York

Sennett R (1977) The fall of public man. Penguin Books, London

Sieyès EJ (1988) Qu'est ce que le tiers-état? Preface by JD Bredin. Flammarion, Paris

Terpstra M (2011) Democratie als cultus. Over politiek en religie. Boom, Amsterdam

Winterer C (2016) American enlightenments. Pursuing happiness in the age of reason. Yale University Press, New Haven/London

Philosophy of Friendship

Antoon Vandevelde

Abstract In his work, Jan Broekman has consistently put into question social contract theory and the central position of the individual human subject. This position has inspired us in our analysis of some of the seminal texts on friendship that philosophers and mythologoi, narrators, have transmitted to us. Friendship as mutual goodwill, anchored in the experience of vulnerability, a friend as heteros autos, always present in my most intimate reactions, friendship as a disposition fed by active gift giving in frequent interaction, but also friendship as mutual tolerance of otherness: these are the strands of thought that we explore in this article.

> Gut ist es, an Andern sich zo halten. Denn keiner trägt das Leben allein.—Hölderlin, *Die Titanen*

For so many years, Jan Broekman has argued that most contemporary social philosophy is profoundly—although implicitly—influenced by social contract theory. In this view, society is seen according to an atomistic model as a sum of individual actions, communication as the result of individual intentions along a speaker-hearer model and law as the external regulation of the interaction of supposedly completely free subjects. The dialogical philosophy of Martin Buber and Emmanuel Levinas, structuralism and post-structuralism have tried to break away from this frame of thought, but still, in an era when liberalism, rather than Marxism or communitarianism, is the unescapable horizon of our time, this is far from evident. Jan Broekman assigns to philosophy the task of putting into question all of our accepted ideas (Broekman 1971). Genuine philosophy joins a tradition ranging from Socrates and Aristotle to German idealism, critical theory, Jewish religious thought and forms of mysticism in relativizing the central position of the human subject. In this article I start from Broekman's inspiration in order to analyze the difficulties of grasping what can be meant by friendship. This topic seems particularly well suited to challenge the atomistic understanding of social life, but

A. Vandevelde (✉)
Institute of Philosophy, University of Leuven (KU Leuven), Leuven, Belgium
e-mail: antoon.vandevelde@kuleuven.be

F. Fleerackers (ed.), *The Rearguard of Subjectivity*, Law and Visual Jurisprudence 9,
https://doi.org/10.1007/978-3-031-26855-7_13

how a nuanced alternative theory can be devised is less evident. The article starts from a concise analysis of the classical texts of Platon and Aristotle and amends their findings on the basis of a few stories about the lived experience of friendship and with the help of contemporary social and economic theory.

1 Lysis

Notwithstanding a few fragments of pre-Socratic philosophers like Empedocles, stating that friendship is what keeps the cosmos together and what makes it orderly and beautiful, the first thorough account of friendship can be found in Platon's *Lysis*. This is eminently an aporetic dialogue. It starts in a witty mood: a rather stupid person has fallen in love with a beautiful young boy called Lysis and he asks Socrates to teach him a lesson in seduction. Socrates agrees that nothing in the world is so enviable as having good friends: it is better than owning horses, dogs, cocks, money, or honorific positions. He engages in conversation with Lysis, who seems to be immediately fascinated by the clever way of questioning practiced by the philosopher.

However, Socrates leads him and all bystanders into complete confusion. Definitely, friendship is an elusive subject. One could think that friendship is based on similarity and that people seek friends who are interested in the same topics, but according to Socrates this is pointless: why would people be interested in likeminded people? Take for instance bad people: they can never trust each other and hence they can never be friends. Good persons on the contrary are supposed to be more or less self-sufficient (*autarcheia*): they do not need each other. Socrates repeats often the same point: friendship and love are first and foremost desire, and by definition we desire what we lack. This means that, in friendship, we seem to look for difference or for complementarity. A single human being is badly fit for life. According to Socrates, he is very much like a desert longing for rain. Now, the most radical difference is that between a good and a bad person or that between myself and my enemy. Does the love for difference imply that we should develop friendship with our worst enemies? Again this is absolutely counterintuitive. That we should love our enemies may be a Christian precept, but, for the ancient Greeks, it was totally unthinkable.

From this reasoning Socrates concludes that friendship, i.e. love of the good can only emanate from someone who is neither entirely good, nor evil. Now, by miracle, this is exactly the definition of a philosopher. She knows that she is imperfect because she knows that she does not know, but she is not so much blinded that she has abandoned the quest for wisdom. Hence, indeed, she is neither good, nor evil. In the end Socrates seems to be in despair. When Lysis and his young companions are taken home by their supervisors (the *pedagogoi*), the dialogue ends and Socrates has to acknowledge to his friends his failure to find a good definition of friendship. However he has managed to turn the discussion on friendship into an apology of philosophy. The question of the philia is crucial in understanding what philosophy is all about. Not just for extrinsic reasons, because originally philosophy is developed in a dialogical setting, but intrinsically because we yearn to know what is worthwhile in human life. Now the critical reader may wonder whether the turn from friendship among human beings to the love of wisdom is not a diversion. What can we learn from the *Lysis* for understanding human friendship? When Socrates gets stuck with his reasoning, he often appeals to a myth. Let's follow his example.

2 Gilgamesh

The epos of Gilgamesh is one of the oldest literary texts that human history has bequeathed to us. It tells the story of one of the first kings of Uruk, a town in the south of what is now Iraq. Gilgamesh would have lived around 2700 years before JC. For centuries, his exploits have been transmitted orally before being written down in various versions and languages on clay tablets. Around 1800 before JC all these stories have been gathered in the more or less coherent, but still fragmented epos that we can read nowadays.

Gilgamesh is a young and boisterous king. He cannot stop harassing the young women of Uruk and he continuously mobilizes the male inhabitants of the town for dangerous adventures. The people of Uruk complain about all this to the gods and these are willing to help them out. They decide to give Gilgamesh a friend. He will be named Enkidu. He is a wild human being, not born, but created by a female goddess. Enkidu strays in the steppe. He grazes with the antelopes and he drinks their milk. A young hunter spots the Wildman at a watering place, and, as he disturbs his hunting parties, he imagines a trick to get him out of his way. He brings a young woman, a kind of temple prostitute, to the water source with the intention to seduce the natural man. Sjamchat fully succeeds in her task. Enkidu makes love to her during six days and seven nights. Then he wants to return to the antelopes, but they do not recognize him anymore as a member of their herd. Love has alienated Enkidu from his natural origin. Sjamchat introduces him in culture. She clothes him, shaves his hair, learns him to eat bread, to drink bear and to speak the local language. Finally she brings him to the town of Uruk in order to meet Gilgamesh.

Enkidu and Gilgamesh, the natural creature and the demi-God, meet on the public place of Uruk. Enkidu defies the king. They confront each other like young bulls and fight for hours. The walls of the town thrill. Neither of both wants to yield to the other. And like in the Jewish story of the fight of Jacob with the angel, the situation balances into a sudden conversion. The enemies start admiring each other, their wrestle turns into an embrace and they become the best friends. Henceforth the citizens of Uruk can be quiet. From now on Gilgamesh wages his exploits together with Enkidu. They are inseparable. They slaughter the most terrible monsters, but unfortunately, they get overconfident. Gilgamesh insults a goddess and she takes revenge by making Enkidu sick. Enkidu is caught by fever. He raves. At first he revolts against his fate, then he languishes and eventually he dies.

Gilgamesh has done all he could to save his friend, but it is useless. And then something incredible happens. Gilgamesh is distraught. He cries, he tears apart his cloths, he pulls out his hair. The funeral ceremony lasts for days, but Gilgamesh stays disconsolate. Now, he is the one who is running through the steppe, in despair because of the death of his friend. Together with Enkidu he has displayed incredible bravery, but now he is afraid of the lions. He realizes the transience of all that is dear to him. This is his encounter with mortality. The demi-god becomes human in realizing his vulnerability. The death of his friend not only confronts Gilgamesh with mourning, it also pushes him to question his own destiny. Gilgamesh becomes a philosopher. Still he stays a man of action. Desperately he will seek for immortality, but ultimately he will have to accept personal mortality. In the last verses of the epos, he realizes that the stone walls of Uruk, which he has built, will survive himself and the other heroes who had been living in the same town for thousands of years.

In the beginning of his *Politica* Aristotle situates human beings as intermediary beings, in between the gods and the animals. The Gilgamesh story illustrates this, but still, it tells us so much more. It is the love of a woman that saves Enkidu from brute animality, that introduces him into the culture of a community of humans and that makes him develop his abilities in new directions. It is the friendship of Enkidu that teaches Gilgamesh to respect his subjects, that liberates him from solipsism, that makes him discover emotions and that eventually leads him to a reflection that confronts him with vulnerability and mortality. Hence the Gilgamesh story broadens the teaching of Platon's *Lysis*. The desire for wisdom—philosophia—finds its origin in the consciousness of a lack of perfection, in the awareness of one's incompleteness. Gilgamesh shows us how friendship is rooted in the much more general human experience of vulnerability.

3 Koinonia

Aristotle devotes two of the ten books of his *Nicomachean Ethics* to the virtue of friendship. He wholeheartedly joins Socrates in his praise of friendship: 'It is one of the most indispensable requirements of life. For no one would choose to live without friends, but possessing all other goods' (1155a 1–6). At the end of Book IX (1170 a 15–1170 b 19), he situates friendship at an ontological level. I paraphrase here Aristotle's reasoning. At first sight it seems rather classical, but there will be a sudden turn that makes it less so. The Philosopher starts by stating that human beings are characterized by their capacity for thought. This is the *differentia specifica* that distinguishes them from animals, who are only capable of perception and sensation. 'If one who sees is conscious that he sees, one who hears that he hears, one who walks that he walks, and similarly for all the other human activities there is a faculty that is conscious of their exercise (1170 b 28–33). Hence human beings are conscious of all faculties that make possible their most diverse activities, not just their sensations, but also the very fact that they are thinking beings, able to think before, and even more while acting. Now the consciousness of our sensations and thoughts implies the consciousness of our being, of the fact that we are living. After all for Aristotle 'life in the full sense is sensation or thought' (1170 a 19–20). Moreover, for a virtuous person, life is pleasant and desirable. This is not the case for people who lead a vicious or corrupt life, or one that is painful, because such a life lacks a focus or a goal. The meaning of their life, the direction they want to go is indefinite, and, for Aristotle, this is characteristic of evil. However for a virtuous person it is a pleasure to be alive. For him or her, life is an end in itself.

Then comes what is for our purpose a crucial passage in Aristotle's text. If, for a virtuous person, life is intrinsically valuable, we should not understand this in an individualistic way. For the virtuous person consciousness, (aisthanestai) is always *synaisthanestai.* This means, it is hardly possible outside a community with other persons. By living together virtuous people develop a common consciousness. As friends they experience a common pleasure in being alive. 'If the virtuous man feels towards his friend in the same way as he feels towards himself (for his friend is a second self) – then, just as a man's existence is desirable for him, so, or nearly so, is his friend's existence also desirable' (1170 b 4–7). According to this text, the basis for friendship consists in *synaisthanestai*, something like feeling together, in old French 'consentir', what could be called sympathy, the sharing of passions. 'Therefore a man ought also to share his friend's consciousness of his existence and this is attained by their living together and by conversing and communicating their thoughts to each other' (1170 b 10–12).

In his discussion of this passage Giorgio Agamben emphasizes that the Aristotelian definition of a friend as 'heteros autos', here translated as 'a second self', has connotations that differ from the canonized Latin translation as an 'alter ego' (Agamben 2007). The friend is not a stranger outside myself. He is not another self. Alterity resides within myself. As a friend I look at myself with the eyes of the other. Even more: in the reflection on my activities, on my seeing, hearing, walking, sensing, thinking and being, the other is always already present. It is no accident that Aristotle develops in this passage the theme of friendship in connection with the position so fiercely advocated by Socrates that human beings are reflexive beings, and that a life without reflection would hardly be worthwhile. Philosophy is articulated reflection, and as the other is already present in my most personal reflection, once again this explains why friendship is a matter belonging to the heart of philosophy. It can be called 'consubstantial' with philosophy, so much that the term philosophy already contains the word philia.

By the way, the Christian concept of joy refers to the same Aristotelian strain of thought. The French philosopher Jean-Louis Chrétien defines 'la joie' as an 'acute consciousness of being' (Chrétien 1980). Again, this refers to the basic structure of the human condition. We feel joy when we prefer to be rather than not to be. Within a Christian perspective, like for Aristotle, this is not a purely individual feeling. Typically it is mixed with a profound sense of gratefulness for being allowed to be alive. Gratefulness towards God in a Christian tradition, towards friends who make our life worthwhile in more secular strains of thought.

4 The Existential Need for Friendship

In the beginning of the fifth century, for unknown reasons, a number of monks coming from the Syrian desert settled as hermits in the most solitary valleys in the Italian region of Umbria. They were common people, sometimes simple camel drivers, who wanted to devote their life to God. Local people in Umbria admired them for their piety and some of them followed their example. This was the start of the monastic tradition in Italy, as it has been recalled in a chronicle written by pope Gregorius the Great.

In the valley of Valcastoriana, near a place called Campli, a first *canobium* was formed, a loose settlement of monks, guided by the blind Santo Spes. In the neighbourhood, two hermits, Santo Eutizio and Santo Fiorenzo, lived together in a small *oratorium*—a place of worship—in the mountains. Santo Eutizio was an activist. He travelled from one village to another to convert local people to Christianity. Santo Fiorenzo on the contrary mostly stayed home and led a life of praying. The story reminds us of Maria and Martha in the Gospel of Lucas: the former engaging into an active life and the latter leading a life of prayer and contemplation. In 510 Santo Spes passed away and the monks of his abbey insisted that Santo Eutizio would succeed him as their abbot. He accepted the offer and he entrusted to Santo Fiorenzo the care for the oratorium where they had been living together for a very long time. However Santo Fiorenzo suffered from loneliness. He missed his friend. He begged God for relief in his distress and God answered his prayer by sending him a bear as a companion. Santo Fiorenzo educated the animal so well that he could let him herd his sheep. Hence Santo Fiorenzo is always depicted with four sheep and a bear at his feet.

In general, the early hermits in Umbria, doubtlessly champions in solitary living, were quite aware of the existential need for friendship and they managed to deal with it. During week they lived in almost complete solitude, except for a rare traveler passing by, but on Sundays hermits from different valleys came together to celebrate mass. Afterwards, they had a frugal dinner in community and they spent the rest of the day walking together, accompanying each other to their respective hermitages.

The existential need for friendship has been denied in a most spectacular way by Jean-Jacques Rousseau. In a strange thought experiment, he imagined human beings in the state of nature living in almost complete isolation (Rousseau 1965). Males and females would occasionally meet for sex and when they have children, they would take care of them, but strictly no longer than needed for their survival. This means that they would send their children away as soon as possible in order to resume their solitary way of life. This is similar to the way in which moles live, but Rousseau himself knew quite well that this is not a realistic picture of the human condition. In another version of the state of nature he imagines young boys and girls meeting at water sources and trying to seduce each other, a somewhat romantic story that we easily recognize as more appropriate than the picture of human beings as fierce wild men running through the steppes. However, even in his *Second Discourse* (Rousseau 1969) Rousseau presents his state of nature not as actual reality, but only as a hypothetical supposition, telling us how things could have been in a counterfactual world. Ultimately the image of completely self-sufficient individuals in the state of nature only serves as a rhetorical devise in his plea for a society without any division, in which all citizens would be immediately socialized. In his *Social Contract* Rousseau seems to defend an oversocialized, rather than an undersocialized anthropology.

5 The Aristotelian Definition of Friendship

Aristotle dares to do what Sokrates and/or Platon were unable to do in the *Lysis*. He offers a definition of friendship (Aristotle 1962). In its most concise version, it is defined as 'mutual goodwill' (1155b 34) or as 'reciprocal affection' (1156 a 9). First of all, friendship is benevolence: friends want the good of the other(s). At the same time, friendship is more than mere goodwill. Friendship requires that all parties are *aware of* mutual goodwill (1155b 34–1156a 4). Hence it is not sufficient that people are generally well-disposed towards each other, they must actively seek each other's company and aim at entertaining their relation. Reciprocity makes that friendship is not just good for the other, but also for myself. At least in principle. Of course misunderstandings are possible. When our conceptions of the good diverge, paternalism can threaten the equality of both partners. Aristotle acknowledges that what is good for me, is not necessarily good absolutely (1155b 23–26).

Aristotle is well-known for distinguishing three kinds of friendship according to three definitions of what is lovable and worth pursuing: in friendship we can seek what is *useful, pleasant*, or *good in itself.* Definitely, there is a hierarchy in these motivations. *Friendship of utility* is the lowest kind, because utility is a quality of means and these are subservient to reaching particular ends. That the end is always superior to the means is a basic axiom for Aristotle. If we aim at utility we love a person not for himself, but because of the advantages this can yield to him and to us. Commercial relations belong to this type.

Friendship of pleasure is already higher ranked in Aristotle's mind, as pleasure can be a goal in itself. The Philosopher seems to think here of spending time in good company, 'a society of witty people' (1356a 13). We know that the classical Greek philosophers thought that common meals were important for forging social bonds within the polis, although there was disagreement about whether tax money could be used for funding them. Probably, two thousand years later, Kant was inspired by these passages in Platon and Aristotle when, in his third *Critique*, he praises 'die Geselligkeit' (Kant 1968). Although this term is difficult to translate in non-Germanic languages, it could mean something like sociability, and it seems to refer to the 'friendship of pleasure' that is enjoyed when taking dinner in good company. To some extent, pleasure as a motive of friendship is ambivalent. At first sight, it can be labeled as predominantly selfish, but the pleasure of an enjoyable evening with friends is typically a collective good. However, like utility, pleasure is also a contingent good and relations based on it are easily broken up.

For Aristotle, *friendship of virtue* is the highest form because it aims at the good of both partners. Here the friend is loved for what (s)he is and not for some advantage or for a passing form of pleasure. Only this kind of friendship is long lasting and aims at permanence. It takes time to engage into intimacy and to entertain it.

However, Aristotle's definition of friendship does not solve all problems. Definitely, there is some tension between the two main aspects of it: goodwill and mutuality, benevolence and reciprocity. While one element refers to the good of the other, the other seems to refer to self-interest. If reciprocity happens, then benevolence is also in my self-interest. However, should real friendship, friendship of virtue, not be totally disinterested? Doubtlessly this is the case in friendship between two perfectly virtuous persons. Here friendship seems to obey to the highest ethical norms.

However, on this point, Aristotle's thought is less straightforward. In his conception, friendship is not just indispensable because human beings are political beings, able to reason and speak, or because we need each other for survival, it is also desirable because it is noble ('kalos'). And the nobility of a person is revealed by the extent of the gifts (s)he offers to others. Indeed, the art of gift giving has an important place in Aristotle's theory of virtues and in his theory of friendship. 'In its essence friendship seems to consist more in giving than in receiving affection.' (1158a 28) It is remarkable that while Aristotle never mentions craftmanship, honesty or commercial qualities as virtues, he abundantly praises the virtues of *liberality*, giving small gifts, and of *magnificence*, the sponsoring of public events or the funding of great monuments. In the first book of his *Politics* Aristotle even defines *oikonomia* as the art of *spending* wealth, which he appreciates as much more noble than the *chrematistikè technè*, the art of *acquiring* wealth.

The background of Aristotle's philosophy of giving makes his definition of true friendship, friendship of virtue, somewhat ambivalent. When it aims only at the good of the other, it looks like being totally disinterested, but when it manifests itself in magnificent gifts, it may still be anti-economic, in the sense of being opposed to the concern for material self-interest, but at the same time noble gift-giving confers upon the beneficent person social prestige or 'symbolic capital' as Pierre Bourdieu calls it. In this second taking, noble gift giving, characteristic of friendship of virtue is far from being totally disinterested. In order to understand this ambivalence we should remember that Aristotle does not make a clear cut distinction between facts and values. Definitely, his conception of ethics is not an anticipation of the Christian praise of altruism, i.e. the purest forms of altruism. Aristotle's concern is for example not about poverty relief, but about social prestige. For him it is clear that it is a much better situation to be able to give than to be obliged to receive, although from a naïve materialist perspective it can be seen as better to receive than to have to share one's wealth. Hence, Aristotle's friendship of virtue hovers between the pure forms of altruism that we nowadays associate with ethical behavior and magnificent gift-giving that yields social prestige.

6 From Aristotle to Mauss

Now the aim of this article is not to present an exegesis of Aristotle's texts, but rather to shed light on the notion of friendship as we understand it today, based on more recent insights in the nature of social life. In this paragraph I want to amend Aristotle's analysis from two different perspectives, first by appealing to contemporary philosophy of gift giving and second by presenting a new evaluation of markets and economic exchange.

First, in his famous *Essai sur le don*, Marcel Mauss expands the logic of gift-giving that Aristotle presents more or less explicitly in his theory of friendship into a general sociological theory (Mauss 1950, see also Caillé 2000 and Godbout 1992). Mauss makes it possible to go beyond Aristotle's analysis and to distinguish between two different concepts of reciprocity.

1. The reciprocity that is typical of economic exchange is strict and immediate, explicitly stated and intended. Ideally, at the moment of the transaction, a contract is devised that specifies all that is important for the interaction between the economic partners: price, conditions of delivery of the good or service, instances of appeal in case of dispute or non-compliance with the requirements of the contract.
2. However, common social interaction is characterized by a much more informal reciprocity. When I invite a colleague for dinner, probably, at some later moment, I will be invited at my turn by the invitee. *When* this will happen is not fixed in advance: probably not too soon, otherwise it could seem that my colleague wants to get rid of all obligations towards me, but also not too late, because then it will look as if he is free riding on my benevolence. There is a right time for devising a counter invitation—the Greek notion of *Kairos* applies here—but that is not precisely defined. Also, what form the counter gift by the receiver will take on is not specified: it could be a dinner, but also an evening at a theatre. And finally, I cannot sue my colleague for ingratitude when, beyond the appropriate time, (s)he has not returned the gift. In all societies, ingratitude is recognized as one of the worst vices, but in most cases it is not legally but only socially sanctioned—by some forms of ostracism. Social pressure, the willingness not to lose one's face, the quest for prestige, or simply friendship are more common motivations in social interaction than a narrow economic calculation of personal gain.

Economists will object that, from an empirical perspective, one can hardly see any difference between an economic exchange and a gift exchange: in both cases, there is a transaction from A to B followed by a more or less equivalent return. For informal gifts economists are able to calculate the shadow price of the interaction. However, from the point of view of the persons involved in the game of gift giving, things look totally different. Although the beneficiary of a gift feels obliged to return what (s)he has received, (s)he has the impression that this is a voluntary choice. Reciprocity is probably the strongest social norm among human beings (and even among some animals). There is a hidden law in social life saying that one always gets back what one has given: love and friendship as well as contempt and distrust. The reciprocity in the gift exchange is more implicit than explicit (Bourdieu 1997). In general I do not give with the aim of getting back, although in the back of my mind I know that this will probably happen. In this informal setting, gift giving looks like an almost perfect marriage of freedom and necessity. The obligation to return a gift is masked by the time interval between gift and countergift. Hence we have the impression that the gift we offer or receive is an expression of genuine appreciation, while it is also a way of escaping to the shame of not being able to reciprocate. Under Mauss' inspiration, Caillé and Godbout present the gift exchange as a third model of social interaction, beyond the opposition of altruism and egoism. As Aristotle's idea of the nobility of friendship of virtue also points at a model of giving that is partly altruistic and partly aiming at social prestige, it looks very much like the model proposed by Mauss and by the sociologists belonging to his school of thought.

I come to my second amendment to Aristotle's analysis. It is well known that in the first book of his *Politics* Aristotle is very negative about commercial relations and about the *chrematistikè techné*, the art of making money (Aristotle 1972). Once money making starts to be the primary aim of people, they will tend to skip all ethical and social considerations. Even nowadays many philosophers share this dismal view according to which all actors on the market are merely self-interested. However, it is very well possible to conceive of them as aiming at *mutual interest* rather than at pure unmediated self-interest. Look at what actually happens on the market place: the seller of a good or service tries to convince potential buyers that it is in their interest to engage into a transaction with him or her. Of course this is somewhat hypocritical: it is also in the seller's interest to do so—and the buyer has no doubts about this state of affairs—but the idea is that both agents will be better off through the sale/purchase. In view of this interpretation of market behavior, Aristotle's thesis that transactions aiming at utility embody already a form of friendship, although not the highest form of friendship, becomes more acceptable.

An additional argument in favor of a more positive evaluation of market transactions is that markets can only be beneficial for society if economic actors have interiorized in their 'habitus' the respect for some basic norms of honesty. Not all moves are allowed on the market place. Commercial actors have to respect the rules of the game. If they do not, then the beneficial effects of markets as explained by economic models will vanish rapidly. In fact markets are a mixture of competition and cooperation. If economic competition degenerates into war, that means that all elements of friendship in the Aristotelian sense have disappeared from the economic realm and that market behavior has become self-destructive. Of course Aristotle is still far away from conceiving of something like an invisible hand, leading economic actors unknowingly to the common good, but certainly the idea that commercial relations embody some form of friendship, as it is developed in the *Nicomachean Ethics*, is more positive than the rejection of chrematistics in the *Politica*.

On the basis of Mauss' suggestions and with a view on contemporary insights borrowed from economics we can now amend Aristotle's distinction of three forms of friendship. The highest form of friendship would be genuinely ethically motivated. It would appeal to pure altruism without any expectation of reciprocity. A second form of friendship is based on informal gift exchanges: reciprocity is not a goal of individual action, but in most cases it is achieved on the basis of interiorized social pressure: not returning a gift is considered to be shameful and magnificent gifts yield social prestige. The third form of friendship relies on the economic model of exchange, where a strict equivalence between gift and countergift is aimed at. Stressing the nobility of the gift, Aristotle tends to mix up ethics and the search for prestige in his characterization of friendship of virtue. In my proposal both motivations are separated. Moreover, my example of inviting friends for dinner can serve as an illustration of the logic of gift giving, as well as of Aristotle's idea of friendship of pleasure. Finally I have presented some considerations making the idea of friendship of utility more acceptable and less of a contradiction in terminis.

Friendship as mutual goodwill, anchored in the experience of vulnerability, a friend as *heteros autos*, always present in my most intimate reactions, friendship as a disposition fed by active gift giving in frequent interaction: this characterization of friendship, inspired by Aristotle and Mauss, yields us quite valuable insights, but is probably still incomplete. I illustrate this with another almost mythical story of a remarkable friendship.

7 Rumi and Shams of Tabriz

Maulana Jalaluddin Rumi lived in Iran and Turkey in the thirteenth century, at the time of Thomas Aquinas. He was born in a family of learned theologians and still nowadays he is one of the most important sources of inspiration for mystical Sufi-brotherhoods in the Middle-East. 'Seldom you will meet a saint during your lifetime. So, if it happens to you, make sure that you do not miss the occasion', is one of his famous quotes. In 1248 Rumi meets Sham-I Tabriz, an itinerant mendicant. The somewhat dull theologian is very much impressed by the encounter with the wayward monk. He invites him at home, gives him a woman in order to motivate him to stay longer and engages into a dialogue with his guest. They continue their conversation for months, almost day and night. Rumi is so much absorbed by his discussions with Sham that he loses all interest in his school and in his disciples. We hardly know what they have been talking about, but apparently they have developed a most exalting and almost mystical friendship. Then, suddenly, on an evening, during a philosophical discussion, Shams leaves the room and never comes back. There are various versions of what happened. Some pretend that Rumi's disciples have thrown Shams in a pit and murdered him out of jealousy, others say that Shams just left and resumed his former way of life as a begging monk. Rumi is left in complete despair. He travels from town to town searching for his friend, but, like Gilgamesh, he will have to accept his disappearance and he will cherish the memory of his friend for all his life.

The friendship of Rumi and Shams was very intense and exclusive. It looks like an extreme attempt to reach something like fusional friendship, where the individuality of both friends is fading away. To some extent that was also the case in the friendship of Gilgamesh and Enkidu or in the friendship of Montaigne and Etienne de la Boétie, another famous topos in the philosophical literature on friendship. In the Gilgamesh epos, an external intervention by the gods has destroyed friendship. And Montaigne recalls the history of his perfect friendship with de la Boétie ten years after the death of his friend. Probably time has helped to purify their friendship from all blemishes. However the story of Rumi can be read as an intrinsic failure of his friendship with Shams. Rumi seems to have aimed at a complete identification with his friend, in a relation that was totally detached from the outside world.[1]

Now I agree with Paul Van Tongeren that these almost mythical stories of friendship are largely misleading, not just for empirical reasons, because they describe an ideal of perfect friendship that is hard to realize, but also for more principled reasons (Van Tongeren 2021). Actually, as no single person is perfect, neither can this be the case of friendship. Sooner or later we are always confronted with the idiosyncrasies of the other, with his or her obsessions, strange habits, unacknowledged neuroses, irritating character traits, unintended awkwardness. Hence, as Paul Moyaert has pointed out, genuine friendship that survives the contingencies of daily life and that aims at permanence always appeals to patience and tolerance, as much as to a spontaneous communication of sentiments (Moyaert 2015). The difficulty of defining friendship that Platon has highlighted and that Derrida has theorized in his famous book on *Politiques de l'amitié* (Derrida 1994) is not fortuitous, but corresponds with the difficulty of finding a proper combination of fellow feeling and social distance.

8 Friendship and Otherness

Probably most of the philosophical tradition has gone too far in idealizing friendship. Look again at Aristotle. He quotes the proverb saying that 'friends have everything in common'. Maybe this can approximately be put in practice within abbeys, within some families, among very close friends, but it is difficult to implement this dictum in the other forms of friendship that Aristotle enumerates. Indeed, he does not restrict friendship to personal relations. He explicitly says that also the polis is held together by some form of friendship. Without friendship justice would hardly be possible (1155a 25–30). Even better, he thinks that 'a natural affinity and friendship exist between man and man universally' (1155a 20–23). This is one of the first formulations of the idea of cosmopolitism, even before the stoics. And Aristotle characterizes even the most general and most abstract form human relations can take as a form of friendship. Moreover, remember that commercial relations are also said to rely on some form of friendship. Clearly it is very difficult to associate all these relations with common property, all the more as we know that Aristotle has severely criticized Platonic communism.

[1] 'A worldless love': that was how Hannah Arendt has characterized her relation with Heidegger, which was (inter alia) a way to say that this was an impossible love.

Now, Aristotle was right in stating that human beings interiorize social patterns of thought and action, not just in their intimate relations, but also at a societal level, and maybe even at the level of humanity. However the suggestion that friends have to share everything with each other and that friendship can only survive when there is maximal similarity between the partners is simply wrong. One of the primary experiences in friendship, and also in love, is that of the otherness of our partner. This is not necessarily negative. Doubtlessly, it is pleasant that our partner can surprise us and that he or she is not totally predictable, but of course, as we have recalled already, when we live closely together with a friend, we are also confronted with irritating features of his character.

The illusion that someone is totally admirable or that he or she is completely tuned to my own sentiments easily crops up when someone falls in love. However infatuation is largely ignorant of the real other. Rather it is directed towards an idealized version of the beloved. Hence, ideal friendship can only survive in the absence of the beloved, for instance after his or her death, or during long absences. To a naive person the confrontation with the real other will always be disappointing. Friends do give each other a lot of pleasure. They do have common tastes, that is why they long for each other, but even among the dearest friends, there is never a complete coincidence of reason and emotions. If friendship is defined as mutual goodwill or as reciprocal affection, it also means that we do not abandon our friend at the slightest dispute and that we stick to friendship although we disagree in some of our judgments. Friendship is not to be confused with fusional love. It is a combination of close proximity and distance, and this explains that friendship can survive disagreements, long periods during which the friends do not meet, and even episodes of bitter conflict.

Let's summarize our argument. In describing friendship as the experience of the other as *heteros autos* Aristotle is in tune with Broekman's advocacy of the abrogation of the central position of the human subject in social life. As Hölderlin said, no human person is able to live on his own (Hölderlin n.d.). We need various forms of community to sustain us. Lucid persons know that the meaning of my life crucially depends on social recognition, on the appreciation by others, elusive social 'things' that cannot be produced or enforced: in my bright moments I know that 'I am another' and that I will never be able to measure the extent of all social determination in the formation of my identity. This is most obvious in genuine friendship, which is rooted in the experience of our vulnerability and mortality, but it also applies to all other forms of social embeddedness that not just make possible our survival, but also explain our most intimate thoughts and reactions.

References

Agamben G (2007) L'amitié. Payot, Paris
Aristotle (1962) Nicomachean ethics (trans: Rackham H). Harvard University Press, Cambridge
Aristotle (1972) Politics (trans: Rackham H). Harvard University Press, Cambridge

Bourdieu P (1997) Méditations Pascaliennes. Le Seuil, Paris
Broekman J (1971) Strukturalismus: Moskau, Prag, Paris. Kolleg Philosophie. Alber, Freiburg i. Br./München
Caillé A (2000) Anthropologie du don – le tiers paradigm. Desclée De Brouwer, Paris
Chrétien JL (1980) La joie d'être. Revue Thomiste:57–73
Derrida J (1994) Politiques de l'amitié. Galilée, Paris
Godbout JT (en collaboration avec Caillé A) (1992) L'esprit du don. La Découverte, Paris
Hölderlin F (n.d.) Sämtliche Werke. Emil Vollmer Verlag, München
Kant I (1968) Kritik der Urteilskraft. Suhrkamp, Frankfurt (1786)
Mauss M (1950) Essai sur le don. in Sociologie et anthropologie. PUF, Paris (1924)
Moyaert P (2015) Lankmoedigheid: de waarheid van de liefde. In: Becker M, Brugmans E, Hermens J (eds) Rondom vriendschap – Filosofische beschouwingen. Klement, Zoetermeer, pp 91–109
Rousseau JJ (1965) Discours sur l'origine et les fondements de l'inégalité parmi les hommes, Gallimard Paris (1755)
Rousseau JJ (1969) Essai sur l'origine des langues, A.G. Nizet, Paris (1781)
Van Tongeren P (2021) Doodgewone vrienden – Nadenken over vriendschap. Boom Amsterdam

From Life to Law: Towards an Evolving Conception of Ecocide

Anne Wagner and Sarah Marusek

> *The rules of our world are laws, and they can be changed.*
> *Laws can restrict or they can enable.*
> *What matters is what they serve. https://twitter.com/EcocideLaw/status/1384802479678894080/photo/1*

Abstract Our contemporary world gives agency to Law as the source of determining right and wrong. With a global history of increasingly, seemingly justifiable human destruction of the natural environment for political and economic cause, Law is empowered to step in and declare 'no more'. At the level of courts and national governments, Law is a higher figure, compelling action on a global scale to label and adjudicate acts of ecocide. Yet, even Law must reflect on its role as accomplice or objector to the ongoing realities of manmade environment calamity and destruction.

1 Dual Circuit of Law

Law is like an integrated circuit with two main lines of development, at times autonomous, at others conflicting with each other to reveal a new vision of reality. This integrated circuit thereby enables the Law to grow with the life surrounding it, while simultaneously reviving concepts sometimes far too deeply rooted in a predetermined time period. Yet the Law as a living organism has the ability to territorialize a concept, while also creating alternative trajectories or

A. Wagner (✉)
University of Lille, ULR 4487 - CRDP - Centre de recherche Droits et Perspectives du Droit, Lille, France

S. Marusek
Department of Political Science, University of Hawai'i Hilo, Hilo, HI, USA
e-mail: marusek@hawaii.edu

F. Fleerackers (ed.), *The Rearguard of Subjectivity*, Law and Visual Jurisprudence 9,
https://doi.org/10.1007/978-3-031-26855-7_14

deterritorialization routes for more modern and contemporaneous visions.[1] In this way, this two-stage integrated circuit may be a source of either promise or struggle in addressing and understanding new visions of the Law. Hence, we need to speak about these lines of resistance—i.e., refusal/hindrances of evolution or adaptation, as well as about these lines of transformation—i.e., acceptance of an evolving world with new conceptions of the past living reality.

> Out of this emerges a restored or modified situation, a new situation. Everything is individuated: the milieu as a particular spacetime, the situation as determining and determinate, the collective as well as the individual character (Deleuze 1986, p. 142)

For both Deleuze and Guattari,[2] the milieu consists of the combination of three meanings "surroundings", "medium", and "middle". As such, it is situated at the intersection of these trajectories in a dynamic and evolving space, also referred to as the "rhizome theory", whose multiplicity of meanings can result therefrom:

> The rhizome operates by variation, expansion, conquest, capture, offshoots[3]

Understandably, this milieu is far from being homogeneous, as it is subject to inner and outer forces that both constitute or divide it, thus requiring a number of important adjustment variables. Such variables are intermediate states, enabling pre-existing realities to be addressed or re-created in a more contemporary milieu, "which shatter its continuity, fragment its ring, and break it down into gradation",[4] being referred to a "cubistic or kaleidoscopic transformational kind of representation".[5] Law is constantly adjusting to social changes, but some lines of resistance may surface that hamper deterritorialization, thereby generating either non-intentional inertia, intentional inertia or slow shifts.[6] As a result, a hold in a given time and space may emerge, blocking the progress of the law. Tensions within this dual circuit may therefore arise, causing limitations in transferring "ecocide" to other dimensions and so alienating it from lines of transformation, which means that

> Knowledge is based on interpretation of a "something" as a "something mediated through signs [. . .] It means, that concrete knowledge is always based upon semiotic transformations [. . .]".[7]

Our chapter not only revolves around this concept of ecocide but also around its contemporary shift to different dimensions of legal reality. In the law, the concept of ecocide is firmly rooted along historical and political lines of resistance, while remaining flexible and adaptable to the passage of time (i.e., lines of transformation)

---

[1] Deleuze and Guattari (1987).

[2] Deleuze and Guattari (1987), p. 18.

[3] Deleuze and Guattari (1987), p. 42.

[4] Deleuze and Guattari (1987), p. 71.

[5] Kevelson (2015), p. 215.

[6] Mootz (2011), pp. 5–20.

[7] Broekman (2010), p. 58.

by multiple variations. This dual circuit of law should work "in unison, in the sum of their relations".[8]

2 Lines of Resistance

Ecocide derives from the root "eco" meaning in Greek "ΟΙΚΟΣ" (house, dwelling place, habitation) and "cide" from the Latin "occidere" that signifies killing. Originally, ecocide referred to the deliberate intent to destroy an ecosystem, by means of the complete depletion of an area's resources, the endangerment of its ecosystem, or the international trafficking and smuggling of protected species living in this area. Ecocide, as defined by the Larousse, is "a serious attack on the environment, resulting in significant damage to one or more ecosystems, which may lead to their destruction" (our translation).[9] Cambridge dictionary defines it as "the destruction of the natural environment of an area, or very great damage to it",[10] associating it with global warming and acid rain, amongst others. In the dictionary of Environment and Conservation, ecocide is "a planned effort to eliminate all or part of an ecosystem". However, these variables are gradually moving ahead, namely when considering the definition provided by the Encyclopedia of Religion and Nature where both ecocide and Holocaust

> depend on highly developed technology and large, impersonal bureaucracies; and both reveal how irrational modernity can be. They disclose a **profound inability to empathize with other people and other forms of life and express a vision of human relationships keyed to domination and exploitation**. That is why the Holocaust and ecocide both call into question many of the basic premises of our civilization. [our emphasis][11]

Ecocide's grasp and encapsulation over the Vietnam War became a norm, alienating it for a long time from any other meaning. Indeed, "there is no life that is not embedded in what we notice as being potentially significant".[12] As such, ecocide became deeply rooted with the American military's use of Agent Orange. The US military developed a powerful defoliant—Agent Orange—knowing full well that it was extremely hazardous given its dioxin content:

> James Clary, a U.S. Air Force (usaf) scientist stationed in Vietnam, noted in 1988 in a letter to former senator Tom Daschle, "When we initiated the herbicide program in the 1960s, we were **aware of the potential for damage due to dioxin contamination in herbicides**. We were even aware that the 'military' formulation had a higher dioxin concentration due to the

[8]Deleuze and Guattari (1987), p. 121.

[9]https://www.larousse.fr/dictionnaires/francais/écocide/186327. Accessed on 7 July 2021.

[10]Entry "Ecocide" in https://dictionary.cambridge.org/fr/dictionnaire/anglais/ecocide. Accessed on 7 July 2021.

[11]Entry "The Holocaust and the Environmental Crisis" in Taylor (2006).

[12]Citation of Peirce quoted in Broekman (2011), p. 3.

> lower cost and speed of manufacture. However, because the material was to be used on the enemy, none of us were overly concerned. [our emphasis][13]

From 1961 onwards, warplanes dropped large white trails over the southern part of Vietnam, known as the Operation Ranch Hand.[14] It is estimated that 76 million liters of chemicals were released in Vietnam over a ten-year period, as well as along the Cambodian and Laotian frontiers. Over 20% of the Vietnamese southern part was defoliated. Vegetation was dying, exposing people to devastating levels of dioxin, including cancers, malformations, and depriving them of basic livelihoods. As such "ecocide" became coined with US history and ecological warfare:

> This environmental warfare has been conducted without any broad examination of the question whether any cause can legally or morally justify the deliberate destruction of the environment of one nation by another.[15]

Galston, a plant biologist, strongly protested against the use of Agent Orange by the US military, employing for the first time the term ecocide associating it with "humanity genocide" as a weapon of mass murder. Galtson made the following statement on February 1970 at the conference titled "War Crimes and the American Conscience":

> After the end of World War II, and as a result of the Nuremburg trials, we justly **condemned the willful destruction of an entire people and its culture, calling this crime against humanity *genocide***. It seems to me that the **willful and permanent destruction of environment** in which a people can live in a manner of their own choosing ought similarly to be considered as a crime against humanity, to be **designated by the term *ecocide***. I believe that the most highly developed nations have already committed autoecocide over large parts of their own countries. At the present time, the United States stands alone as possibly having committed ecocide against another country, Vietnam, through its massive use of chemical defoliants and herbicides. [our emphasis][16]

Still in 1970, on December in Orsay (France), at the International Meeting of Scientists on Chemical Warfare in Vietnam, a resolution was issued associating ecocide to genocide and introducing "biocide" as a new variation to the concept "ecocide", as follows:

> The volume of human loss and the widespread destruction of nature lead us to the conclusion that we are not only faced with genocide but *biocide*.[17]

This line of resistance towards a kind of Code of Crime Against the Peace and Security of Mankind proved a slow and lengthy road to completion, leading half way to the 1977 Protocol to the Geneva War Conventions on ecological warfare:

> Article 35 – Basic rules

[13] Weisberg (1970), p. 8.

[14] Zierler (2011).

[15] Cook et al. (1970), p. 94.

[16] Weisberg (1970), p. 19.

[17] Weisberg (1970), p. 20.

> 3. It is prohibited to employ methods or means of warfare which are intended, or may be expected, to cause widespread, long-term and severe damage to the natural environment.[18]
>
> Article 55 – Protection of the natural environment
>
> 1. Care shall be taken in warfare to protect the natural environment against widespread, long-term and severe damage. This protection includes a prohibition of the use of methods or means of warfare which are intended or may be expected to cause such damage to the natural environment and thereby to prejudice the health or survival of the population.
>
> 2. Attacks against the natural environment by way of reprisals are prohibited.[19]

Despite this limited achievement of the Geneva Protocol, many other countries used similar techniques to counter insurgencies in Borneo and West Kalimantan in the 1960s,[20] guerrilla warfare in El Salvador in the 1980s and even during the 1991 Gulf War. With ecological warfare, the intent was to dislodge the enemy from their territory without leaving any hiding place and end the war more quickly. In 1991, the United Nations Security Council held Iraq liable for ecocide:

> liable under international law for any direct loss, damage, including environmental damage and the depletion of natural resources, or injury to foreign Governments, nationals and corporations, as a result of Iraq's unlawful invasion and occupation of Kuwait.[21]

For that period, the international Studies Encyclopedia re-defined ecocide as "a scorched earth reality":

> The environment can also suffer during war as part of a **scorched earth policy**, also known as "ecocide" (**killing of the earth**"), which is intended to render the area uninhabitable. Probably the most well-known and egregious example of ecocide in recent armed conflict occurred during the 1991 Gulf War [our emphasis][22]

Another line of resistance began with a waltz of uncertainty about how to prepare the draft Code of Crimes against the Peace and Security of Mankind on December 1981. In an attempt to break down this line of resistance, British lawyer Polly Higgins broadens the concept of ecocide to the protection of the planet, which she submitted to the UN Law Commission in 2010:

> Ecocide is extensive loss, damage or destruction of ecosystems of a given territory(ies) ... such that **the peaceful enjoyment of the inhabitants has been or will be severely diminished.**[23] [our emphasis]

---

[18] https://ihl-databases.icrc.org/applic/ihl/ihl.nsf/ART/470-750044?OpenDocument. Accessed on 14 July 2021.

[19] https://ihl-databases.icrc.org/applic/ihl/ihl.nsf/ART/470-750070?OpenDocument. Accessed on 14 July 2021.

[20] Peluso and Vandergeest (2011), pp. 252–284.

[21] United Nations Security Council Resolution 687. 3 April 1991: http://unscr.com/en/resolutions/doc/687: 14. Accessed on 10 June 2021.

[22] Entry "Environment and Security" in Denemark and Marlin-Bennett (2017).

[23] https://www.theguardian.com/environment/damian-carrington-blog/2011/sep/29/ecocide-oil-criminal-court. Accessed 10 June 2021.

Higgins and her team termed ecocide as "the missing 5th crime against peace"[24] with "human caused and naturally occurring ecocide".[25] As pointed out by Falk, "[...] state system[s are] inherently incapable of organizing the defense of the planet against ecological destruction".[26]

3 Lines of Transformation

Ecocide requires transcending these lines of resistance embedded in the past to achieve a more comprehensive framework in which this concept can gain momentum. The crime of ecocide is gaining greater recognition in national laws. In this sense "a dozen foreign law [...] have introduced into their criminal codes the crime of ecocide, defined as the act of massively destroying fauna or flora, contaminating the atmosphere or water, and, more generally, committing any act likely to cause an ecological disaster" [our translation].[27] In 1990, Vietnam included in its Criminal Code ecocide as a crime against humanity committed by destroying the natural environment, in times of peace as well as in times in war. Ten States already listed ecocide in their national legislation, such as Russia, Kazakhstan, Ukraine.

A concept is a fragment of contemporaneous culture and appears in "perpetual disequilibrium or bifurcation".[28] Indeed,

> [Concepts] *evolve,* and evolve mainly through verbal and lingual interaction, above all through the never-ending shifts of authority from speaker to hearer, who themselves are components of a community, which is in its turn a fragment of culture[29]

As components of a community, and so as parties involved in the constitution of this fragment of culture, French citizens were asked their opinion and a citizens' climate convention[30] was set up on October 2019, out of which they presented proposals to the Government for consideration on June 2020. One of them was to define ecocide as a crime,[31] criminalizing it in the context of the 9 planetary boundaries,[32] and

---

[24] Gauger et al. (2012).

[25] Higgins et al. (2013), p. 262.

[26] Falk (1971), p. 20.

[27] Neyret (2015), p. 338.

[28] Deleuze (1997), p. 83.

[29] Broekman and Fleerackers (2018).

[30] https://www.conventioncitoyennepourleclimat.fr. Accessed 19 June 2021.

[31] Convention citoyenne pour le climat. (10 April 2020) https://www.conventioncitoyennepourleclimat.fr/wp-content/uploads/2020/04/Contribution-de-la-CCC-au-plan-de-sortie-de-crise-1.pdf: 144–148. Accessed 20 June 2021.

[32] https://www.stockholmresilience.org/research/planetary-boundaries/the-nine-planetary-boundaries.html. Accessed 20 June 2021.

integrating a duty of vigilance and negligence.[33] A debate occurred about the meaning of "crime" or "offence", for which the latter was considered less serious compared to the former being related to the most severe illegal activities in France. Éric Dupond-Moretti, the French Minister of Justice, declared that:

> We will introduce a general offence on pollution. Fines will be adjusted depending on the perpetrator's deliberate intent. Sanctions would vary from three to ten years' imprisonment depending on whether it was a negligent offence, or, above all, a deliberate offence.[34]

It is a gradual and uneasy transformation, one that is influenced by the vicissitudes of time, the will of politicians, and the way society perceives these issues. It is a living reality, in constant flux, at times controversial, at others questionable. This slow line of transformation led to the removal of an ecocide crime and its replacement by "aggravating circumstances" when the law was enacted by the Parliament on 21 July 2021.[35]

These lines of transformation are roads paved with pitfalls whose aim is to gain the most acceptance from a community to guarantee its feasibility. They are always filled with the best intentions, although these intentions do not really enter into the equation, rather the legal feasibility of their implementation without them being permanently challenged. On 22 June 2021, a committee of international experts recently suggested that the crime of ecocide be defined to complete this slow, difficult and contested line of transformation. It would then constitute the 5th crime, so much sought after by late Polly Higgins, and would fall under the jurisdiction of the International Criminal Court:

> Chair of the Stop Ecocide Foundation and convenor of the panel, said:
>
> This is an historic moment. This expert panel came together in direct response to a growing political appetite for real answers to the climate and ecological crisis. The moment is right - the world is waking up to the danger we are facing if we continue along our current trajectory.
>
> The drafting work, she explained, "was high-level, collaborative and informed by many experts as well as a public consultation comprising hundreds of legal, economic, political, youth, faith and indigenous perspectives. The resulting definition is well pitched between what needs to be done concretely to protect ecosystems and what will be acceptable to states. It's concise, it's based on strong legal precedents and it will mesh well with existing laws. Governments will take it seriously, and it offers a workable legal tool corresponding to a real and pressing need in the world."[36]

The main challenge would be for the International Criminal Court, which prosecutes individuals. Lines of resistance will again appear in which Governments may be reluctant in setting up a mechanism that would lead to the criminal liability of

---

[33] Convention citoyenne pour le climat. (10 April 2020) https://www.conventioncitoyennepourleclimat.fr/wp-content/uploads/2020/04/Contribution-de-la-CCC-au-plan-de-sortie-de-crise-1.pdf: proposition SN7.1: 145. Accessed 20 June 2021.

[34] Enault and Ceaux (21 November 2020).

[35] See art. 68 Loi Climat et Résilience to be published soon on the official French website.

[36] https://www.stopecocide.earth/expert-drafting-panel. Accessed on 25 June 2021.

Governments, CEO of multinational companies for instance. Alex Whiting, former International Criminal Court prosecutions coordinator, expresses his thought:

> Defining the crime is a first step on a path of discussion, debate, and, one day, ratification. The hope is that the process will energize states to think about how to use international criminal law to target the most grave environmental crimes while at the same time deploying domestic criminal and regulatory law to address a broad range of environmental harms that threaten our planet.[37]

Yet, even the defined criminality of ecocide on an international scale exposes the unwillingness of some states to conform to global pressures. One example is the United States, who, under President Trump, reinforced the construction of the wall between the U.S. and Mexico. Defiling the kaleioscopic array of American environmental legislation, the Trump Administration waived over thirty-seven federal laws to continue building this fence/wall in the desert.[38] In striking political alignment, the United States Supreme Court refused to hear challenges to the construction of the border wall.[39] The transfer of power from Trump to Biden ended, albeit most likely temporarily, construction. Meanwhile the building of border walls between nations continues elsewhere, with continued destruction to the environment and amplified effects of ecocide on local populations.[40]

4 Conclusion

The prospective goal of our discussion is to call attention to the role of law either as protector of the planet against ecocide or as complicit agent in furthering ecocide. Law, as a global institution comprised of international courts and state actors, must self-reflect to stop the destruction of our planet. Law must rally in unison around the world to defy political trends, cultural wars, and economic exploitation if our planet and way of life will continue. In their envisage of the anthropocene as a "geohistorical event", Christophe Bonneuil and Jean-Baptiste Fressoz urgently invite us to

> take a political grip on the institutions and oligarchies, the powerful symbolic and material systems that led us into the Anthropocene: military apparatuses, the system of consumerist desire and its infrastructure, the gaps of income and wealth, the energy majors and the financial interests of globalization, the technoscientific apparatuses when these work in commodity logics or silence criticisms and alternatives.[41]

[37] https://www.stopecocide.earth/press-releases-summary/top-international-lawyers-unveil-definition-of-ecocide. Accessed on 25 June 2021.

[38] Schwartz (2019).

[39] Wolfe (2020).

[40] Jones (2012, 2017).

[41] Bonneuil and Fressoz (2017), p. 291.

References

Bonneuil C, Fressoz J-B (2017) The shock of the anthropocene. Verso, New York

Broekman JM (2010) Firstness and phenomenology - Peirce and Husserl on attitude change. In: Wagner A, Broekman JM (eds) Prospects of legal semiotics. Springer, Dordrecht, Heidelberg, London, New York, pp 37–78

Broekman JM (2011) Introduction. In: Broekman JM, Mootz Francis J (eds) The semiotics of law in legal education. Springer, Dordrecht, Heidelberg, London, New York, pp 2–4

Broekman JM, Fleerackers F (2018) Legal signs fascinate: Kevelson's research on semiotics. Springer, Dordrecht, Heidelberg, London, New York

Convention citoyenne pour le climat. (10 April 2020). https://www.conventioncitoyennepourleclimat.fr/wp-content/uploads/2020/04/Contribution-de-la-CCC-au-plan-de-sortie-de-crise-1.pdf. Accessed 20 June 2021

Cook RE, Haseltine W, Galston AW (1970) What have we done to Vietnam? In: Weisberg B (ed) Ecocide in Indochina: the ecology of war. Canfield Press, San Francisco, pp 89–94

Deleuze G (1986) Cinema 1: the movement-image (trans: Tomlinson H, Habberjam B). University of Minnesota Press, Minneapolis

Deleuze G (1997) Essays critical and clinical. University of Minnesota Press, Minneapolis

Deleuze G, Guattari F (1987) A thousand plateaus - capitalism and schizophrenia. University of Minnesota Press, Minneapolis

Denemark RA, Marlin-Bennett R (eds) (2017) The international studies encyclopedia. Wiley and Blackwell, London

Enault M, Ceaux P (21 November 2020) Barbara Pompili et Eric Dupont-Moretti: nous créons un délit d'écocide. https://www.lejdd.fr/Politique/barbara-pompili-et-eric-dupond-moretti-nous-creons-un-delit-decocide-4007210. Accessed 25 June 2021

Falk RA (1971) This endangered planet: prospects and proposals for human survival. Random House, New York

Gauger A, Pouye Rabatel-Fernel M, Kulbicki L, Short D, Higgins P (2012) The Ecocide Project - 'Ecodice is the missing 5th Crime Against Peace'. https://sas-space.sas.ac.uk/4830/1/Ecocide_research_report_19_July_13.pdf. Accessed 10 June 2021

Higgins P, Short D, South N (2013) Protecting the planet: a proposal for a law of ecocide. Crime Law Soc Changes 59:251–266. https://doi.org/10.1007/s10611-013-9413-6

Jones R (2012) Border walls: security and the war on terror in the United States, India, and Israel. Zed Books, New York

Jones R (2017) Violent borders: refugees and the right to move. Verso, New York

Kevelson R (2015) Things I: property: the legal 'thing' as artwork. In: Broekman JM, Catá Backer L (eds) Signs in law - a source book: the semiotics of law in legal education III. Springer, Dordrecht, Heidelberg, London, New York, pp 213–226

Mootz FJ (2011) "Die Sache": the foundationless ground of legal meaning. In: Broekman JM, Mootz Francis J (eds) The semiotics of law in legal education. Springer, Dordrecht, Heidelberg, London, New York, pp 5–20

Neyret L (dir) (2015) Des écocrimes à l'écocide: le droit pénal au secours de l'environnement. Bruylant, Paris

Peluso N, Vandergeest P (2011) Taking the jungle out of the forest. In: Peat E, Robbins P, Watts M (eds) Global political ecology. Routledge, London, pp 252–284

Schwartz MS (2019) "Government Can Waive Environmental Laws to Build Border Wall Prototypes, Court Rules", National Public Radio (NPR). https://www.npr.org/2019/02/12/693777466/government-can-waive-environmental-laws-to-build-border-wall-prototypes-court-ru. Accessed 28 July 2021

Taylor B (ed) (2006) The encyclopedia of religion and nature. Continuum Publisher, London

United Nations Security Council Resolution 687. (3 April 1991). http://unscr.com/en/resolutions/doc/687. Accessed 10 June 2021

Weisberg B (ed) (1970) Ecocide in Indochina: the ecology of war. Canfield Press, San Francisco

Wolfe J (2020) "U.S. Supreme Court Spurns Environmental Challenge to Trump's Border Wall". Reuters. https://www.reuters.com/article/us-usa-court-border/u-s-supreme-court-spurns-environmental-challenge-to-trumps-border-wall-idUSKBN2401RY. Accessed 28 July 2021

Zierler D (2011) The Invention of Ecocide: Agent Orange, Vietnam and the Scientisit who changes the way we think about the environment. The University of Georgia Press, Athens & London

Anne Wagner is Research Associate Professor at University of Lille, ULR 4487 - CRDP - Centre de recherche Droits et perspectives du droit, F-59000 Lille. Anne's research focus on the Semiotics of Law, Law and Visual Jurisprudence, Legal Translation, Jurilinguistics, and Legal Philosophy.

Sarah Marusek is Professor of Public Law in Political Science at the University of Hawai'i at Hilo (USA). Sarah's research and teaching focus on everyday jurisprudence, legal semiotics, and legal geography.

Subject and Self

Jan M. Broekman

Abstract Rearguard battles concerning the position of the subject show how the relationship to the object plays a leading role even if the object changes as the subject does! Experience the discussion of a sensitive situation via your iPhone. You cannot, that instrument is not a component of the situational sensitivity. What widens our grip on reality and a fitting object? The question also touches the relation of subject and text. The contemporary praxis of data-management parallel to writing seems to threaten the concept of language, which is in this case of fundamental importance. Indeed, rearguard battles around the subject seem to continue, even in phoning, reading, writing or looking at another person. The lives of subject–object relations continue despite any battle.

Who am I? And who are you? No, that are not outcries in an urgent psychological disorientation. Western cultures posed the question since their Greek parents formulated them during multiple and various theatric and other social positions. Today we live with the remainders of the unfamous process named cogito resp. cognition. Our horizon is in fact colored by tensions between components of that activity, the I and You located far beyond the dualist notions of Martin Buber and his followers. The two words still dominate our thoughts, and their utterance relates to insight, knowledge and interest as well as our own position when we try to pursue any type of cognition. What do we mean with words like 'subject' and 'self'? One could write a cultural history of the two and never truly finish that text!

One of the many connotations is that the first, the word 'subject', seems fixated by the multiple patterns of thought and related structures at backgrounds which determine our lives. An explorative connection with the original Latin term 'submitting' seems evident—but what type of evidence is at stake? The second, the expression 'self', seems on the other hand to set us free from the strong ties of patterning or the structuring fragments of knowledge. It gives us an unknown enjoyment of freedom.

J. M. Broekman (✉)
Pennsylvania State University, University Park, PA, USA
e-mail: janm.broekman@kuleuven.be

F. Fleerackers (ed.), *The Rearguard of Subjectivity*, Law and Visual Jurisprudence 9,
https://doi.org/10.1007/978-3-031-26855-7_15

Yet, the two are equally determinative. indeed, there is no Self without a contrasting or otherwise related Other. Contrasts or other types of relation are indeed basic for understanding Otherness. But that is no longer the acceptable theoretical or philosophical basis for a contemporary understanding of the Self.

Take your iPhone and click one of the many options the instrument offers: with each choice you become a somewhat different *subject* because of the consequences of your click. All clicks make you responsible, participating, liable and—for short—making law: via your usage of the click, not of a word. That is because you are in the patterns of your phone a subject created by law that creates law. However, you may have wanted to do something else: to photograph a nice situation, a portrait of yourself walking with others or in the middle of beautiful flowers: your face wonderfully framed by great roses: to create a 'Selfie', as we call it today.

Yes, your phone allows you a distinct form of your self's image—in ways that were not recognized some ten years ago. But it is still not identical with any self-image you cherish! Mind and self were reduced to moments of your brain's activity before your phone and its digital world existed. Today, *subject and self come together again*—as if this togetherness creates a new social and cultural event. But the Selfie is only a fraction of the Self we know and accept as component of our identity. My smartphone makes me into a complicated and above all multiple personage: I am a subject in its social as well as legal sense, but also a self to be introduced in social relations! Hence our introduction of the term 'Self-E', where the Self became central in digital patterns of thought and experience.[1]

Victoria Lady Welby, who is known from her intense correspondence with the US philosopher Charles S. Peirce, stated already in 1911 that the Self acquired a unique position in her thoughts—long before it became as popular as is the case today in the light of digital notions. Yet, there remains a most remarkable truth when she writes: "What is our greatest gift and prerogative? The mortality of our *selves*." And she adds, as if warning us: "As nothing but a self was *born*, so nothing but a self can *die*. And that blessing is secured to us..." She added more meaningful words in the remark: "For the first time we emerge into the *answer-world* which has prompted our question and stimulated our discontent ... It is true of course that the term 'self' was originally equivalent to 'same' and 'ego'. But now a self is what You *have* and are apt selfishly you pamper and work for. And what you have you cannot in the full sense be."

Note her quotation. Note the words: "for the first time we emerge into the answer-world." That emergence is precious and suggests a distance from either the relative passivity in cases of repetitious structures or the dependency of two components in case of a dialogue world, which are the I and the You. The fact that we do not seem to depend on identity-less structural moments and not on solely two figures of personality. This underlines her thoughts as well as ours. We should, indeed, not! Notice how our concerns are focused on what is called "de-subjectivation[2]" although our

[1] See Broekman (2023), Ch. 1., Ch. 8.

[2] Svantner (2016), p. 95 ff.

power and interest is in contrast a search for the responding other! Victoria Lady Welby noticed our ability of self-identification that *widened* the difference between Subject and Self—which is the opposite of the modern de-subjectivation. She writes: "Our selves in the end are *ours*, not *us*; they were born, they die. If we will, they will obey us; if we will, if *we* loyally deny and train them, they will grow not only in faithful servants, but also into magnificent instruments . . ." Indeed: our selves are *ours*, not *us*; they can be treated and can function by means of differentiating our existential assets!

An important moment of relativity is implied here: the individuality of the recipient (which implies the hearer in the answer-world) has the same value as the speaker, the orator in that world. The Self of the two is a mediator among them. Relations between both must be understood as functional. The roles of speaker and hearer change constantly: the reciprocal relations create a field of tensions *among* them, and not in two separated specialized fields. Those tensions are thus never a domain that is mainly possessed by one of the two. Speaking subjects are de-centered by their speech-activity, as your smart-phone indicated! Their function unfolds in the fields among them, which they partially constitute by their simple presence. Your phone should bring communication, but it can only function thanks to well-defined and accepted positions. It does not create a domain or community. A Self is in our digital days an attempt *to de-center what needs to be a center* to function. For example, try to discuss a sensitive situation via your iPhone. You cannot since that instrument is not a component of the situational sensitivity. Why did we construct and worldwide accept emojis as a substitute?

The same is, surprisingly enough, valid for a *text* and for a *subject.* Roland Barthes described already in the early days of structuralism, in 1968, how a text closes itself and thus becomes a specific unity, so that a same text can become interpreted in accordance with other, if not all, cultural values. Any text represents in his eyes a threefold pact with reality. First, a text always collaborates with vested social institutions, Barthes claimed.[3] For instance, the *event* of a birth becomes an *act* of a Civil Status. The latter implies the documentation of a name, of family relations, dates as well as hours, and the like. Second, a text does fervently want to be understood in accordance with its *surface* structure. The denial of any surface being the result of an in-depth structure would annihilate its independence and thus become non-valid. Third, a text always closes a pact with its inherent signs, so that the letter of the text becomes fixated before any analysis can take place. These three forces influence our understanding of text and language in general—they determine personal and cultural heritage in many regards! So, language and linguistic activity (like socially classified utterances) do *not* coincide and are *not* equal forces in the light of social determinations.

Barthes thus touches essentials: the human being is in an exemplary manner *client* as well as its *delivering party* of any speech activity. This double sense is in all regards mirroring the position of a human being in philosophy. Plessner provided in

[3]Barthes (1968).

earlier years, in 1928, a formula: a human being is in essence an *eccentric* being.[4] Every thought, move, activity, relation, word, understanding is in that view resulting from a '*point over the shoulder*' and never the result of *whatever fixated totality* we could imagine. A human is deeply, firmly and existentially 'what he is not', he is namely: not complete but growing and continuously changing, in search of another identity, committing himself to other norms and values. There is always freedom and space to be different, to create the unexpected, the surprising or the alienating, the addictive, the dark side of the light. You take your phone to convert or to confirm your situation? No wonder that *otherness* and *alienation,* the *other* person, that is: the *beloved* as well as the *hatred,* seem to outlive sameness in one concept of a *self*! The *Self* is a metaphor for the wealth of inner positions, which were created during the same Self's continuous positioning and re-positioning in life.

The Self makes clear that accepting a moment of *discontinuity* determines the flow of life on the planet—its globalization, climate change and interstellar positioning included.[5] It occurs today, that our sciences do no longer embrace special relations with unities of norms and values made in located townships, world cities or laboratories. The CERN in Geneva is not an issue of Swiss culture, or the Massachusetts MIT of USA culture. The same goes for modern democracies: several EU democracies seem in fight with nationalist tendencies; but they are *not* fully determined by local problems and insights! On the contrary: *the profiling of the human mind* is at stake. Whoever limits his or her observations to political boundaries will be the jester of terrestrial regions with different names, sounds or contexts of what we experience as a Self. Whoever brings features of individual words or speech in question as *data,* challenges the limits of analog norm systems and reaches out to abolish any ambiguity of morals. Bringing such features back to analog expressivity is not the same as restoring a legal system and its state concept as the basis for a post-critical democracy. The digital culture creates *flows that operate at distance* from a litigious society: *one 'dike' fights another*—that's life! Subject and Self are enjoying their uninterrupted mutual conversions.

Indeed, *the world seems a composition of selfies which are functioning as Self-E's.* In that world we live and look: here I was, look at that! The positioning has a strong mimetic character. So, there it looks like I was paying attention. Give it a look: this position I had yesterday here! You see me now, but that's only today—it all looks as if, but whenever or wherever you look more closely, you change your impression. The whole of the Self as sign in all visual contexts is now offered by today's smartphone that remembers yesterday's positions. The Self is here and here; it is not there and will never submerge into an unknown composition—it is here, and it is the Self. This perception is the result of an "infinite mirroring," the philosopher Walter Benjamin observed when he walked through Passages in Paris during the mid-twentieth century which he perceived as essential parts of what he called a City of Mirrors.

[4]Plessner (1928), p. 288 f.

[5]Broekman (2023), Ch.9, §5.

In that light, the rearguard battles around the subject continue to rage. There appear to be no forces nor positions developed which open the relationship between culture and criticism. Multiples continue to be reduced to a summation of positions and correlations between mutually distinct scientific and cultural phenomena. The praxis of data-management seems very nearby! But the concept of language, which is in this case of fundamental importance, should be explicit. What remains of the mimetic, of sign and meaning, of the work of art and the foundation of science, that characterizes the new age? Is a language and its subject tenable in the context of a science in which the opposition between natural science and humanities is outdated and the problem of knowledge revolutionized in the natural sciences themselves? Is it not precisely the case that in any discourse the principle of foundation is to be understood as a mimetic achievement? Any position within the investigation of the documents of culture is important. After all, it is ultimately about what experience as such means and implies. Experience springs from history and leads it to distance itself from itself, to let go of itself.

That also provides a crossing of boundaries between speech and silence, or what Foucault called a "se déprendre". This does not imply an exclusively hermeneutic understanding of social praxis. The boundaries of the increasingly historical are constantly being crossed. Thus, the question of which are the documents of culture cannot possibly be answered in the traditional subjunctive-objective chemistry of the speaker-hearer model. It grasps much deeper and indicates that the ever historical, in which the instantaneous is present, always possesses the dimensions of the more embracing concept of history. This question indicates that there is no fixed relationship between the present and the past, and as a result one can never retreat to formal rationalities. The extraordinary always determines the ordinary; the other always determines the self. Any experience of the other is present in a way that differs from any formal rationality. That positioning characterizes the Subject and the Self in all periods of cultural determination, as our ancestors already documented in multiple forms of life.

References

Barthes R (1968) Texte (théorie du -). In: Encyclopaedia Universalis, Paris, vol XV

Broekman JM (2023) Knowledge in change. In: The semiotics of cognition and conversion. Springer Nature

Plessner H (1928) Die Stufen des Organischen und der Mensch [The steps of the organic and the human]. W. de Gruyter & Co, Berlin/Leipzig, p 288 f

Svantner M (2016) De-subjectification in semiotics: argumentations, self-defense and signs of opposing forces. Pragmatism Today 7(2):95 ff

MIX
Papier aus verantwortungsvollen Quellen
Paper from responsible sources
FSC® C105338

If you have any concerns about our products,
you can contact us on
ProductSafety@springernature.com

In case Publisher is established outside the EU,
the EU authorized representative is:
Springer Nature Customer Service Center GmbH
Europaplatz 3, 69115 Heidelberg, Germany

Printed by Libri Plureos GmbH
in Hamburg, Germany